The Rise of Spanish Multinationals

T0300545

Since 1992, Spanish companies in a variety of industries have acquired a prominent presence in the global economy, especially in Latin America and Europe. Companies such as Telefónica, Banco Santander, Repsol-YPF, and Inditex (the owner of the Zara brand) have become major international competitors in a short space of time, making Spain one of the world's ten largest foreign direct investors. Mauro Guillén offers not only an explanation of why this has happened, but also an assessment of the economic, financial, political, and social consequences for Spain and for Europe. In this analysis, he also addresses the weaknesses of the Spanish multinationals, especially their lack of proprietary technology and their primary focus on Latin America, arguing that the next step should be to consolidate their European positions through mergers and acquisitions, opening up new possibilities for further expansion in North America and Asia.

MAURO F. GUILLÉN holds the Dr. Felix Zandman Endowed Professorship in International Management at the Wharton School of the University of Pennsylvania, and the Fundación Rafael del Pino Chair, which funded this research. An expert on globalization and on the multinational firm, he is a visiting faculty at Instituto de Empresa, Guggenheim Fellow, and Member in the Institute for Advanced Study, Princeton.

The Rise of Spanish Multinationals

European Business in the Global Economy

MAURO F. GUILLÉN

CAMBRIDGE UNIVERSITY PRESS
Cambridge, New York, Melbourne, Madrid, Cape Town,
Singapore, São Paulo, Delhi, Tokyo, Mexico City

Cambridge University Press
The Edinburgh Building, Cambridge CB2 8RU, UK

Published in the United States of America by Cambridge University Press, New York

www.cambridge.org
Information on this title: www.cambridge.org/9780521402713

First published 2005
Reprinted 2006
First paperback edition 2011

A catalogue record for this publication is available from the British Library

Library of Congress Cataloguing in Publication data
Guillén, Mauro F.
The Rise of Spanish Multinationals: European Business in the Global Economy / Mauro
F. Guillén.
p. cm.
Includes bibliographical references and index.
ISBN 0 521 84721 4
1. International business enterprises – Spain. 2. Spain – Foreign economic relations.
I. Title.
HD2887.G84   2005
338.8'8946 – dc22   2004057107

ISBN 978-0-521-84721-6 Hardback
ISBN 978-0-521-40271-3 Paperback

Contents

Preface

NOT too long ago, a book on the Spanish multinational enterprise would have been regarded by many as a work of fiction. Nowadays, however, Spanish companies are making a dent in international competition just like firms from other European countries. This book tells the story of how exactly this has happened, after decades of relative isolation from the global economy, and analyzes the consequences for Spain's economy, society, foreign policy, and international image. The book also delves into the implications for Europe as a whole, given that the international success of Spanish firms has introduced new dynamics in a number of continental industries.

This book has been in the making since early 1993. The original stimulus came from a panel discussion organized by the Economist Intelligence Unit at the MIT Sloan School of Management, when I confronted the skepticism of Dean Lester Thurow and Harvard Professor Andreu Mas-Colell concerning the international visibility of Spanish firms. Back then I argued that there were perhaps a couple of hundred Spanish firms that could be regarded as "multinational" in nature. Fortunately, today there are nearly one thousand. I very much hope that the evidence and the arguments presented in this book will help give credit to the Spanish firms that have become competitive enough to operate internationally in their own right.

My greatest debt is to the Fundación Rafael del Pino for its generosity in appointing me to the Cátedra Rafael del Pino, which made it possible for me and my family to live in Madrid during the 2003–4 academic year and to focus the better part of my scholarly energies on the writing of this book. The Foundation also provided funds to hire research assistants and conduct interviews. I am especially indebted to its Director, Amadeo Petitbò, for his constant encouragement, and to its President, Rafael del Pino, for his leadership and example.

My home institution, the Wharton School of the University of Pennsylvania, was kind enough to grant me sabbatical leave. I am also indebted to the Instituto de Empresa and its Dean, Angel Cabrera, for providing me with a forum in which to present and discuss my ideas as well as with office space. I have made many presentations of this work at these and other institutions, and have benefited from the comments and suggestions of many scholars and students. I am also grateful to Emilio Lamo de Espinosa and Javier Noya, from the Real Instituto Elcano, for including in their public opinion survey questions relating to the foreign activities of Spanish firms. At the Fundación para el Análisis y los Estudios Sociales, directed by Baudilio Tomé, I had the opportunity to present early drafts to an audience of government officials, who politely disagreed with several of my points of view. A radio interview with Miguel Angel Fernández Ordóñez, later to become Secretary of State for Finance, helped me clarify several of the key arguments.

This book combines insights drawn from business economics, sociology, and political science to understand the complex consequences of the rise of the Spanish multinational firm. Professor Alvaro Cuervo of the Universidad Complutense de Madrid has taught me much of what I know about Spanish firms. Professor Jesús M. de Miguel of the University of Barcelona has helped me understand Spanish society in ways that have also been helpful to the writing of this book. Finally, Professor Juan J. Linz of Yale University remains my best teacher of Spanish politics, which are inextricably related to the activities of many of the firms discussed in the book. José Manuel Campa, Esteban García-Canal, William Chislett, Julio García Cobos, Sofía Pérez, Sandra Suárez and Carlta Vitzthum gave me innumerable comments and suggestions. Donald Lessard of MIT read the entire manuscript and provided excellent advice. I am also grateful to Adrian Tschoegl, who has collaborated with me on several articles concerning the Spanish banks. A long list of research assistants have helped me conduct interviews, collect and organize data, and iron out many of the details in the book: Kwame Abrah Mia Adelberg, Balbina Alvarez Toral, José Asturias, Patricia Gabaldón Quiñones, Rut González Alonso, Paloma Martínez Almodóvar and Diego Vargas Yábar.

It tends to be the case that a writer's most immediate family feels most intensely the consequences of the prolonged effort of bringing a book to life. I therefore dedicate the book to my wife Sandra and my daughters Daniela and Andrea. They figured out early on that, whenever they found me sitting in front of the computer, it was better to leave me alone so that I could finish and return to them as quickly as possible.

1 | *Spanish firms come of age*

> Spain is not so different, so special as it is
> manipulatively said to be. We must stamp
> out once and for all the idea that Spain is an
> anomalous country . . . a case apart, an
> exception that justifies any action.
>
> Julián Marías, philosopher and
> sociologist (1965)[1]

D URING the last decade of the twentieth century a number of
Spanish firms catapulted themselves to worldwide visibility.
In banking, BBVA and Grupo Santander became the largest
financial institutions in Latin America, within the top five in the
eurozone, and among the twenty-five largest in the world, while
Telefónica became the world's eleventh-largest telecommunications
provider (the top firm in Latin America) and Repsol-YPF the ninth-
largest oil company. In consumer goods, Freixenet became the largest
producer of sparkling wines, and Inditex (the owner of the Zara
brand) one of the leading apparel designers, makers, and marketers. In
industrial goods, Ficosa International and Grupo Antolín led the
world in the production of certain automobile components, and
several of the worker-owned cooperatives of Mondragón Corporación
Cooperativa expanded throughout the world as if they were regular
capitalist enterprises. And in security services, unfortunately a key
industry for the twenty-first century, Prosegur became one of the two
or three top global firms. Since 1993, Spanish firms have invested
abroad nearly $200,000 million (€180,000 million). As a result of this
remarkable process of international expansion, the Spanish economy,
the financial system, foreign policy, the labor market, and society have
been transformed in profound ways.

---

[1] "España no es tan diferente, tan 'especial' como interesadamente se dice.
Hay que deseterrar de una vez para siempre la idea de que España es un
país anómalo . . . que constituye siempre un caso especial, una 'excepción'
al amparo de la cual puede hacerse lo que convenga." I thank William
Chislett (2003) for calling my attention to this quote.

The rise of multinational firms from Spain poses a number of questions, because their process of international expansion is, to a certain extent, paradoxical. Spain is not among the most advanced countries in the world in terms of per capita income or technological development. Virtually no Spanish firm has global brand appeal. Yet hundreds of them are making formidable inroads into the global economy. This book aims to tell and analyze the story of the opportunities and problems produced by the enhanced stature of Spain in global economic and political affairs as a result of foreign direct investment (FDI) by Spanish firms.

After decades of international isolation, backwardness, and dictatorship, Spain entered the twenty-first century as a relatively "normal" country, boasting a relatively high degree of integration with the rest of the world, a vigorous economy, and a consolidated democracy. Since about 1980, the country and its firms have undergone a quite extraordinary process of change, including deregulation, privatization, enhanced competition, and increasing exposure to imports and inward foreign investment. In 1987, just one year after becoming a member of the European Union, the stock of cumulative inward foreign investment in Spain started to exceed the level for the average country in the world, adjusting for the size of the economy. Spain had become more attractive than the average country as a destination for foreign investment. Starting in 1992 Spanish firms responded to the growing arrival of foreign firms and to the creation of the European single market by stepping up their own foreign investments, a process that led to a unique situation in recent history: by the end of 2000, just as the twentieth century was drawing to a close, the cumulative stock of foreign direct investment by Spanish firms exceeded that of foreign firms in Spain for the first time in recent history (see figure 1.1). In 2002 Spain's stock of outward FDI reached the equivalent of 35 percent of GDP, up from less than 1 percent in 1980. Tellingly, Spanish firms have invested abroad more than those from the average high-income country. While in 1980 Spain was the twentith-largest foreign direct investor in the world in absolute terms, by the end of 2002 it had become the tenth-largest, behind the United States, the United Kingdom, France, Germany, the Netherlands, Hong Kong, Japan, Switzerland, and Canada, after having surpassed several countries that had been more important investors in 1980 (Belgium, Denmark,

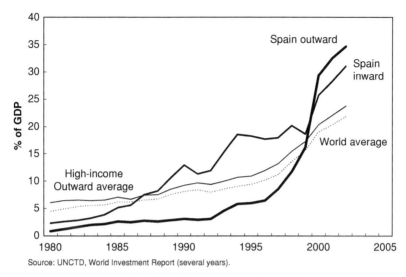

Source: UNCTD, World Investment Report (several years).

Figure 1.1. Spain's foreign direct investment stock position, 1980–2002.

Greece, Italy, Sweden, Australia, South Africa, Argentina, Brazil, Mexico, and Singapore).[2]

While Spanish multinational firms have been rather idiosyncratic in terms of the industries (mostly public utilities and financial services) and geographical regions (mainly Latin America and the European Union) in which they have expanded internationally, the reasons why they proceeded to invest abroad can be readily explained by established theory. I will make systematic use of economics, management theory, sociology, and political science to demonstrate that the logic underpinning the process of international expansion of Spanish firms has been, for the most part, sound, and in several instances simply brilliant.

[2] UNCTAD (2003: 262–5). The figures reported in figure 1.1 do not take into account the effect of "transit capital," i.e. when instrumental security-holding companies (entidades tenedoras de valores en el extranjero, in Spanish) are used to take advantage of certain tax incentives in Spain. When foreigners set up these companies, both inward and outward direct investment flows are artificially inflated. The companies were allowed after a 1995 reform of the Corporate Tax Law (Fernández-Otheo 2003). The timing around 2000 of the moment when outward investment stock exceeded inward stock is not affected by this effect.

However, I will also point out that many Spanish multinational firms are still far from the global frontier in terms of financial, organizational, managerial, and technological capability. Similarly, the country and its government seem relatively lacking and unprepared when it comes to coping with the economic, financial, diplomatic, political, and social consequences that increased outward foreign investment entails. The international financial community, the media, and business schools have increased the amount of attention they devote to Spanish firms, though not as much as one would predict given the growing importance of Spanish foreign direct investment. Thus, my main argument is that, while Spain has indeed become a "normal" country from the point of view of its integration with the global economy, it continues to be a second-rate country, aspiring but unable to join the club of the most advanced and powerful countries in the world. I argue that the gap separating Spain from the elite club of countries is not merely quantitative, as such simple statistics as gross domestic product per capita reveal (see figure 1.2). Spain finds itself behind the truly advanced countries in a *qualitative* way: one that has to do with power and influence. I shall offer some cardinal ideas as to how to close this other kind of gap.

Three myths about the Spanish multinationals

There are three widely held, albeit somewhat inaccurate, beliefs about the remarkable process of internationalization of Spanish firms over the last decade: (1) the process was driven by the adventurous investments of a small cadre of "new conquistadors"; (2) Spanish firms have invested mainly in Latin America, the reason being the shared language and culture; and (3) Spanish foreign direct investment is "anomalous" (and perhaps doomed to ultimately fail) because Spanish firms lack the requisite technological and managerial skills to succeed in the global economy. One of the purposes of this book is to address these myths. Let me preview the reasons in turn.

The myth that the Spanish multinationals are merely brave conquistadors who did not know what they were getting themselves into, but nonetheless managed to strike gold, is completely inaccurate. First of all, most people forget that there are nearly one thousand Spanish firms with investments abroad (UNCTAD 2003:222), and while some may have made wild investment decisions, it would be

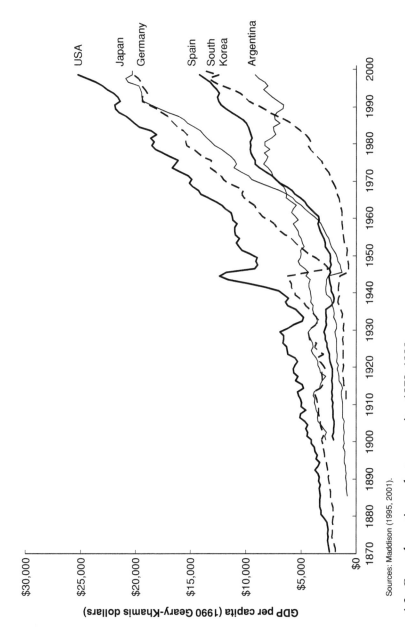

Sources: Maddison (1995, 2001).

Figure 1.2. Gross domestic product per capita, 1870–1999.

hard to believe that *all* of them were equally careless. Neither have all Spanish multinationals been able to strike gold. A second fact that undermines this myth is that dozens of articles and several books published over the last few years by Spanish and foreign scholars demonstrate that patterns of Spanish foreign investment can be readily explained with theories that also happen to account for the patterns observed for other, richer countries.[3] Thus Spain is hardly any different as far as the foreign investment decisions made by its firms are concerned.

The second belief, that Spanish foreign investment was to be expected as a "natural" projection of its firms into a linguistically and culturally similar region, such as Latin America, is simply fallacious. If that were the only, or the main, reason why Spanish firms invested abroad, why did they wait until the mid-1990s to do so? Why was Spanish investment south of the Rio Grande negligible during the period between the loss of Cuba and Puerto Rico back in 1898 and the early 1990s? There is, in addition, another fallacy related to this myth, namely, that most Spanish foreign investment has had Latin America as its destination. In fact, only 43 percent of net investment since 1993 has had Spain's former colonies as its destination, 60 percent if one excludes holding companies from the data (Fernández-Otheo Ruiz 2003:74; see also Fernández 2003). The European Union accounts for another 43 percent of net investment. (Moreover, since 1997 more than one third of Spanish investment in Latin America has arrived in Brazil, a *Portuguese*-speaking country that represents 40 percent of the region's economy. Far more Spanish entrepreneurs and managers speak English than Portuguese.) Clearly, a common language and culture help in managing foreign subsidiaries, transferring products and services, and relocating expatriate executives and their families. Language and culture can be *facilitators*, but they can hardly be the main reason, or a prime cause, why Spanish firms invested some $90,000 million over ten years in the region. It is also worth considering that the reaction of the stock market has been more

---

[3] See, among others: Alguacil and Orts (2002); Campa and Guillén (1996a, 1996b, 1999); García Blandón (2001); García Canal (1996); García Canal, Valdés Llaneza, and Ariño Martín (2003); García Canal and Valdés Llaneza (1997); Guillén (2001c); López Duarte and García Canal (1998, 2001, 2002a, 2002b); and Molero (1998).

positive in the case of investments in OECD countries other than in Latin America (López Duarte and García Canal 2003), probably because of the higher risk associated with operating in emerging economies.

The third myth strikes at the heart of a major problem looming large over Spain's future: the relatively weak technological capabilities of a country that nonetheless aspires to be rich and influential on the global stage. It is indisputably true that Spanish firms account for a tiny fraction of worldwide patents, and that the country devotes meager resources to R&D (less than 1 percent of GDP). However, more than half of Spanish foreign direct investment is in banking, public utilities, telecommunication services, and construction, activities in which managerial know-how and "project-execution capabilities" are more important than technology, which can be readily acquired in the marketplace (Amsden and Hikino 1994). Besides, successful multinationals tend to possess proprietary assets, of which technology is just one. Another important source of proprietary competitive advantage is brands, and Spanish firms do have valuable trademarks (see chapter 8). Lastly, it is important to remember that aggregate figures are always misleading: there are Spanish firms at the leading edge of technological innovation, especially in metals, industrial machinery, and transportation equipment and components, as identified by an OECD study published just before the beginning of Spain's outward foreign investment boom (Archibugi and Pianta 1992). Like any "normal" country, Spain has specialized in certain technological areas, although the process is still in its infancy.

Dunning and Narula (1994) proposed that the relationship between foreign direct investment, on the one hand, and the ownership, location, and internalization (OLI) factors that underpin foreign investment decisions, on the other, changes according to the country's stage of economic development and sophistication. In other words, the relative weights and roles of the three elements of the OLI or eclectic approach to international production vary as countries (and their firms) become richer, shift from natural to created assets, and become more embedded in the world economy (Dunning 1979, 1981, 1988).

In 1996, José Manuel Campa and I stated that "the case of Spain may be taken as representing a group of middle-income countries that, in spite of being early industrializers and having achieved relatively high standards of living, have not moved far in what has been termed the 'investment development path'" (Campa and Guillén 1996a:207). At the time, Spain was still receiving more FDI than it was sending to the rest of the world. Spain's attractiveness to foreign investors up until the mid-1990s had to do with what Dunning and Narula (1994) call natural assets, such as relatively cheap labor and a large domestic market. The very scarcity of created assets such as brands and technology was said to be preventing outward FDI from reaching higher levels. However, the phenomenal increase in foreign investment by Spanish firms since the mid-1990s does not seem to fit the predictions of the investment development path in that Spain has become a fully developed country from the theory's point of view, while lagging seriously behind other major countries in terms of technological and marketing expertise.

The (recent) history of Spanish foreign direct investment

As is true of many other countries, the FDI cycle in Spain has historically been affected by domestic political events and upheavals as well as by economic developments.[4] Liberal trade policies in the mid-nineteenth century set the stage for the arrival of French, Belgian, and (after 1870) British investments in railways, mining, wineries, banking, insurance, and public utilities. The return of protectionism and legal restrictions to foreign investment after 1891 slowed down the inflows. Meanwhile, Spanish investments abroad paled by comparison, with Cuba and Argentina as the major destinations (Tortella 1994:128–34; Nadal 1975:25–53, 87–121).

The 1920s witnessed the rise of American, German, and French investment in electrical machinery, chemicals, autos, and telecommunications despite growing restrictions on foreign investment and trade (Campillo 1963). Over this early period of industrialization, Spain attracted foreign investment at increasing rates, albeit with many ups and downs dictated by political financial, or economic crises. Most of these early inflows of FDI had to do with the exploitation of either natural assets such as mineral deposits and unique agricultural products (wines in particular), or the development of the markets for

---

[4] This section relies heavily on Campa and Guillén (1996a).

transportation, communication, banking, insurance, and basic industrial goods. During the first two decades of the century, Spanish investment abroad was negligible except for the mostly speculative flows during World War I.

The Great Depression was shallower in Spain than elsewhere in Europe or America, but nonetheless devastating for FDI. The Civil War of 1936–9 represented a further setback to foreign investment and trade. After the war, the authoritarian government of General Franco became dominated by a group of populist and staunchly nationalist economic policy-makers who implemented a series of foreign-exchange controls and protectionist measures, and encouraged import-substitution investments in industry, while the Allied powers imposed a trade embargo that remained fully in place until the late 1940s. A restriction of foreign ownership to a maximum of 25 percent, the overvaluation of the currency, the intricate system of multiple exchange rates, mounting inflation, and economic stagnation provoked capital flight and close to zero inward FDI. However, Spanish firms did invest abroad in mining and construction projects, especially in Morocco and some Latin American countries.

From liberalization to EU membership, 1959–1986

The liberal economic reforms of 1959 assigned foreign capital several roles to play: supplementing the meager level of domestic savings, generating much-needed hard currency, and facilitating technology transfers (Varela Parache et al. 1972; Muñoz et al. 1978:45–60). The reformers also introduced changes into the protectionist regime: very steep tariff barriers were substituted for non-tariff barriers to trade. The punitive taxation of imports of industrial and consumer goods in a domestic market of considerable growth potential attracted inward FDI during the 1959–73 period. During the 1960s and early 1970s, annual inward FDI flows ranged between 0.15 and 0.59 percent of GDP, while outward FDI stayed under 0.10 percent of GDP, i.e. twenty-five to thirty times smaller than inward FDI. By the mid-1970s, and despite the reduction in foreign activity in Spain, inward investment was still about four times higher than outward investment.

Spanish investments abroad during the 1960s had to do with: (1) the access to raw materials (uranium, paper pulp, petroleum, various metals, fisheries), (2) the creation of distribution channels for Spanish fish, beverages, and food products, (3) construction and engineering projects (especially in Latin America and the Arab world), and (4) banking. Manufacturing FDI based on firm-specific advantages was not significant until the early 1970s. While manufacturing investments were initially worth 20 percent of total outward FDI, by the mid-1970s they represented nearly 40 percent. Firms in the chemical, paper, mechanical, electro-mechanical, textile, and beverage industries invested in manufacturing activities abroad (COCINB 1973:25; Muñoz et al. 1978:352–3). Most analysts agree that the government did little to facilitate outward FDI during this period. Exchange controls were too tight and state subsidies to help create distribution channels abroad were not very effective (Varela Parache et al. 1972; Moreno Moré 1975:106–7). One destination of intense Spanish outward FDI in the early and mid-1970s was the relatively depressed French department of the Pyrénées Orientales (the historic Roussillon), to the north of one of Spain's most developed industrial regions, Catalonia (Castellvi 1973; Raurich et al. 1973). Catalan firms in the textile, clothing, appliance, chemical, beverage, and food-processing industries invested there to secure access to the European Common Market, given that the 1970 Preferential Agreement with Spain failed to significantly reduce tariffs for labor-intensive manufactured goods. This specific location was selected for its geographical proximity and relatively lower labor costs than in other European areas.

The world economic crisis of 1973 and the Spanish transition to democracy after 1975 slowed down FDI. By the late 1970s, however, both outward and inward flows resumed their upward trend, albeit with significant annual ups and downs until the mid-1980s due to the second oil shock, the 1981 world recession, and the initial uncertainty over the Socialist Party's electoral victory in 1982. In 1985 outward and inward flows represented 0.16 and 1.00 percent of GDP, respectively, more than three times the rates for the early 1970s. This upward trend since the mid-1970s was in part facilitated by regulatory changes. The agencies that had tightly controlled foreign transactions since the 1940s were dismantled as the Ministry of Commerce assumed the authority over foreign investment authorization and control (De Erice 1975). In 1973–4 and 1976–7 procedures for inward FDI were clarified and simplified (Muñoz et al. 1978:45–60), while similar changes were introduced for outward FDI beginning with the first comprehensive legislation of 1973 and several liberalizing decrees in 1978 (De Erice 1975; Marín 1982; Aguilar Fernández-Hontoria 1985; Nueno Iniesta et al. 1981).

EU membership and the inward FDI boom, 1986–1992

The 1986–92 period featured economic liberalization in the context of membership of the European Union (EU), rapid economic growth (by 1992 Spain's per capita income was 80 percent of the UK's), expansion of private enterprises in both manufacturing and services, huge inflows of FDI peaking at 4.2 percent of GDP in 1991, and the coming of age of outward FDI, towering also in 1991 at 1.2 percent of GDP. Membership of the EU has meant that both the origin of inward FDI and the destination of outward FDI accounted for by other EU countries has almost doubled to roughly two-thirds of the total, compared to between 30 and 50 percent prior to 1986 (Secretaría de Estado de Comercio 1993:228–33). Flows from the United States or to Latin America fell in relative terms, while destinations such as France, the Netherlands, and Portugal became increasingly popular with Spanish firms. Outside Europe, Morocco attracted manufacturing investment, but Japan remained a minor source or destination of FDI (Portillo 1994).

Most of the surge in outward FDI after 1986 took place in industries such as public utilities, telecommunications, and financial services. Outward manufacturing FDI as a percentage of GDP trebled after the mid-1970s. Acquisitions were more common than greenfield operations. Since 1988 most Spanish acquisitions abroad have taken place in Latin America and the EU, targeting firms in utilities, banking, plastics, and oil and gas (Durán Herrera 1992:227–8). The goals sought by outward investments prior to 1992 were, in decreasing order of importance, market access, asset-seeking, factor-seeking, and, lastly, investments related to the procurement of raw materials. By comparison, between 1975 and 1978 investments in search of cheaper labor or raw materials were four times higher than market-seeking FDI (Nueno Iniesta 1981:152–3).

Despite the increase in outward FDI between 1986 and 1992, inward investment stole the show, with much of its fast growth taking place through acquisitions of Spanish firms. The most active acquirers were firms based in the UK and France, while the most targeted industries were food, beverages, chemicals, and pharmaceuticals (Durán Herrera 1992:227). One important difference from outward FDI was the relative importance and growth of manufacturing investment. Inward manufacturing FDI increased after the mid-1980s although less rapidly than total inward FDI, and its share of the total fluctuated annually between 35 and 65 percent. Given that the Spanish economy was becoming less protected, many of these acquisitions had to do with other kinds of barriers of entry defined at the industry level of analysis, including difficulties in accessing distribution channels.

Coming of age at the turn of the century

As chapters 4 and 5 will explain in detail, the coming into force of the European Single Act in January 1993 set in motion a chain of events leading Spanish firms to look for growth opportunities abroad, especially in Latin America and the rest of the European Union. During the 1998–2001 period, Spanish firms invested abroad in financial services (20 percent of the total), transportation and telecommunications (19 percent), energy, water, and oil (18 percent), marketing and distribution (13 percent), and manufacturing (13 percent). Overall, services came to account for two-thirds of net Spanish investments abroad. Still, starting in 1998 Spanish firms have invested in foreign manufacturing plants more than foreign firms have invested in manufacturing plants in Spain. In fact, in 1999 and 2000 there was a net divestiture of foreign manufacturing in Spain while outward manufacturing investment skyrocketed.

As mentioned above, Latin America and the rest of the European Union account for 40–44 percent of total outward investment each, depending on the year. In Latin America, only 7 percent of all net investments by Spanish firms between 1993 and 2001 have been in manufacturing. In the European Union, by contrast, the proportion has been 38 percent. Investment in the United States has fluctuated between an average of 7 percent of the total in the 1990s and almost 15 percent in 2000–2. Asia accounts for less than 1 percent of Spanish investment. Within Latin America, Brazil has become the leading destination of Spanish investment (more than one-third of the total in the region), with Argentina a strong second (30 percent of the total), followed by Chile and Mexico at 11 percent each (Fernández-Otheo

2003:68, 74, 76, 78, 86–7).[5] By the turn of the century, the international presence of Spanish firms had consolidated in two main areas – the European Union and Latin America – and in a wide array of service and manufacturing industries.

Plan for the book

In spite of the fact that no more than two-thirds of total Spanish direct investment has gone to Latin American countries or had to do with recently deregulated and/or privatized industries, most available research monographs on the subject of the Spanish multinationals have exclusively dealt with those countries and sectors. Toral (2001) offers the most theoretically grounded analysis, while Chislett (2003), in a more descriptive vein, devotes some attention to the consequences of the rise of the Spanish multinational firm. Casilda Béjar (2002) and Giráldez Pidal (2002) are perhaps the best treatments of the context in which Spanish firms invested in Latin America. More balanced in geographical coverage, though less analytical, is the study by the Cátedra SCH (2003). Like those focused on Latin America, however, it does not fully address the consequences of the massive wave of Spanish foreign investments. Lastly, Durán and his collaborators (Durán 1996, 1997, 1999) offer a range of company case studies. None of these books ascertains in a systematic way the impact that government policies have had on Spanish outward foreign investments, and vice versa.

In their books on the Spanish economy during the twentieth century, economic historians have noticed in passing the rise of outward foreign direct investment during the 1990s, without analyzing either the causes or the consequences. Only the macroeconomic risk associated with massive investments in Latin America has deserved their attention (García Delgado and Jiménez 2001:186; Tortella 1994).

This book's treatment of both the causes and the consequences of Spanish outward direct investment shifts back and forth between the business and government sectors. Equipped with the theoretical apparatus developed in the second chapter, and based on statistical

---

[5] Statistical data on Spanish foreign direct investment can be found at www. mcx.es. A discussion of sources of data appears in Merino de Lucas and Muñoz Guarasa (2002).

information, archival material, secondary sources, and over a hundred interviews with key decision-makers, I document and explain the process by which different types of Spanish firms have become multinational in scope, and assess the consequences for the country and for Europe as a whole. In chapter 2 I review the main theories of the multinational enterprise, concluding that they explain very well why and how Spanish firms invested abroad. After the two introductory chapters, Part I of the book focuses on the phenomenon of multinational firms and its causes. Chapter 3 analyzes in depth the reasons why family-controlled firms and worker-owned cooperatives have pursued foreign markets and production opportunities, while chapter 4 deals with the large multinationals in oligopolistic sectors such as energy, water, telecommunications, and oil and gas. Chapter 5 specifically deals with the international expansion of the Spanish banks because of its peculiar implications for the role of the country in global finance.

Part II of the book addresses the consequences. Chapter 6 assesses Spain's new financial role in the global economy and the impact of the crisis in Argentina, while chapter 7 focuses on the foreign-policy implications. Chapter 8 deals with the continuing image problems that beset Spanish firms and brands when competing abroad. The relatively subdued response elicited by public opinion and by the labor unions is documented and analyzed in chapter 9. Finally, chapter 10 summarizes the overall evidence and argument, suggesting future evolutionary paths and policies to enhance Spain's chances of becoming a country that truly counts in the global arena. While my overarching goal is purely to make a contribution to scholarship, to what we know about both multinationals in general and Spanish multinationals in particular, a sound, theoretically driven analysis of the consequences of the phenomenal international expansion of Spanish firms has the potential for providing the foundations for making political and policy choices. I also wish to contribute to this debate.

2 | Theories of the multinational firm

> Control of the foreign enterprise is desired
> in order to remove competition between
> that foreign enterprise and enterprises in
> other countries. Or the control is desired in
> order to appropriate fully the returns on
> certain skills and abilities.
>
> Stephen Hymer (1960: 25)

B EFORE we are in a position to assess the strengths and weaknesses of Spanish firms, and of their process of international expansion, one must review why multinationals exist, how they operate worldwide, and what the consequences of their activities are. Thus, in this chapter I review the most important theories of the multinational firm. Drawing on economics, management theory, sociology, and political science, I review the reasons that lead firms to invest abroad, the strategic-organizational arrangements that they put in place in order to do business around the world, and the political and sociological impact of their operations.[1]

No matter what their home country, multinational firms are a peculiar form of organization. By straddling different countries, they come into contact with a variety of institutional contexts. Understanding the reasons for their existence is a necessary step prior to assessing the consequences of their actions. The key insight is that the multinational firm possesses certain kinds of advantages that set it apart from purely domestic firms. In reviewing a variety of theories, I wish to establish the economic advantages of the multinational firm, describe the various strategies and organizational structures that can be used to maximize its advantages relative to local firms in the foreign countries in which it operates, and outline the various sociopolitical issues that it needs to attend to in order to successfully operate in a foreign market.

---

[1] Parts of this chapter draw on Guillén (2001a, 2001b).

The multinational firm is one of the most pervasive types of firm in the global economy. If we define it as a firm with assets or employees in more than one country, there are more than 60,000 companies in the world that qualify as multinationals, and they control nearly a million subsidiaries worldwide. Some of them are relatively small, and employ fewer than 250 workers. Others are sprawling organizations with more than 250,000 employees scattered around more than 100 countries. The world's 500 largest multinationals account for about 25 percent of world product, and nearly half of total world trade. Multinationals own most of the technology in the world, and they receive about 80 percent of all technological royalties and fees. Multinationals are becoming more important relative to the size of the global economy, about three times as prominent today as twenty years ago. More than 85 percent of all multinationals are based in the rich countries of Western Europe, the US, Canada, Australia, and Japan. During the last decade, new multinationals have emerged from countries such as South Korea, Taiwan, Mexico, Argentina, Brazil, and, of course, Spain.

Managing a multinational enterprise requires a different set of conceptual tools than a purely domestic firm. In particular, it is important to understand the fundamental economic, strategic, organizational, and sociopolitical issues that have an impact on the process of international expansion of the firm, on the linkages between foreign subsidiaries and corporate headquarters in the home country, and on the relationship between the multinational firm and interest groups in the foreign countries, including the government, labor unions, and suppliers.

Economic advantages of the multinational firm

Multinational firms exist because certain economic conditions make it possible for a firm to profitably undertake production of a good or service in a foreign location. It is important to distinguish between vertical and horizontal foreign expansion in order to fully understand the basic economic principles that underlie the activities of multinational firms. Vertical expansion occurs when the firm locates assets or employees in a foreign country with the purpose of securing the production of a raw material or input (backward vertical expansion) or the distribution and sale of a good or service (forward vertical expansion). The necessary condition for the occurrence of an act of vertical expansion by a multinational firm is that there is a comparative advantage in the foreign location. The advantage typically has to do with the prices and productivities of production factors such as capital, labor, or land. For instance, a clothing firm might consider production in a foreign location due to lower labor costs, as many Spanish firms in this industry have done, especially in the Maghrib.

It is important, though, to realize that the mere existence of a comparative advantage in a foreign location does not mean that the firm ought to expand vertically. The necessary condition of lower factor costs or higher factor productivity, or both, is not sufficient. After all, the firm may benefit from the comparative advantage in the foreign location simply by asking a local producer to become its supplier. The sufficient condition justifying the act of foreign investment by the firm refers to the possible reasons encouraging the firm to undertake foreign production by itself rather than rely on others to do the job. The main two reasons are uncertainty about the supply or asset specificity. If uncertainty is high, the firm would prefer to integrate backward into the foreign location so as to make sure that the supply chain functions smoothly, and that delivery timetables are met. Asset specificity is high when the firm and the foreign supplier need to develop joint assets in order for the supply operation to take place. In that situation the firm would prefer to expand backward in order to avoid the "hold-up" problem, i.e. opportunistic behavior on the part of the foreign supplier trying to extract rents from the firm. The cases of Spanish oil and fishing companies lacking the needed natural resources in the home country are good examples of backward vertical expansion. These necessary and sufficient conditions also apply in the case of forward vertical expansion into a foreign location. Uncertainty and asset specificity with, say, a foreign distributor, would compel the firm to take things into its own hands and invest in the foreign location in order to make sure that the goods or services reach the buyer in the appropriate way and at a reasonable cost. The distribution investments by Spanish consumer-goods firms in the European Union would be an example of forward vertical expansion. These relationships are summarized in figure 2.1

Horizontal expansion occurs when the firm sets up a plant or service delivery facility in a foreign location with the goal of selling in that market, and without abandoning production of the good or service in

Type of foreign expansion:	Necessary conditions for the existence of the MNE	Sufficient conditions for the existence of the MNE
Vertical	• Cost and productivity of production factors (theory of comparative advantage)	• Asset specificity • Uncertainty
Horizontal	• Transportation costs • Trade protectionism • Exchange rate shifts • Need to customize	• Intangible assets: patents, brands, know-how, and other firm-specific skills

Adapted from: Caves (1996).

Figure 2.1. The economic view of the multinational enterprise (MNE).

the home country. The decision to engage in horizontal expansion is driven by forces different than those for vertical expansion, a point that many managers tend to forget. Production of a good or service in a foreign market is desirable in the presence of protectionist barriers, high transportation costs, unfavorable currency exchange rate shifts, or requirements for local adaptation to the peculiarities of local demand that make exporting from the home country unfeasible or unprofitable. As in the case of vertical expansion, these obstacles are merely a necessary condition for horizontal expansion, but not a sufficient one. The firm should ponder the relative merits of licensing a local producer in the foreign market against those of committing to a foreign investment. The sufficient condition for setting up a proprietary plant or service facility has to do with the possession of intangible assets – brands, technology, know-how, and other firm-specific skills – that make licensing a risky option because the licensee might appropriate, damage, or otherwise misuse the firm's assets.[2] Examples of Spanish firms that have expanded horizontally include those in telecommunications, banking, electrical appliances, and automobile components, among others.

In addition to the fundamental necessary and sufficient conditions for vertical and horizontal expansion summarized in figure 2.1, there

[2] For a summary of the basic economic model of the multinational firm, see Caves (1996). Stephen Hymer (1960) was the first to observe that firms expand horizontally to protect (and monopolize) their intangible assets.

are four other important economic aspects to the activities of multi-national firms that deserve careful attention. First, foreign investment tends to occur more frequently among firms that compete in an oligopoly in the home country. Thus, firms in highly concentrated industries such as oil, chemicals, automobiles, semiconductors, or banking have been observed to follow each other to foreign locations once one of the oligopolists makes the first move. A pattern of action–reaction or move–countermove results from the dynamics among firms in industries with only a limited number of (large) competitors. Oligopolistic reaction is driven by the fear that if the foreign investment undertaken by one of the firms in the oligopoly is not matched by the others, a permanent loss in competitive advantage might occur.[3] Examples of oligopolistic reaction in foreign direct investment abound. The "seven sisters" in the oil industry, the "big three" automobile makers in the US, Coke and Pepsi in the cola industry, the three German chemical giants (BASF, Bayer, Hoechst), and the largest banks in the Netherlands (ABN, AMRO, ING), Spain (BBVA and Santander), or Switzerland (Credit Suisse, Swiss Bank, UBS) have over the years made foreign investment decisions driven by oligopolistic reaction. A number of other Spanish firms also conform to this pattern (see chapters 4 and 5).

A second important economic aspect of the multinational firm is that the process of foreign expansion is often, though not always, driven by product life-cycle dynamics. Firms tend to come up with ideas for new products and services based on stimuli coming from their home markets. They do not pursue foreign markets until the home market has become saturated. Given that the good or service reflects features of the home market, the firm pursues foreign opportunities in a sequential way, targeting first those foreign markets that are most similar to the home market. The reason is that it is in relatively similar foreign markets that home-grown innovations are most likely to succeed and be profitable. One important implication of this way of looking at foreign expansion is that the firm ought to approach it as an incremental, gradual, one-step-at-a-time process. Thus multinational firms would be wise to increase their commitment

---

[3] The classic statement of the oligopolistic reaction thesis appears in Hymer (1960). The most complete elaboration is by Knickerbocker (1973).

to foreign markets slowly, starting perhaps by exporting, considering licensing before they set up a plant, and building up their knowledge and presence in foreign markets over time (Vernon 1979). It is important to note that the slow and cautious process of foreign expansion derived from product life-cycle theory may not be appropriate when the firm competes in an oligopoly, or when the industry is characterized by strong first-mover advantages due to technological or marketing peculiarities. Under these circumstances, moving fast may be a more appropriate response. A large number of Spanish firms have expanded abroad following the dynamics of the product life-cycle, especially those in the consumer-goods industries.

One of the most intriguing aspects of the recent internationalization of Spanish firms is utterly consistent with the product life-cycle approach. In many instances, the first Spanish firm in a given industry to expand abroad was not the largest one but the underdog. Thus, the internationalization of Spanish sparkling wines was pioneered by Freixenet, still wines by Miguel Torres, foodstuffs by Nutrexpa and Viscofán, confectionery by Chupa Chups, autoparts by Ficosa, electrical appliances by Fagor, steel by Acerinox, pharmaceuticals by Ferrer Internacional, magazines by Hola, banking by Santander, ground transportation by ALSA, construction and concessions by Ferrovial, clothing by Cortefiel, and railway rolling stock by Patentes Talgo. None of these firms was the largest in their respective industry in Spain at the time they started to internationalize. Often, however, they grew so quickly that they eventually surpassed their larger domestic competitors on the basis of their worldwide operations and sales. To be sure, there are several exceptions to this pattern (e.g. Telefónica, Repsol, Tabacalera, Pescanova). Still, the "underdog hypothesis" merits special attention because it demonstrates that access to foreign resources and exposure to international competition often lead to enhanced competitiveness in the long run.

A third distinctive economic aspect of multinational firms is that they may benefit from their "multinationality" in that it is only firms with operations in several countries that can use their network of subsidiaries to arbitrage differences in prices or adverse shocks, such as a sudden currency realignment. From this point of view, multinational firms ought to consider foreign expansion as a process by which the firm acquires "real" options. Like financial options, real options give the firm the right, but not the obligation, to use an asset in the future. Real options are particularly valuable under conditions of uncertainty. One important implication of an options-based theory of the multinational firm is that the option value of a foreign plant or service delivery facility is higher the greater the uncertainty associated with the foreign location. This logic runs contrary to the traditional prescription that the multinational firm ought to calculate country risks carefully, and either avoid dangerous locations or protect itself against the possible materialization of the risk. According to the real-options perspective, however, the firm will benefit from exposing itself to uncertainty and volatility (Kogut and Kulatilaka 1994). It is per-haps a bit too early to ascertain whether Spanish firms with extensive global operations are benefiting from their multinationality in the sense that real-options theory suggests.

Finally, the economic literature on the multinational firm has de-voted a great deal of attention to the issue of the mode of entry into foreign markets, which varies in terms of the degree of control that the firm exercises over its foreign subsidiaries: alliances with a foreign partner, minority joint ventures (or partial acquisitions), majority joint ventures, and wholly owned acquisitions or greenfield investments. In the case of vertical expansion, the firm will prefer a greater degree of control the higher the asset specificity and/or the uncertainty. In the case of horizontal expansion, it will prefer greater control the more valuable and difficult it is to protect its proprietary intangible assets (Caves 1996). Product life-cycle theory also makes a contribution to entry-mode choice by arguing that firms will progressively shift from less to more control as they accumulate experience (Vernon 1979; see also Aharoni 1966; Johanson and Vahlne 1977).

The economic theory of the multinational firm outlined above explains patterns of Spanish outward foreign direct investment very well, as recent empirical research has shown. The higher the level of intangible assets and the size of the firm, the more it invests abroad and the more control it exercises over foreign operations (Campa and Guillén 1996b, 1999; García Blandón 2001; García Canal 1996; García Canal and Valdés Llanza 1997; García Canal, Valdés Llanza and Ariño Martín 2003; López Duarte and García Canal 2001, 2002a, 2002b; Molero 1998). These findings hold regardless of whether the empirical data were collected cross-sectionally or longitu-dinally, at the level of the investment project, the firm, or the industry. In addition, using aggregate data at the industry level, Campa and

Guillén (1996a) confirmed that Spanish firms that invest abroad to
acquire assets they find lacking in Spain do so in countries that are
more advanced, that they look for natural assets in countries that lack
created assets, and that they invest in distribution channels in countries to which they export. Thus, we do not need a Spanish theory of
the multinational firm in order to understand why Spanish firms have
invested abroad. Readily available theory, which explains patterns for
firms in other countries, does a beautiful job.

Strategic-organizational configurations of the multinational firm

All multinational firms need to make two fundamental strategic decisions in order to ensure that they have a competitive advantage over
purely domestic firms. First, the firm must decide where to locate
assets and employees. This decision can be fruitfully approached from
an economic perspective, as summarized in figure 2.1, and will lead
the firm to be more or less geographically dispersed throughout the
world. Second, the firm must decide whether its operations dispersed
throughout the world need to be managerially coordinated or not.
Depending on the degrees of geographical dispersion and organizational coordination, the firm will adopt one of four possible strategies
(see figure 2.2a).[4]

The simplest strategy for a multinational firm is to be a global
exporter (cell 1 in figure 2.2a). This strategy entails a relatively low
degree of dispersion (the firm produces in one country) and a high
degree of coordination of the marketing and sales activities that the
firm undertakes with its own employees in foreign markets. If foreign
markets are very different from each other the firm may think about
an exporter strategy with decentralized marketing, whereby production is still largely concentrated in the home country but marketing
and sales managers in foreign markets are given autonomy so that they
can adapt to local market conditions in terms of price, advertising,
promotion, and service (cell 2). Functional organizational structures –
in which purchasing, manufacturing, sales, and service are the key
departments – or worldwide product divisions are the ideal organizational structures to pursue an exporting strategy. Many Spanish

[4] For the full exposition of this approach, see Porter (1987).

(a) The Dispersion-coordination framework

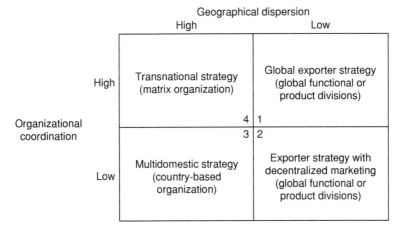

Adapted from: Porter (1997: 27–5).

(b) The integration-responsiveness framework

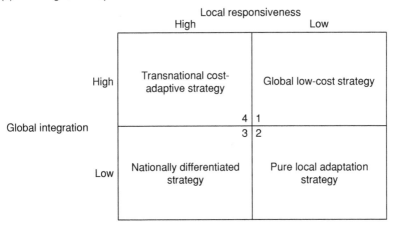

Adapted from: Prahalad and Doz (1987).

Figure 2.2. The strategic view of the multinational enterprise (MNE).

multinational firms in the consumer-goods industries have adopted this strategy.

If the multinational firm, however, needs to disperse operations because of the necessary and sufficient conditions identified in figure 2.1, then the issue of coordination of the dispersed activities calls for managerial attention. A multidomestic strategy enables the firm to focus on local adaptation because cross-border organizational coordination is kept to a minimum (cell 3). The downside is, of course, that many activities will be replicated in each country and redundancies may proliferate, with the associated escalation in costs. Multidomestic strategies are best implemented with a country-based organizational structure in which self-standing national subsidiaries are headed by an autonomous country manager. Many Spanish firms operating in Latin America – especially those in regulated industries that are very different from country to country – follow the multidomestic strategy. Finally, a transnational strategy allows the multinational to simultaneously pursue local adaptation and global coordination (cell 4). This strategy, however, requires a complicated matrix structure in order to work.[5] Few, if any, Spanish firms have made an effort to become transnationals.

The managerial tradeoffs between the various strategy-structure configurations in figure 2.2a are important to note. Exporting strategies based on functional or product divisional structures are relatively simple but inflexible in response to changes in the economic or political environment (e.g. a sudden currency realignment or a regulatory change). Multidomestic strategies and country-based organizational structures help the firm adapt to local circumstances but are limited when it comes to learning and cost control. Finally, transnational strategies based on the matrix organizational structure are costly and conflict-prone, but very good at gathering and integrating information from various locations.

The tension between local responsiveness and global integration can be more thoroughly examined with the diagram in figure 2.2b Multinationals are presented as organizations designed to strike some kind of a balance between two conflicting sets of demands. On the one hand, every multinational firm needs to deliver what the customer wants, even if this requires costly local adaptation and responsiveness. On the other, multinational firms seek to improve the efficiency of their operations by integrating across borders so as not to be outperformed by local players in each national market (Prahalad and Doz 1987).

---

[5] For a discussion of the virtues and pitfalls of a transnational strategy based on the matrix structure, see Bartlett and Ghoshal (1989).

When adapting to local peculiarities represents the key competitive advantage, and few gains can be obtained from global integration (because national markets are large enough to reap the benefits of economies of scale, for instance), multinational firms pursue a strategy of national differentiation (cell 3 in figure 2.2b). Branded packaged goods such as consumer non-durables, food, and beer are good examples of this situation. Product or service characteristics, however, may be such that there is no real need to be locally responsive, while efficiency pressures on a global scale are the main source of competitive advantage. Consumer electronics products tend to be presented as an example of this situation. Firms in this industry tend to adopt a strategy geared towards global integration in order to achieve cost reductions and be able to invest large sums of money on R&D (cell 1). Cells 1 and 3 in figure 2.2b pose no intrinsic managerial dilemma to the extent that competitive advantage derives only from global integration, or only from local responsiveness.

When both integration and responsiveness are equally important sources of competitive advantage, then the firm needs to strike a strategic and operational balance between the two (cell 4). The telecommunications equipment industry is generally presented as an example of such competing demands on the firm. Finally, when neither local responsiveness nor global integration provide competitive advantage, a strategy of pure local adaptation is generally followed, the example being commodity products such as cement (cell 2; see Guillén 2002).

Sociopolitical aspects of the multinational firm

Managing a multinational firm requires not only realizing its economic advantages and adopting an appropriate strategy-structure configuration, but also understanding the role that its foreign subsidiaries play in the foreign countries in which it operates. Local actors such as the government, labor unions, suppliers, and the community have tended to keep a critical eye on foreign multinationals because of their unrivaled ability to develop technology, reap economies of scale, avoid high wages, reduce transaction costs, shift from saturated to emerging markets, exploit tax loopholes, and leverage their power in negotiations with governments, labor unions, local communities, suppliers, and customers. Spanish firms, especially those operating in Latin America, are confronting these issues on a daily basis.

There is one important contrast between advanced and developing countries that needs to be borne in mind. The debate over the presence of foreign multinationals tends to be more heated in developing countries than in advanced ones. There are three main reasons for this. First, developing countries tend to be rich in natural resources and/or cheap labor that multinationals find lacking in their home countries. This resource asymmetry typically results in conflicts over how to divide up the pie between the providers of natural resources or labor, on the one hand, and the owners of technology and capital, on the other. Second, during the post-World War II period many developing countries were ruled by authoritarian regimes. Dictatorships tend to repress labor and mollify its political and economic demands, in part to satisfy local and foreign business interests. There is hard evidence, for example, indicating that multinationals obtain higher rates of return in developing countries ruled by an authoritarian regime than in those in which the political system is democratic. In addition, the presence of multinationals frequently boosts the international legitimacy of an unpopular authoritarian regime. Not surprisingly, labor unions in countries ruled by authoritarian regimes often accuse the government of allying itself with the multinationals for mutual gain. The fact that most multinationals tend to be headquartered in democratic countries tends to add insult to injury. And, third, developing countries often perceive multinationals as limiting national sovereignty or being the agents of neocolonialism.

Only a thorough understanding of the role that multinationals play in different development contexts can guarantee an effective management of the relationships between the local subsidiary and local interest groups. Two dimensions are especially relevant to understanding the level and operational mode of multinational activity in a given host country. The first dimension is whether the host government's economic strategy pursues export-led growth or import substitution. Under export-led growth, costs and incentives are aligned so that local production is competitive in global markets in terms of either price or quality, or both. Under import substitution the goal is to generate economic growth by replacing imports with local production. The second dimension is whether policies toward foreign multinationals are permissive or restrictive. For example, host governments often restrict multinational activity by imposing a certain level of domestic ownership, limiting profit repatriation, demanding minimum local

Policies towards MNEs	Strategy of economic development	
	Export-led growth	Import substitution
Permissive	Foreign MNEs seen as "partners" in outward oriented economic development. Acquisitions in mature industries. Wholly-owned in growth industries. MNE labor requirements: Flexibility, skill formation, stability. 4	Foreign MNEs seen as "necessary evils" in the effort to sustain and deepen import-substitution. Joint ventures (JVs) in mature industries. Wholly-owned or JVs in growth industries. MNE labor requirements: Enhanced purchasing power, stability. 1
Restrictive	3 Foreign MNEs seen as "arm's length collaborators" to obtain the technology and marketing skill needed to increase exports. Export Processing Zones (XPZs). Manufacturing contracts (OEM); Minority JVs. MNE labor requirements: Low wages, docility, union avoidance.	2 Foreign MNEs seen as "villains" to be avoided so as to preserve national sovereignty and independence. Exodus of MNEs in the face of hostile incentives, expropriations or nationalizations.

FDI: Foreign direct investment.   SMEs: Small and medium enterprises.
JVs: Joint ventures.   SOEs: State-owned enterprises.
MNEs: Multinational enterprises.   XPZs: Export processing zones.
OEM: Original equipment manufacturing.   Adapted from Guillén (2001c).

Figure 2.3. The sociopolitical view of the multinational enterprise (MNE).

product content and technological transfers, or requiring production to be exported. figure 2.3 lays out the four contexts that result from cross-classifying these two dimensions, each associated with a different view, image, or ideology about the multinational firm (Haggard 1990; Guillén 2001c).

Import-substitution policies can be accompanied by permissive or liberal foreign investment policies (cell 1 in figure 2.3). In this situation multinationals gain access to a protected domestic market in exchange for import-substituting investments that create jobs and save hard currency. The arrival of foreign multinationals to invest jointly with local businesses as "necessary evils" is justified because import-substitution in growth or new industries – e.g. automobiles or electronics – usually requires technology and capital that the average developing country lacks. The cases of Indonesia and Spain during the 1940s and 1950s, or of India, Brazil, Argentina, and Mexico until the early 1980s illustrate this situation. In this context, multinationals expect an industrial relations system that promotes adequate levels of purchasing power inside the protected domestic market, given that exports of local production are not encouraged. However, multinationals attracted to an import-substitution environment will rarely make the most innovative products, transfer the most sophisticated technology, or spend large sums on worker training given that trade protection allows them to sell at high prices and thus obtain large profit margins even with mature or plainly obsolete products. The multinationals' readiness to enter into coalitions with other inward-looking interest groups to preserve protectionist measures or even to perpetuate friendly governments in power regardless of their legitimacy may also cause tensions with labor unions, which feel excluded from the political process.

Countries pursuing an import-substitution strategy sometimes give way to nationalist sentiment and prevent multinationals from operating in the country. They justify such policies by reference to autarkical versions of dependency and world-system theories. This is the situation captured by cell 2 of figure 2.3. Countries as diverse in their resource endowments as Argentina, Venezuela, Mexico, or India periodically adopted utterly restrictive policies towards the multinationals. In this situation, multinationals are depicted as "villains" that plunder the country's riches, thwarting its economic potential and limiting its national sovereignty. Typical policy initiatives are expropriations of the subsidiaries of foreign multinationals, especially in such highly visible industries as oil, mining or public utilities. At least in the short run, workers and their unions have often celebrated the wage increases and enhanced job security afforded by state ownership, especially when compared to the shortsighted attitudes of multinationals under import-substitution conditions.

Like import substitution, the export-oriented strategy can also be accompanied by either permissive or restrictive policies towards the multinationals. Export-led growth with restricted foreign direct investment (cell 3) typically takes the form of export processing zones, supply contracts (original equipment manufacturing or OEM), and minority joint ventures.[6] These special arrangements allow multinationals to take advantage of the natural resources or cheap labor so plentiful in developing economies but impose on them a number of limitations on the production process and the sale of the output, as proposed by late-industrialization theory. Under such restrictive export-oriented conditions multinationals become "arm's length collaborators," precisely because the state prefers to follow a strategy of "indebted" industrialization rather than one based on the attraction of equity capital, i.e. foreign multinationals. Multinationals are attracted to this situation by low wages, labor docility, and the absence of unions. The cases of South Korea and Indonesia stand out as instances of this strategy. The emphasis on exporting products manufactured with cheap labor will often lead to friction between workers and multinationals over wages and working conditions that may escalate into serious political conflict, especially under repressive authoritarian regimes.

An export-led strategy accompanied by permissive policies towards foreign multinationals results in the "partner" image (cell 4). This context is only feasible in countries that are willing to ignore or downplay ownership issues and to pursue full integration with the global economy or trade blocs in exchange for economic growth and job creation, as preached by modernization and neoclassical theories of development. The cases of Singapore, Puerto Rico, Ireland, Spain, and, more recently, Mexico illustrate the image of multinationals as partners. Multinationals will stay in an export-oriented country only if they can develop a long-term labor strategy geared towards flexibility, skill formation, and stability, i.e. they can invest in a workforce capable of adapting to changes in the global economy. Tensions may also arise in this context. The government, labor unions, and other interest groups may feel that multinationals are not fulfilling their part of the partnership contract if they decide to cut jobs or divest altogether. Another area of friction might be acquisitions of domestic firms by multinationals, which could restrict competition in the host industry.

---

[6] Foreign firms in export-processing zones hire local workers to assemble components of foreign origin for reexport. By contrast, in an original equipment manufacturing (OEM) contract a foreign firm supplies a local company with the technology and most sophisticated components so that it can manufacture goods that the foreign firm will market under its own brand in international markets.

Case	Before investing	After investing
Extractive investments	Large and long-term investment helps MNE extract commitments from host government, unless there is competition to invest.	Balance of power shifts to host government as it learns about the production process and investment cost is sunk.
Import-substituting investments	MNE is weak because host government can decide who can establish operations inside the protected market.	Balance of power shifts to MNE as it develops links to suppliers, buyers, and joint-venture partners.
Export-oriented investments	Host government is weak if labor cost is the locational advantage; somewhat stronger if investment is capital-intensive.	Balance of power does not shift so long as locational advantages do not change, and assets are mobile (e.g. machinery).

Adapted from: Haggard (1990: 220 2).

Figure 2.4. The bargaining power of the multinational enterprise (MNE) relative to the host government in the foreign country

The conceptual scheme summarized in figure 2.3 helps us better understand the different roles that multinationals play in various country contexts. This approach can also be used to elucidate the most important issue of bargaining power between a local government and the multinational. The key idea is that the multinational possesses assets – technology, brands, capital, skills – that give it leverage to the extent that the assets are critical to the foreign subsidiary's success but are not accessible to the host country. Conversely, the host country has leverage over the foreign multinational to the extent that it possesses resources desired by the foreign investor, including a large domestic market, inexpensive and/or skilled labor, and natural resources. The host's bargaining power also increases with the degree of competition among foreign firms for access to these resources.

It is imperative to distinguish between extractive, import-substituting, and export-led foreign investments in order to fully understand the relative bargaining power of the multinational relative to the host government. In addition, the multinational's bargaining power also depends on whether the investment is already in place or not (see figure 2.4; Haggard 1990: 220–2). In extractive industries the interests of multinationals and home countries are inherently in conflict, but there is still the possibility of mutual benefit. Bargaining occurs over the distribution of the benefits. Once the initial fixed investment is made by the multinational the balance of power shifts in favor of the host-country government. When the foreign investment is in manufacturing, however, a shift in the balance of power towards the host country is less likely or occurs more slowly than in the case of extractive industries. In the case of manufacturing investments that seek to substitute local production for imports, the balance of power shifts in favor of the multinational after the investment is made because suppliers, distributors, consumers, joint-venture partners, and labor provide a political base of support for the multinational. In the case of export-oriented manufacturing investments, the balance of power favors the multinational throughout the investment cycle to the extent that such investments are relatively small and the assets involved mobile. Large fixed-asset manufacturing investments tend to give the host government a little more bargaining power after they have been undertaken (figure 2.4).

There is one last political issue associated with the multinational firm that deserves our attention because of its ramifications in the case of Spain. The branch of political science known as international relations has also made contributions to the study of the multinational firm. Much debate in this field over the last twenty years has focused on who are the key actors in international relations. Realist scholars assert that states are the only actors of importance, while multinational firms, non-governmental organizations (NGOs), international labor union confederations, and multilateral agencies (such as the UN or the IMF) are just instruments of governments or states. By contrast, the proponents of the world-politics paradigm (also referred to as international pluralism) conceive of international relations as the complex interplay between multiple actors who are relatively independent of each other. More recently, other scholars have proposed looking at international relations from a constructivist perspective, one that relegates material interests to the background and highlights shared or negotiated norms for appropriate behavior in the international arena (for a review, see Tarrow 2001).

The international-relations literature reports ample evidence of both multinationals being used by their own governments to achieve foreign-policy objectives and multinationals using their home governments to obtain certain advantages abroad, especially in countries run by authoritarian regimes (Oneal 1992). The classic example of the former is Secretary of State Henry Kissinger's policy towards the USSR, and, of the latter, ITT's role in the fall and demise of the democratically elected President of Chile in 1973 (Gilpin 1987: 231–45). Thus, there is evidence in favor of the realist, pluralist, and constructivist views. Part II of this book, on the financial, diplomatic, and social consequences of the rise of Spanish foreign direct investment, will use the insights of these theories to ascertain to what extent Spanish multinationals have changed Spain's predicament and stature in the international-relations system.

The challenges of a fast-moving global economy

Multinational firms possess certain economic advantages over purely domestic firms. Understanding the necessary and sufficient conditions to sustain those advantages over time is the first step for any multinational manager to take. Economic fundamentals, however, are not enough to successfully manage a multinational firm. Managers have to decide to what extent foreign operations need to be coordinated across borders. The key managerial dilemma facing multinational managers is that of the balance between local responsiveness and global integration. Identifying and implementing the correct strategy structure configuration in terms of responsiveness and integration is perhaps the most important task for multinational managers to accomplish. They also need to pay attention to the dynamics of the relationship between the firm and local interest groups in the foreign countries in which they operate, including the government, labor unions, suppliers, and the community. The distinction between extractive, import-substitution, and export-led investments is useful when assessing the relative bargaining power of the multinational firm over the investment cycle.

   The management of the multinational firm must obey certain fundamental economic, strategic, organizational, and sociopolitical principles. Globalization and new information technologies are not undermining such principles, but rather creating new opportunities and threats to multinational firms. Globalization has erased differences across countries because of falling trade barriers and convergence in technical standards, but also sharpened certain key political, social, and cultural differences in the world. The fact that foreign direct investment by multinational firms has increased markedly over the last two decades indicates that the effects of globalization do not affect countries uniformly – firms still find it useful and profitable to locate assets and employees in various countries, often replicating operations and creating redundancies (Guillén 2001a).

New information technologies have enabled multinationals to gather and diffuse knowledge more effectively and more quickly than in the past. An obvious consequence of this technological revolution has been the acceleration of the cycle of development and the introduction of new products in different markets throughout the world. While during the 1960s the typical multinational would take between five and ten years to introduce a new product in more than fifty national markets worldwide, today the cycle has been reduced to less than three years, and in many cases multinationals launch new products simultaneously in dozens of markets. There has also been a reduction in the time that a firm would take to have a significant share of its assets, employees, and revenues located outside its home country, as illustrated by several Spanish firms as well as many others from all over the world. In the recent past, it would take two generations of managers for the firm to fully develop its foreign operations. Nowadays, some firms become full-fledged multinationals within a few years, very quickly reaching the critical threshold of having more than half of their assets and employees outside the home country.

Clearly, the speed at which international business takes place has increased, but the basic principles governing the dynamics of foreign expansion remain relevant. In fact, multinational managers need to pay more attention to economic, strategic, and organizational imperatives than in the past because the cost of making a mistake is much higher today than it used to be twenty or thirty years ago. The cost of reversing a wrong decision – for example setting up a plant in a given foreign country, or not establishing the plant – is today much more onerous precisely because of the higher speed of international business decision-making. When the firm and its competitors move fast, mistakes are much more expensive than when things move more slowly. While the firm fixes the problem, the competitors will surge ahead. Thus avoiding mistakes – and learning from the failures as well as the successes – becomes terribly important. Only a careful consideration of the economic, strategic, organizational, and sociopolitical principles driving foreign expansion can help the firm avoid costly mistakes in a fast-moving global economy.

Managing across borders is not easy. The international dimension complicates the already difficult issues of strategy formulation and implementation in purely local firms. Multinational managers, however, should try to find and exploit the opportunities hidden in the complexities of international situations. It is precisely because multinationals tap into such opportunities that they successfully expand throughout the world, and develop a sustainable competitive advantage over local firms. The following chapters will show how Spanish firms in a variety of industries have managed to pursue international opportunities, meeting both success and failure.

PART I

The process

3 | The family-controlled and worker-owned multinationals

> Technology and specialization . . . are
> necessarily and distinctively associated with
> large-scale organizations . . . [Economic
> activity is] carried on by large-scale
> enterprises which require extensive
> coordination of managers and the managed.
> Clark Kerr et al. (1960: 21)

> I was brought up on the theory of the
> "economies of scale" – that with industries
> and firms, just as with nations, there is
> an irresistible trend, dictated by modern
> technology, for units to become ever bigger.
> Ernst F. Schumacher (1975: 64)

WHILE family firms and worker-owned cooperatives are said to have certain advantages in terms of personal incentives, commitment, loyalty, reduced agency costs (to the extent that family or cooperative members get along with each other), even altruistic behavior, they are frequently denigrated because of their alleged inability to attain enough scale to operate efficiently and to be technology leaders. Family firms and worker cooperatives are assumed to be victims of a vicious circle, in which their limited ability to raise capital prevents them from growing and from acquiring or developing the best technology; insufficient scale and lack of leading-edge technology puts them at a cost disadvantage relative to firms with other governance structures; and higher costs and shrinking earnings, to close the circle, make it hard for them to allocate enough capital to grow (for a review of the arguments and counterarguments, see Galve Górriz and Salas Fumás 2003).

It is important to note, however, that the negative impact of being family- or worker-owned can be minimized in at least four ways, which may turn these firms into formidable competitors: (1) by focusing on a niche market of sufficiently small size that a modest family firm can operate profitably; (2) by competing on the basis of quality and product differentiation as opposed to cost; (3) by listing part of the firm's equity without the family losing effective control, as happens so frequently in South Korea (Chang 2002) and other countries around the world, and in the case of cooperatives by organizing a savings bank; and (4) by collaborating with other small firms in "industrial districts" (Marshall 1919; Piore and Sabel 1984; Sabel and Zeitlin 1985) or networks (Hamilton and Biggart 1988; Perrow 1992). Some scholars argue that small firms, which are frequently family- or worker-owned, may be more flexible, adaptable, innovative, and socially desirable because they spread wealth (Schumacher 1975; Granovetter 1983; Naisbitt and Aburdene 1990; Perrow 1992; Snodgrass and Biggs 1996: 11–12). As we shall see in this chapter, many Spanish family- and worker-owned firms have apparently surmounted their scale and financing disadvantages and succeeded not just in their home country but around the world. Others, unfortunately, have not, and face formidable challenges.

For the purposes of this chapter, family firms are companies that are either owned or controlled by the members of a family, who wish to transmit ownership or control of the company from one generation to the next. Thus I am using a relatively broad definition in that a family firm can have part of its equity listed, as long as the family retains effective control. Most importantly, I am not imposing the condition that the firm be managed exclusively by the family members themselves. It could well be that professional management is in place (with or without family executives at the top), while corporate governance is fully run by the family. Following this definition, family firms account for more than half of GDP and employment in most countries around the world, and it is true that they tend to be disproportionately small in size. Whether their size inescapably puts them at a disadvantage or not is one of the key topics of this chapter.

Economic development scholars of the most varied stripes have been skeptical of the potential of family firms and worker-owned cooperatives in the global economy because of their inability to grow big enough to take advantage of technology and economies of scale. During the 1950s, modernization scholars argued that traditionalism was the main impediment to economic growth, and that development could only occur if modernizing elites – social, political, economic, financial – acted as agents of change (Kerr et al. [1960]; Rostow 1960: 4–12, 26, 31). They were adamant that "technology and specialization . . . are necessarily and distinctively associated with large-scale organizations." Economic activity is "carried on by large-scale enterprises which require extensive coordination of managers and the managed" (Kerr et al. [1960]: 21; see also Rostow 1960: 9–11, 40). Family firms and cooperatives were explicitly predicted to disappear as traditional patterns of behavior are replaced by modern ones (Kerr et al. [1960]: 67, 227). Dependency scholars, although ideologically and theoretically opposed to the modernization paradigm, pointed out that the small-scale local bourgeoisie would be swallowed by the powerful combination of the "triple alliance" of foreign capital, large-scale domestic capital, and the state (Evans 1979; see also Frank 1967; Cardoso and Faletto [1973]: 163, 174, 213). Late-industrialization scholars – who proposed Japan and South Korea as examples to emulate – also raised doubts about small-scale enterprises, although they did not take issue with family control per se (Amsden 1989; Amsden and Takashi 1994).

Neoclassical economists, for their part, with their emphasis on comparative advantage, specialization, and free exchange within and across borders have criticized both "industrial gigantism," and family or worker ownership. They see an important role for small enterprises to play, albeit merely "servicing" larger firms (Sachs 1993: 18–20, 82–3). However, as market failure is rampant in newly industrialized countries, economists expect the rise of business groups that internalize inefficient markets for managerial talent, worker skills, capital, and intermediate goods until adequate markets are developed (Caves 1989; Leff 1978, 1979).

In this chapter I review the predicament of family firms and worker cooperatives in Spain, focusing on whether their size prevents them from competing in the global economy. I will illustrate their pattern of international expansion with case studies drawn from a series of industries in which varying combinations of comparative advantage, technology, and marketing skill are the key to competition. This evidence will suggest that family firms and worker cooperatives are not necessarily at a disadvantage when it comes to pursuing opportunities in the global economy.

The predicament of family firms in Spain

Family firms abound in Spain, as in any other country. Although they tend to be relatively small, they are doing extremely well in terms of technological development, marketing know-how, and international orientation. According to the Survey of Business Strategies (ESEE), undertaken periodically by the Fundación Empresa Pública,[1] only 6 percent of manufacturing family firms in 1998 employed more than 500 people, compared to 94 percent of non-family firms. Back in 1991 slightly more than 10 percent of family firms were above that threshold, so the average size seems to be on the decrease, perhaps as more and more of the owners of relatively large family firms have sold their companies, frequently to foreigners. Interestingly, it is more likely for a family firm to surpass 500 employees early in its life (especially during its first three years) while the opposite is true for non-family firms. Family firms are more prevalent in industries characterized by strong comparative advantages of a locational kind, namely, metal working, textiles and clothing, leather and footwear, and wood and furniture, in which they represent over 40 percent of the number of firms (Galve Górriz and Salas Fumás 2003: 81–6).

Spanish family and non-family firms differ in terms of their use of capital, labor, and production technologies. Regardless of size, family firms are about 30 percent less capital intensive. They have unit labor costs that are approximately the same as for non-family firms, although they generate less value added per employee. They compensate for their lower labor productivity with lower labor unit costs. One-third of all family firms and two-thirds of those with more than 500 employees use computer-aided design. About 17 percent of all family firms use robotics and/or flexible manufacturing systems. The prevalence of these production technologies is actually higher among family firms than

---

[1] The ESEE collects information on a representative sample of manufacturing companies with ten or more employees located in Spain. The definition of family firm is based on a question asking whether members of the owning family play an executive role in the company.

non-family firms. For instance, a greater proportion of family firms with more than twenty employees use computer-aided design than non-family firms. More family firms with 51 to 500 employees use robotics or flexible manufacturing systems (Galve Górriz and Salas Fumás 2003: 108–9; see also MICYT 1992: 39, 130).

Most importantly, Spanish family firms fare well in terms of intangible assets. They make an R&D effort comparable to that of non-family firms, although they obtain somewhat inferior results. About half of all family firms undertake R&D activities (90 percent for those with more than 500 employees). Those that do R&D spend an average of 2.2 percent of sales, compared to 1.8 in the case of non-family firms. These figures are obviously low compared to those in other, more advanced countries. Slightly more than 38 percent of all family firms report having implemented production process innovations (compared to 41 percent for non-family firms); 22 percent of all family firms report having obtained a product innovation (compared to 30 percent for non-family firms); family firms, however, patent at a rate that is one-fourth that for non-family firms. Family firms with more than 500 employees spend 6.5 percent of sales on advertising, compared to just 3.1 percent for non-family firms, a difference that has widened during the late 1990s. Regardless of size, family firms spend less than non-family firms (Galve Górriz and Salas Fumás 2003: 110–11; see also González Cerdeira 1996: 34). Most importantly, the technology areas in which Spain holds a comparative advantage within the OECD – fabricated metals, industrial machinery, and transportation, primarily auto parts and railway equipment (Archibugi and Pianta 1992: 69, 76–7) – tend to be heavily populated with sophisticated family firms. Spanish medium-sized firms (300–499 employees), many of them family-owned, are also more committed to their workers, spending about 50 percent more per employee on training than either smaller or larger firms (Mineco 1994: 269, 290–4).

In part due to their proprietary technology and brands, family firms in Spain with more than 500 employees are more internationally oriented than their non-family counterparts: 18 percent of the former sell outside Spain compared to only 11 percent of the latter. They are similarly export-oriented. Those that export sell abroad 32 and 33 percent of total sales, respectively (Galve Górriz and Salas Fumás 2003: 114; see also: MICYT 1992: 63; Moreno and Rodríguez 1996: 35). In addition, medium-sized manufacturing firms have traditionally invested more in foreign production activities than larger firms, although the reverse is true when it comes to investments in distribution and sales subsidiaries (Alonso and Donoso 1994: 28–41; Campa and Guillén 1996a, 1996b, 1999; MICYT 1992: 115). As of the mid-1990s, thirty-four of the fifty largest foreign direct investors from Spain (i.e. multinationals) were family firms (Guillén 2001c: 98).

Taking into account the above figures, it should not come as a surprise that the overall performance of family firms in Spain is strikingly similar to that of their non-family counterparts. No matter what indicator of economic or financial returns is used, and taking into account differences by industry, Spanish family firms listed on the stock exchange (fifty-seven of them during the 1990s) perform at strikingly similar levels to those attained by non-family firms. As detailed econometric analyses show, family firms enjoy higher alloca-tive efficiency in the use of resources, but this advantage is offset by lower scale efficiencies, resulting in similar performance levels when compared to non-family firms (Galve Górriz and Salas Fumás 2003: 121–55).

The reality of a vibrant, internationally competitive sector of rela-tively small family firms in Spain stands in stark contrast to the traditional complaint of economic historians, policy-makers, and labor leaders alike that the lack of true entrepreneurs and the small size or *raquitismo* of Spanish firms have retarded the country's devel-opment.[2] It is true that family firms, and small firms in general, were hurt by the creation of privileged financial circuits during the 1960s. The unusually high borrowing costs of the 1970s also wreaked havoc on them (Guillén 2001c, chapter 7). During the 1980s and 90s, however, family firms and small and medium-sized firms in general have thrived as state-owned enterprises have lost ground and foreign multinationals have established export-oriented operations in Spain, using small local firms as suppliers and transferring technology and know-how.

As noted above, some Spanish family firms have established them-selves in a variety of countries, mostly in the form of horizontal

---

[2] On the economic historians, see Tortella (1994: 179–95); on policy-makers see Martín Aceña and Comín (1991: 79–84); on labor leaders see chapter 9.

investments driven by their intangible assets (brands, technology) and forward vertical investments into distribution channels in foreign markets. In the following sections I will review the cases of firms in a variety of industries, including wines, food-processing, textiles, clothing, railway rolling stock, and automobile components. I have chosen industries in which natural comparative advantages and brands are of fundamental importance (e.g. beverages, food-processing), others in which both technology and brands are key (textiles and clothing), and yet a third in which technology, though not brands, is essential (automobile components, rolling stock). In wines I will describe and explain the pattern of international expansion of Freixenet, the world's leading maker of sparkling wines (€383 million in sales, 1,258 employees), and Miguel Torres, a still winemaker (€144 million; 820). In food-processing I will cover Nutrexpa, the maker of the instant cocoa drink Cola-Cao (€268 million; 818), and Chupa Chups, the inventor and the world's largest maker of the lollipop (€344 million; 1,900). In textiles and clothing, I will focus on two cases: Inditex, one of the world's leading clothing manufacturers and marketers (€3,972 million; 32,535), and Pronovias (approx. €100 million; 650), the world's largest bridal wear multinational. Finally, in automobile components I will highlight Ficosa (€711 million; 6,200) and Grupo Antolín (€1,006 million; 7,100), the world's biggest maker of interior liners for car roofs; and in rolling stock Talgo (€177 million; 991), whose high-speed trains run in Europe and the United States.

The wineries

Together with France, Italy, and California, Spain has one of the world's largest wine industries. It includes some 6,000 wineries owned by about 3,800 separate companies employing 20,000 people. While foreign markets are important to the industry, they represent only 1 percent of total Spanish exports. Spanish wines have been improving in quality. While production of standard-quality table wine has decreased at an average annual rate of 3.7 percent over the last fifteen years, wine bottled under some denomination of origin has increased at a rate of 1.9 percent. Twenty years ago there were twenty-eight denominations of origin in Spain – Rioja, Ribera del Duero, and Penedès being the better known. Today there are sixty. Quality has improved as Spaniards, especially in the south, have substituted beer for wine. In the 2000s annual consumption of wine per head was just 33 liters of wine per head, down from 70 liters during the 1970s.[3]

It is relatively rare, however, for a successful winery to become a multinational firm. Although wine companies may export a high percentage of their production, they seldom invest in their own pro-prietary distribution channels, let alone produce wine abroad. Several Spanish wineries, however, have become multinational firms as a result of both forward integration into foreign distribution channels and horizontal expansion. I will review the cases of Freixenet in sparkling wines and Miguel Torres in still wines.

Spanish sparkling wines did not succeed in international markets until the 1980s (Mínguez Sanz 1994). French producers traditionally held sway in world markets, especially in the premium segment. Italian and (later) Californian producers could only hope to sell lower-quality sparkling wine, enjoying much thinner margins. By the mid-1990s one Spanish firm, Freixenet, had turned the world of sparkling wine upside down, increasing their production to over 100 million bottles annually. Freixenet also became the leading exporter into the world's largest market, the United States, selling 12.6 million bottles, closely followed by Martini Rossi's 11.2 million and leaving far behind the traditional export leader, Moët Chandon at 8.5 million. The firm is the world's largest sparkling wine company (about 130 million bottles) and one of the top ten wine groups overall.

Technically speaking, Freixenet does not make "champagne" but "cava," which is the official denomination for sparkling wines pro-duced in Spain along the Ebro valley and, most importantly, in the Penedès *comarca* located to the west of Barcelona, where production first began in 1892. Thus Spanish firms in the sparkling wine business have always had to surmount the comparative *dis*advantage of not being a producer based in the famous French champagne-producing regions, where the *méthode champenoise* was first developed some three hundred years ago (Prial 1996). Up to the 1970s, the lower quality and weaker brand reputation of the Spanish producers could only be compensated by lower labor costs than in France – and by tariff barriers. Spanish cava output was mostly sold in the domestic market. By the early 1990s, however, 40 percent of Spanish produc-tion was sold in the United States, Germany, the UK, the CIS, Sweden,

---

[3] *Cinco Días*, 3 February 2003.

Switzerland, Canada, and other countries (Bonet 1993; Mínguez Sanz 1994). Freixenet accounts for 70 percent of total Spanish wine exports, even though it has traditionally been the second-largest Spanish producer. Codorníu, its bigger, neighboring rival, has been much slower than Freixenet to become an exporter, an investor in distribution channels abroad, and an acquirer of vineyards and production facilities in the US and Latin America.

Freixenet is a family-controlled and -run company, now in the third generation. Its origins date back to 1889. In 1935 it opened a short-lived US sales subsidiary. Beginning in the 1950s it pioneered exports to the US and Europe, but by the late 1970s export levels were still quite small. The big push came with the creation in 1980 of Freixenet USA and in 1984 of Freixenet Alemania GmbH, located in the two largest export markets for sparkling wines. Freixenet's market entry strategy in the US was absolutely masterful. First, they studied the different market segments and decided to target the one for champagne priced between $4 and $9. Below that segment one could find the Californian low-quality competitors. Above it were the Italian and Californian high-quality producers, while the French premium champagnes dominated the uppermost end of the market. Then Freixenet introduced a new brand specifically for that intermediate segment, the *Cordón Negro* or "black bottle," which was supposed to appeal to the young professional class. They supported the launch of the new label with a massive advertising campaign, eventually turning the firm into the third-largest sparkling wine advertiser in the US market. Freixenet became the US market leader in volume within a short period of time, selling more bottles than all of the French producers combined (Adams/Jobson 1996: 71–4). The *Cordón Negro* was still, however, a wine produced and bottled in Spain, and exported to the US and other major markets, thus suffering from a reputation disadvantage relative to the French labels.

Although they spend about 12 percent of sales on advertising, massive and astute marketing is not enough to account for Freixenet's success. Technological choice also played a decisive role. Freixenet was torn between adopting industrialized methods of sparkling wine production which use large metallic containers, and emulating the traditional *méthode champenoise*. The former is very efficient, but the quality of the wine suffers greatly. Understanding that its success depended on producing champagne of medium-to-high quality at low cost, Freixenet began spending 1 percent of its revenues on R&D, and developed an automated procedure based on *jaulas* or "cage-like" racks for the second fermentation of the wine in the bottle, which produces its characteristic sparkling character. These devices hold a great number of bottles, making it possible to automate the daily operation of turning each bottle so as to shake up the sediment of dead yeast cells that accumulate in the neck of the bottle. This operation was traditionally performed by hand. For a high-volume firm producing 130 million bottles annually, automation represented a major advantage, especially at a time when labor costs in Spain were rising quickly. This production innovation has allowed Freixenet to mass-produce sparkling wine of consistent medium-to-high quality at low cost.

After developing its brand image and improving its production methods, Freixenet transformed itself into a full-fledged multinational firm. In 1985 it founded Freixenet Sonoma Caves in California (1 million bottles of the Gloria Ferrer label), and acquired the third-oldest (1757) French champagne house, Henri Abelé of Reims (400,000 bottles), in a clear attempt to learn about new trends and technologies in the industry. In 1986 it created the Sala Vivé vineyard in Mexico (400,000 bottles). These and other domestic acquisitions allowed Freixenet to almost double its production capacity in a matter of two years and position its new brand offerings in the higher segments of the market.[4] In the late 1980s and early 1990s Freixenet opened marketing and sales subsidiaries in France, Russia, Mexico, Australia, Japan, and China, in addition to its grape- and wine-producing facilities in the US, Mexico, and France. Its latest acquisitions have focused on still wines, including Yvon Mau in Bordeaux, the Wingara Wine Group in Australia, and several wineries in the Spanish grape-growing regions of Ribera del Duero, Rias Baixas, Priorat, and Penedès. Freixenet nowadays has a presence in terms of production or distribution companies in more than 120 countries.[5]

---

[4] In 1984 Freixenet acquired three domestic producers being privatized by the government after the nationalization of the Rumasa business group: Segura Viudas (11 million bottles), Castellblanch (13 million bottles), and René Barbier (10 million bottles).

[5] *Wall Street Journal*, 29 December 1994, pp. 1, 5; *Dinero*, 21 June 1993, pp. 70–1, 74–6; *Expansión*, 27 August 1993, p. 3; *El País Negocios*, 4 June 1995, p. 10; *El País Negocios*, 7 December 1997, p. 6; *Advertising*

Freixenet's success is built on a rare combination of capabilities. It certainly has benefited from a judicious application of the concept of economies of scale. However, the firm has refused to grow indiscriminately and to diversify, even into beverages other than wines. Moreover, Freixenet remains family-controlled and -managed.

Spanish still wineries have not met the same kind of international success as those producing sparkling wines. Historically, only Rioja wines had held sway in foreign markets. In the United States, a key market, Spanish still wines have experienced several years of double-digit growth, especially those from Ribera del Duero (in Castile), Rias Baixas (in the northwestern region of Galicia) and Priorat (on the Mediterranean).[6]

Miguel Torres, whose history goes back to 1800, is certainly not the largest Spanish firm in its industry segment, but it is surely the most international in orientation. Its main vineyards and facilities are located in the Penedès, not far from Freixenet's. In 1979 it set up a winery in Chile (which produces 2 million bottles annually), and in 1982 it set one up in Sonoma County, California. The company is credited with transferring modern winemaking technology to Chile (including stainless steel vinification, cool fermentation, and the use of small oak barrels), whose industry has experienced phenomenal export growth since the mid-1980s. In 1997, after a decade and half of exports, Torres decided to establish a joint venture with the Chinese cooperative Shashen, about 230 km west of Beijing, a plant that was shut down in 2003. In 1999 it established a trading company in Shanghai. The firm has diversified into brandy, vegetable oil, and canned gourmet foods. It is presently owned and run by the fourth generation.[7]

The global success of Freixenet in an industry traditionally dominated by French and Italian producers demonstrates that firms, especially family firms, have the ability to adapt to changing circumstances and adverse conditions. Spanish wineries never received industry-specific subsidies or other forms of state support, with the exception

Age International Supplement, 29 June 1998, p. 13; *Cinco Días*, 27 November 2002; *El País Negocios*, 1 October 2001.

[6] *Nation's Restaurant News* 36(5), 16 December 2002, p. 26.

[7] *Estrategia*, 9 July 2003; *Spanish News Digest*, 9 May 2003; *Cinco Días*, 30 October 2001.

of trade barriers. Moreover, economic policies and conditions during the 1980s and early 1990s tended to hurt the wine producers rather than benefit them: labor costs soared; a strong peseta policy was implemented until 1992 to curb inflation; the adoption of the euro has eliminated the possibility of competitive devaluations; and trade liberalization eliminated tariffs that had protected the industry for years. In the midst of adversity, firms like Freixenet, Codorníu and, in a more limited way, Miguel Torres successfully pursued international opportunities in the Americas, Europe, and East Asia, even though they encountered fierce competition from their better-prepared French and Italian rivals. Thus, they surmounted their relative "prestige" or "image" disadvantage by building on their locational comparative advantage and investing in both technology and marketing skills. They expanded throughout the world on the basis of those location-specific and intangible assets, as the theories reviewed in chapter 2 would predict.

Field interviews strongly suggest that the Spanish wineries have had one key advantage. Firms in the food and beverages industry were long accustomed to competing against foreign multinationals established in Spain on price, quality, and product differentiation. Spain received considerable amounts of foreign investment in consumer goods during the 1960s and 1970s. Multinationals revolutionized marketing and advertising practices in Spanish consumer markets. Moreover, Spanish wineries – especially those making sparkling wines – are located near the industrial belt surrounding Barcelona, home to many domestic and foreign consumer-goods firms. The same kinds of multinational-induced "demonstration" and competitive effects took place in the food-processing industry, to which I now turn.

Food-processing

The food-processing industry is one of the most important in Spain. The country possesses a large agricultural sector, and the variety of climates within the Iberian peninsula – ranging from Atlantic to continental to Mediterranean – offers a rich diversity of products. Agriculture accounts for about 15 percent of total Spanish exports. During the last twenty years much food-processing has become foreign-owned. Still, Spanish-owned firms remain competitive, and they have expanded throughout the world. As is the case for wines, locational comparative advantage is crucial for food-processing firms. But marketing skill is also key.

One of the better-known cases is Nutrexpa which, like Freixenet, has expanded throughout the world on the basis of its intangible assets. It is a diversified group that makes and sells a variety of products, including soluble cocoa, cookies, patés, milk, baby foods, honey and confectionery, among other things. It sells in more than sixty countries in Europe, the Americas, and Asia, and runs production facilities in Chile, China, and Russia. The company, which is based in Barcelona's fashionable Barrio de Gracia, was founded in the 1940s by two brothers-in-law, José Ignacio Ferrero and José María Ventura. The firm is now owned by the second generation of family members, and it has been run by professional managers since the 1970s.[8]

In 1946 Nutrexpa launched its flagship product, Cola-Cao, an instant cocoa mix presented as "cheap, nutritious, delicious." It became a popular product in Spain in 1952 when the company created a famous song (the "Canción del negrito") that was first aired on the SER, Spain's largest radio broadcasting network. In 1964 it made its first major acquisition of another cocoa firm (Phoscao). In 1970 it diversified into cookies (Galletas Plaja), and into honey and other natural products a few years later (Granja San Francisco). In the mid-1980s acquisitions in confectionery (Dulces Unzué) and milk (Palentina Celpa) followed, and in the 1990s it bought a leading paté company (La Piara) and a bread manufacturer (Ortiz), which it sold to Bimbo in 2000, a company it had attempted to acquire from Anheuser-Busch back in 1995. In 1984 Nutrexpa launched Okey, a bottled cocoa drink. In 2002 the firm acquired Nocilla (a chocolate spread) from Unilever. In spite of this pattern of diversification, Cola-Cao accounts for about 40 percent of total Nutrexpa sales. According to Young and Rubicam, the brand is third only to "Spain"

---

[8] The information on Nutrexpa comes from: *Actualidad Económica*, 18 January 1993; 2 July 2001; 6 May 2002; *Cinco Días*, 8 October 2001; 5 February 2003; *El País*, 10 October 1994; 15 October 1994; 28 August 1995; *El País Internacional*, 8 June 1989; *El País Negocios*, 21 April 2002; *Expansión*, 18 September 1997; 6 June 2003; *International Herald Tribune*, 15 June 1994.

and "Coca-Cola" as the most valuable in the country. Nocilla, another Nutrexpa asset, ranks twenty-fourth.[9]

Cola-Cao's first foreign plant was set up in Chile in 1980, followed by another in Ecuador, well before the Spanish economy was opened up to competition after entering the European Union. In 1988 it became one of the first Spanish firms to set up a joint-venture factory in China, at Tianjin, followed by a second plant in 1996, becoming the market leader in soluble cocoa with a 50 percent market share. In 1994 it set up a factory in Warsaw, Poland, and then one in Russia. In each of these markets Nutrexpa has replicated its strategy of low-cost production coupled with strong support of the Cola-Cao brand. In China, for instance, it is called "Gao Le Gao," which translates as "tall, happy and tall." In 2003 the firm made its first important foray into the Middle East with the acquisition of a Jordanian baby food company.

The company's international expansion has not been without pit-falls. In fact, in 2002 the firm was forced to shut down several sales offices, as well as its factories in Ecuador and Poland, after mounting losses. While the Chinese joint venture is hugely profitable, and the Russian operation promises to be so, the firm has encountered some of the typical problems confronting foreign firms in emerging economies, including political turmoil and the need to pay bribes. Nutrexpa is consistently profitable only in China and in Spain, although in the home country it is losing market share to Nestlé.

Given Nutrexpa's product portfolio, the firm effectively competes against some of the most formidable multinational companies: Nestlé in cocoa-based products, Coca-Cola in cocoa drinks, and Unilever and Nabisco in a variety of processed foods, to name but a few. Still, it continues to grow, without losing its family character, and it frequently hires managers away from foreign multinationals.

More internationally successful than Nutrexpa has been Chupa Chups, the company that brought the lollipop to the world, and is the largest maker and seller of the delicious candy (four billion units a year in forty flavors). It sells in over 150 countries, and has established licensing arrangements with makers of clothing, footwear, toys, and

---

[9] In chapter 8 I present data on brand equity that includes, unlike Young and Rubicam's, not only consumer-goods brands but all brands.

personal care products. The firm was founded in 1964 in Barcelona, although the lollipop itself was first produced and sold in 1958. Its first foreign foray was in France, where it set up a plant in 1967 to avoid Spain's 20 percent tax on export sales. By the early 2000s the firm manufactured in France, Brazil, Mexico, Russia, and China. Salvador Dalí designed the firm's logo, and it is the owner of Antoni Gaudí's famous Casa Batlló. In 2003, the Economist Intelligence Unit referred to the company as "one of the world's most legendary corporate globalizers."[10] In spite of its small size, Chupa Chups is the world's second-largest candy company (after Halls), and the tenth in confectionery overall.

Most of Chupa Chups's foreign investments in manufacturing were undertaken during the 1990s, especially after the retirement of the founder and the coming of age of the second generation. By 2003, it became clear that the firm had overinvested, and should have focused on export sales. Big losses in 2001 and 2002 occurred because of currency devaluations in emerging economies, reduced demand for sugar candy, and enhanced competition from powerhouses such as Kraft Foods, Hershey, and Nestlé. The company had accumulated €120 million in debt. In 2002 Chupa Chups decided to hire a Danone executive as CEO, who decided to shut down the French, Brazilian, and Mexican plants. The Chinese operations have been sold to the joint-venture partners. Only the Russian facilities continue to produce and do well, but the firm is transferring more ownership to the local partner. The strategy of the new management team is to concentrate production in Spain, and sell around the world using the firm's network of distribution subsidiaries. Thus Chupa Chups has succeeded as a multinational firm with its forward vertical expansion into foreign distribution channels, though not with its horizontal foreign investments.

Nutrexpa and Chupa Chups are not the only examples of Spanish family-controlled multinationals from the food-processing industry. Others include Agrolimen, Campofrío, Ebro Puleva, and Panrico.

[10] The information on Chupa Chups is based on: *Economist Intelligence Unit Executive Briefings*, 3 February 2003; *Latin Trade*, 1 August 2003; *Actualidad Económica*, 23 June 2003; Cinco *Días*, 7 February 2003; 22 May 2003; *El País*, 6 September 1998; *El País Negocios*, 27 October 2002.

They have expanded vertically and horizontally using their brands and manufacturing know-how as leverage. As in the case of the wineries, their decisions are fully justifiable from the point of view of the theories of the multinational firm outlined in chapter 2.

Clothing

Like wines and food-processing, textiles and clothing comprise one of Spain's oldest industries. Unlike the other two, however, it has never been a major contributor to the country's exports – a mere 4.5 percent of the total. Although Spanish wages are about half those in the most advanced countries of Europe, they are much higher than in the major clothing-producing regions of the world, namely, East and South Asia and Latin America. The industry is populated by family firms that have expanded abroad vigorously both vertically into distribution channels and horizontally. The textile makers Dogi and Tavex (one of the world's largest producers of denim) and the vertically integrated clothing manufacturers and marketers Cortefiel, Inditex, and Pronovias are among the most globally successful firms. I will focus on the latter two.

Inditex (Industria de Diseño Textil), the owner of the Zara brand among others, is perhaps the single most successful family firm in Spain. Its IPO in May 2001 caused a sensation, and turned its founder and majority owner, Amancio Ortega, into the world's eighteenth wealthiest person ($10.3 billion), a quarter the level of Bill Gates.[11] Inditex is a vertically integrated clothing manufacturer and marketer with nearly 2,250 stores outside Spain (Zara, 724; Pull and Bear, 374; Massimo Dutti, 327; Bershka, 300; Stradivarius, 227; Oysho, 104; Kiddy's, 129; Zara Home, 62). Its biggest market is still Spain (46 percent), followed by Europe (31 percent) and the Americas (16 percent). It runs eighteen wholly owned factories in the northwestern city of A Coruña, four others elsewhere in Spain, and two logistics centers, one at headquarters and the other in Saragossa (which employs some 800 workers). The company has been the subject of three Harvard Business School cases that celebrate both its marketing and

[11] As reflected in *Forbes* magazine's annual ranking of billionaires. There are seven Spaniards on the list. See http://www.forbes.com/2003/02/26/billionaireland.html.

technological prowess. In 2003 *Wired* magazine included Inditex on its list of the twenty most innovative firms in the world.

Ortega was born in the province of León into a modest family. His father was a railway employee. The family moved west to A Coruña, in the region of Galicia, when he was little. In 1963 he set up a lingerie workshop with his first wife, and they opened their first store in 1975. They chose the name Zorba, but it was already taken, so they settled for Zara. The firm is not merely run like a family firm, it is a family. The founder and most of the executives are locals and eat regularly with the workers, many of whom own shares.[12]

Inditex's just-in-time manufacturing capabilities have become legendary in the industry. The firm makes about 11,000 different clothing items and accessories every year. While only 20 percent of the fabrics are made in-house, the firm only outsources sewing. Its logistics and vertical integration are so well coordinated that the firm can respond to market trends in a mere three weeks. The stores, most of which are company-owned, are electronically linked to headquarters. Inventories run as low as 7 percent of revenues. The strategy of highly coordinated vertical integration makes perfect sense given the firm's need to cut costs and generate flexibility by reducing the potentially harmful impact of uncertainty and asset specificity along the value chain. Much of this technological wizardry is attributed to CEO José María Castellano, a former full professor at the local university, who worked for a couple of foreign multinationals before joining Inditex. In a fashion world characterized by extensive outsourcing and massive advertising expenditures, Inditex seems to be a stark reminder of the competitive power of efficient manufacturing and logistics. The company is growing fast on the basis of those capabilities while its main competitors (Benetton, GAP, The Limited, Marks and Spencer) are stagnating or deeply troubled. The international financial media have fallen in love with the company.[13]

An equally innovative firm in the clothing industry is Pronovias, the world's largest maker and seller of bridal wear. The company started out in Barcelona, on the classy Paseig de Gracia, back in 1922. It

[12] *Cinco Días*, 9 May 1003; El *País*, 28 February 2003.
[13] *The Economist*, 19 May 2001, p. 56; *Forbes*, 28 May 2001, p. 98; *Wall Street Journal*, 18 May 2001, p. B1.

languished until it presented its first prêt-à-porter wedding collection in 1964. It was perhaps the first company in the world to hit upon the idea of creating a chain of exclusive shops for brides. With annual sales of 480,000 gowns (the equivalent of a 5 percent global market share split between the Spanish and foreign markets), it leads US firms Mori Lee and Alfred Angelo, British Brackenbridge and Brides International, and French Pronuptia. Most of its branded items are made in a factory outside Barcelona, while the accessories and intimate apparel are outsourced in China. It distributes worldwide through a network of 2,500 points of sale in sixty countries, although including only 115 company-owned or franchised stores in Spain, three company-owned in France, and two franchises each in Portugal and Greece. The company has established distribution subsidiaries in several countries. Sever García, the sales director at Pronovias USA, explains what his company's competitive advantage is all about: flexibility and responsiveness. "We can make any style at any price – for any market." The ability to adapt to the local peculiarities of each market is indeed essential because of differences in physiology, custom, tastes, and average age at which women marry.

Like Inditex, the success of Pronovias is not only the result of a keen understanding of markets around the world. There is much design and production know-how accumulated over decades of experience. Spain in general, and Catalonia in particular, have relatively high labor costs. And yet Pronovias offers sophisticated wedding and cocktail dresses with all manner of laces and flounces at relatively affordable wholesale prices ranging from €150 to €3,000. Its current plans are to shift to the €600–10,000 price range, and to integrate forward into the distribution channel by substituting company-owned or franchised stores for arm's-length points of sale. The firm is fully controlled by the second generation of the founding Palatchi family, and is increasingly using professional managers.[14]

The cases of Inditex and Pronovias illustrate the importance of manufacturing skill and flexibility coupled with marketing savvy (though not necessarily massive advertising). Historically, Spain did not play a prominent role in the global textile and clothing industry.

[14] *Actualidad Económica*, 26 May 2003; *Expansión*, 23 February 2001; 28 February 2003; 17 September 2003; "Pronovias Previews Spring." *Women's Wear Daily*, 6 August 2003, p. 12.

But firms such as those discussed in this section are rewriting the rules of competition in their respective market segments. Their pattern of international expansion, however, is not peculiar. As indicated by the theories outlined in chapter 2, they are using their intangible assets as leverage in the quest for foreign markets and integrating vertically into foreign distribution channels so as to reduce the adverse impact of uncertainty and asset specificity.

Automobile components

Spain is best known around the world for its tourist attractions and agricultural products. Most people are stunned to learn that the auto-mobile industry is the country's largest in terms of both production and exports. Spain runs head to head with South Korea as the world's sixth-largest auto assembler, behind the US, Japan, Germany, China, and France. Moreover, since three-fourths of output are exports, Spain ranks as the fourth-largest exporter of motor vehicles, surpassed only by Japan, Germany, and France, and well ahead of the US and Korea. The auto assembly and components industry accounts for 6 percent of GDP and 24 percent of merchandise exports. The components sector comprises over 1,100 firms with 215,000 employees, and exports about half of its production as non-assembled components for the original and replacement markets (García 1998; MIE 1996: 133–43). Moreover, Spanish auto parts plants are among the most efficient in the world, and several Spanish-owned component firms have become multinationals in their own right, with production plants on four continents.

Spain's secret is called foreign direct investment. Her silent rise to prominence in the world automobile industry has to do with the fact that all assembly lines and over three-fourths of component manufac-turing are accounted for by foreign-owned companies, which see their Spanish operations in the context of the European marketplace. Multi-nationals located in Spain must compete among themselves not only for domestic and export sales, but also for skilled workers and supplies. After decades of inconsistent, counterproductive, and largely ineffect-ive import-substitution policies in assembly and components, the state embraced a policy of liberalism and internationalism towards the in-dustry during the late 1970s and 1980s, precisely when the effort at economic integration with Europe was gaining speed. Over the years, multinationals such as FIAT, Renault, Citroën, Peugeot, Rover, Chrysler, Ford, GM, Volkswagen and Nissan took over existing facilities or created new ones, turning the country into an export hub for subcompact cars and certain components (see Guillén 2001c, chapter 6). Although no domestic make survived as an independent firm, and many components firms came under foreign control, a few domestically owned parts manufacturers emerged strengthened from this process, becoming world market leaders in their respective product lines.

The liberal economic policies initiated in the 1970s, and deepened during the 1980s as Spain prepared for European Union membership, had the automobile assembly sector in mind, not components. The shift from import-substitution policies to quite liberal local content requirements took the components sector by storm. More than 20 percent of jobs in auto components were lost during the years of crisis and restructuring. Although diametrically opposed, the liberal policies of the 1980s achieved a result similar to the one produced by the protectionist policies initiated in the late 1940s: a debacle among existing component manufacturers. While in the 1940s and 1950s a relatively autonomous state strangled private initiatives in auto assembly and stymied the growth of components manufacturers, the liberalization reforms of the 1970s and 1980s had the unintended effect of throwing hundreds of auto components firms out of business and placing the industry under heavy foreign control. In 1979, the government approved the first major foreign acquisition, Robert Bosch's takeover of Femsa, the largest domestic components manufacturer at the time. Between 1979 and 1994 – when Exide Corp. of the US acquired the battery maker Tudor, one of the world's largest – dozens of Spanish component firms were bought by foreigners. Overall, the proportion of foreign-controlled auto parts companies, weighted by sales, grew from 37 percent in 1973 to 56 percent in 1983, and to a staggering 71 percent in 1990 (Bolsa de Madrid 1986; *Auto-Revista* 1986: 83, 130, 166–72, 179, 219; MICT 1991; EIU 1996a).

As a member of the European Union since 1986, Spain has become a world center for sub compact automobile and parts manufacturing (Andersen Consulting 1994; Bolsa de Madrid 1986; EIU 1996a). The components industry has attained world standards of competitiveness. According to the OECD, auto parts and other transportation equipment are one of Spain's comparative areas of technological strength, as measured by the number and specialization of patents (Archibugi and Pianta 1992: 76–7). An Andersen Consulting (1994) study – conducted in conjunction with researchers at the universities of Cambridge and Wales – ranked Spanish labor productivity in auto components manufacturing the highest in the world, topping even Japan (*Economist* 1994; EIU 1996a; Sernauto 1996: 37, 45). It is clear, however, that these favorable aspects of the auto components industry in Spain are not only the result of local entrepreneurial initiatives, but also the outcome of the heavy involvement of foreign capital and technology. And the EU's expansion to Eastern Europe threatens some Spanish assembly and components plants.

As a result of changes in government policy and in the economic environment, the Spanish components sector has experienced many bankruptcies. But it has also produced world-class, domestically owned companies thanks to, and not in spite of, the arrival of foreign multinationals. In this chapter I will review the cases of Grupo Antolín and Ficosa International. These companies are among the top thirty automotive suppliers in the world, and command leading global market shares in their respective product lines (García 1998).

Grupo Antolín-Irausa is the world's largest manufacturer of interior liners for automobiles (over 7 million units annually), and a leading maker of seats, door locks, and electrical devices for windows. It is headquartered in the Castilian city of Burgos, north of Madrid, where it was founded in 1959. The second generation of the founding family is now in control. Only 30 percent of the company's revenue is in Spain. Its first Spanish factories were set up near Renault's assembly lines in central Castile during the 1960s. In the 1970s it opened facilities near Ford's new plant on the Mediterranean, and Land Rover Santana's assembly operations in southern Spain. After demonstrating its high quality and reliability, the company was asked by foreign assemblers to set up shop abroad. The firm is present in more than ten countries: it has wholly owned plants in Portugal, France, Germany, the UK, Slovakia, and the Czech Republic; and joint ventures in Turkey, the US, South Africa, India, China, Thailand, South Korea, Japan, Brazil, and Mexico. Three customers (Ford, Volkswagen, and Renault-Nissan) account for almost three-fourths of sales. Others include GM, PSA, DaimlerChrysler, BMW, and Hyundai. R&D centers are located in Spain and Italy, which have produced only a trickle of patents (ten in the US, all obtained since 1999).

Another successful family-owned components company is Barcelona-based Ficosa International, originally founded in 1949. It makes electric wiring and systems, mirrors, door locks, and windshield wipers for Opel (GM), Ford, Volkswagen-Seat, Nissan, Renault, Matra, PSA (Peugeot and Citroën), BMW, and Mercedes-Benz. Almost half of its production in Spain is accounted for by exports. In the 1960s Ficosa started to supply Pegaso (now owned by Iveco), Seat, Renault, Citroën, Barreiros, and Avia (now defunct). In 1976 the company was reorganized into the holding Ficosa International, and the firm expanded into Portugal. The 1980s were the years of European expansion, and during the 1990s Ficosa targeted the Americas and Asia.

Ficosa presently runs production facilities in Europe (Spain, United Kingdom, France, Germany, Italy, Portugal, Poland, Romania, Slovenia, and Turkey), the NAFTA (Mexico, USA), Mercosur (Brazil and Argentina), and Asia (India and South Korea), always capitalizing on its existing relationships with assemblers. In 2002 it acquired a controlling stake in China's second-largest driving-mirror company. Design centers are located in Barcelona and Detroit.

Ficosa has made little R&D effort during most of its history, but it is presently allocating about 5 percent of sales, much more than the average Spanish firm of its size. The firm has only one assigned US patent. One of the innovative products it is developing involves a device to defrost the windshield in less than 90 seconds. Without a sustained innovation record, however, Ficosa will find it hard to remain one of the top thirty automobile suppliers in the world. Another weak point remains its capital structure, which revealed itself as a major limitation in the mid-1990s as the company was expanding throughout the world and had to be assisted by the Spanish and Catalan official credit institutes. Ficosa remains under the control of the Pujol and Tarragó founding families, with UBS Capital (6.67 percent share) and the Landesbank Baden-Württemberg (5.2 percent) as minority partners. Selling the company to a foreign multinational firm is considered by chairman José María Pujol to be "like a heresy."[15]

---

[15] *Actualidad Económica*, 1 July 1996; 1 August 2003; Durán and Úbeda (1996); *Financial Times*, 19 January 1998, p. 19; *Actualidad Económica*, 1 July 1996, pp. 10–14.

Grupo Antolín and Ficosa have enjoyed stable and lasting ownership arrangements that have allowed them to grow organically without taking on much debt or falling into the hands of international investors. Although the arrival of foreign capital to the Spanish components sector could have been regulated in such a way that more domestic companies survived, its generally beneficial effects should not be neglected. Foreign auto parts firms revolutionized production methods and helped raise quality standards. Spain can boast high exports of both assembled cars and components thanks to its ability to attract and nurture foreign investment. Multinationals have contributed to an upgrading of technological and organizational skills, indirectly benefiting the domestically owned sector.

Railway rolling stock

The manufacturing of railway rolling stock and locomotives is generally assumed to be an activity subject to economies of scale in R&D and production, although there is a need to customize products to the diverse technical and design specifications required by different railway companies. Thus, it is an improbable industry for a family firm to succeed in. And yet, with many ups and downs, Patentes Talgo has made a dent in international competition, though it is very much constrained by its small size.

Spain has not been an auspicious platform from which to become internationally competitive in the railway equipment business. The big Spanish railway boom of the 1850s took place thanks to foreign investment, which typically entailed the import of construction materials, locomotives, and rolling stock. As in other countries, the railway industry was subject to sharp ups and downs, speculation, financial crises and panics, and bankruptcies. More often than not, building the railroad and managing the real estate proved more profitable than transporting passengers and cargo. By the turn of the century, the surviving companies had built a network of railway track that linked the most important population, industrial, and commercial centers around the country. Local manufacturers of railway equipment, however, were seriously lagging behind (Nadal 1975).

Although some relatively important companies were founded in the early twentieth century, e.g. La Maquinista Terrestre y Marítima and Fábrica de Vagones, the rolling stock industry did not fully develop until the period of import substitution during the 1940s and 1950s. The 1942 nationalization and merger of the various railway companies into Renfe set the stage for the state's involvement in the industry. Foreign multinationals were persuaded during the 1950s and 1960s to invest in greenfield operations, e.g. Babcock and Wilcox Española, or as minority partners in existing firms – La Maquinista Terrestre y Marítima, Ateinsa, Macosa, and Construcción y Auxiliar de Ferrocarril (CAF, the merger of Fábrica de Vagones with several other smaller firms). The acute industrial crisis of the 1970s and the liberalization of foreign trade and investment during the 1980s resulted in a wave of bankruptcies and mergers. The state-owned enterprise holding company (INI) took over La Maquinista in 1971, Ateinsa in 1973, and Babcock and Wilcox in 1980. As part of GEC-Alsthom's successful bid for the high-speed railway link between Madrid and Seville, the INI state-owned holding transferred majority ownership of La Maquinista, Ateinsa, and Meinfesa to the French multinational in 1989, with Macosa being awarded minority stakes in each company (Martín Aceña and Comín 1991: 234, 401, 508–9, 579–82).

Presently, the biggest players in the Spanish rolling stock industry are CAF (€392 million; 3,180 employees), now controlled by savings banks based in the Basque Country, and Alstom Transporte (€200 million; 1,980), the subsidiary of the troubled French multinational. The most interesting player in the industry, however, is neither of these giants, but rather a medium-sized family firm called Patentes Talgo.

Talgo has traditionally been one of the most innovative firms in Spain. Over the years, it has pioneered the application of aeronautical materials and technologies to the design of railway rolling stock, and the development of special automatic mechanisms allowing trains to adapt to different railway widths without stopping, known as wheel bogies.[16] Two-thirds of its sales come from maintenance work, mostly

---

[16] For geopolitical and technological reasons, several countries have a wider railway track than the international standard, Russia, Portugal, and Spain, among others. Patentes Talgo developed the automatic railway width adaptation technology in the 1960s. In 1993 Talgo licensed Sumitomo of Japan to use this technology. Talgo itself has sold this equipment to the Russian Railways Ministry. See *Kommersant*, 18 January 1995, p. 9.

for the state-owned Renfe railway company and for the German railways system, Deutsche Bundesbahn. Sales of trains represent 25 percent of its total revenues, while sales of maintenance equipment account for the remaining 5 percent. Talgo seems to lack size and financial clout. It is dwarfed by its international competitors – Alstom, Bombardier, FIAT, and Siemens. Analysts have repeatedly declared the firm moribund, but Talgo continues to defy the conventional wisdom in an industry that emphasizes size and economies of scale.

Talgo's unusual trajectory began in the late 1920s, when a Basque railway engineer, Alejandro Goicoechea, challenged the traditional way in which railway cars were built with a series of path-breaking innovations. Instead of making railway cars heavy enough to allow them to make turns at relatively high speeds, Goicoechea sought to minimize the *tara* (equipment's weight) by using materials up to 25 percent lighter and cutting the cars' height by as much as 1 meter or 3 feet. In this way, the center of gravity could be pushed closer to the ground, and the train would not derail when pulled along curves at high speeds. In addition, the cars would be a mere 5 meters long (16 feet), and have only one axle with two wheels at the rear end, while the front end would be mounted onto the next car's axle. Unfortunately, the MZA company – one of Spain's main railways at the time – rejected this project in 1939. A couple of years later, however, one of the country's leading financiers and entrepreneurs, José Maria de Oriol y Urquijo, an industrial engineer by training, liked the idea and provided the startup funds. The first experimental prototype of the *T*rain, *A*rticulated, *L*ight, *Goicoechea and *O*riol (Talgo) became a reality in 1943, in the midst of one of the darkest periods of Spanish history, with international isolation and famine looming large.[17]

The Talgo I prototype proved a performance success. World speed records on the railway track were broken repeatedly. In 1948 the American Car and Foundry Co. of Hoboken, New Jersey, and Wilmington, Delaware, agreed to manufacture three Talgo II trains. Two of them were shipped back to Spain to enter scheduled commercial service in 1950. The third was tested and used for passenger traffic by the New York Central Railroad until 1958 but without much commercial success. Talgo, however, persevered and pumped more

[17] *Motor Mundial* 2 (November 1949): 1–68.

money into R&D, which nowadays represents between 10 and 12 percent of revenues. During the 1950s the newly nationalized Spanish railways, Renfe, turned Talgo into one of its key equipment and maintenance subcontractors. An improved Talgo III design was introduced in 1964, allowing for easy directional reversibility of the train and longer cars. A crucial breakthrough came in 1968 with the Talgo IIIRD, which could travel between Madrid and Paris or between Barcelona and Geneva without having to stop at the border in order to adapt to the different track width. In 1974 the Talgo Camas became the first high-speed sleeper train in the world.

But the most important innovation, the one that sets Talgo apart from its larger foreign competitors, is the 1980 design of the Talgo Pendular, or naturally tilting train. By designing the cars in such a way that the center of gravity lies below the support platform and each wheel has its own axle, the train tilts as it enters a curve, allowing for speeds about 20 percent higher than normal without passenger discomfort. The two other oscillating trains available on the market at the time, FIAT's ETR460 Pendolino and ABB's X2000, required electronic sensors to trigger a complex hydraulic tilting system. The Spanish low-tech design provides risk-free performance levels similar to the high-tech trains of those two powerful multinationals.[18] In the 1990s, Talgo's TPI 200 achieved speeds of over 250km per hour (155 mph) on regular railway tracks during scheduled commercial service, and over 500km per hour at the Munich, Germany, testing track.

In spite of its unique proprietary technology, Talgo's internationalization has been rather limited. The Renfe state railway monopoly accounts for over 90 percent of revenues, and it is a joint venture between Renfe and a Basque manufacturing firm that actually makes the Talgo trains, not the company itself. In 1993 the firm founded Talgo Deutschland GmbH to maintain the six sleeper trains it had sold to the German railways. That same year Patentes Talgo created a joint venture with Deutsche Waggonbau Dessau to make cargo railway cars. In the US Talgo is trying to become a supplier of low-cost, high-speed, high-comfort trains for commuter service along the Atlantic and Pacific coasts' crowded corridors. In 1994 Renfe and Talgo created a joint venture (Renfe Talgo of America) to promote

---

[18] Strohl (1993: 230–2); *Business Week*, 14 June 1993, p. 89.

and test the train. The Washington–Boston project collapsed in the early 1990s in the face of bureaucratic and financial problems. Talgo trains currently service the Portland–Seattle and Seattle–Vancouver lines. The passenger cars were assembled by a company located in Washington state from Spanish-made components, and leased by Talgo to Amtrak. Talgo entered Finland via acquisition in 1999, where it designs, builds, and maintains various types of trains. In 2000 it agreed to make railway truck wheel pairs in Russia and trains in Kazakhstan. Service on the line between Almaty and Astana, the old and new Kazakh capitals, started in September 2003.[19]

In spite of possessing formidable technology, Talgo's problems are legion. Its family-owned character represents an enormous financial constraint in an industry dominated by giant multinational firms, and characterized by excess capacity and the need for huge investments in R&D. Even firms of such stature as ABB and Daimler-Benz had to agree to merge their railway equipment operations (ADTranz) in an attempt to reach economies of scale and scope, and then decided to sell them to Bombardier of Canada. In 2003 Talgo decided to scale back its US operations in the face of uncertainty over railway subsidies in Washington, Oregon, and other states. The company has decided to sell the plant it had acquired in 2000 and to focus on maintenance of the six trains currently in operation.[20]

Talgo's perennial Achilles' heel is its lack of locomotive technology. The company has attempted to surmount this constraint through alliances with other companies. In 1998 it started development of a high-speed train with ADTranz, later acquired by Bombardier. Talgo and Bombardier successfully bid for sixteen of the thirty-two trains that will service the new high-speed link between Madrid and Barcelona. The contract will represent revenues of €338 million for the alliance, of which €202 million will accrue to Talgo. (Siemens will

---

[19] *New York Times*, 11 June 1995, section 5, p. 3; *Handelsblatt*, 8 July 1995, p. 17; *Seattle Times*, 24 May 1995; *Contra Costa Times*, 14 May 1996; *Journal of Commerce*, 17 May 1996, p. 3B, 26 March 1997, p. 8B; *Travel Agent*, 11 May 1998, p. 100; *FT Exporter* supplement in *Financial Times*, 11 May 1998, p. 6; *El País* 5 July 2000; 12 April 2001; *BBC Monitoring Central Asia*, 14 September 2003; *Inzhenernaia Gazeta*, 15 October 2002; *Finnish News Digest*, 19 August 2003.
[20] *El País Negocios*, 24 August 2003; *Trains Magazine*, 1 April 2003, p. 24.

build the other sixteen trains.[21]) Talgo's history is heralded by ingenious sparks of innovation. But the company owns just nine US patents, and does not seem to be spending much on R&D, certainly not enough to stay ahead of the curve in a rapidly changing industry.

The case of Talgo illustrates how a technologically successful medium-sized firm in a capital- and R&D-intensive industry can find a place for itself in the global economy. Talgo, however, is rather unique, not only because of the strong desire of the family not to lose control, but also because of the political-economic conditions in which it grew to prominence. During the 1950s and 1960s Talgo thrived inside a protected domestic market. Since liberalization and EU membership, the firm has benefited from continued ties to the state-owned railway company. To its credit, Talgo has managed to realize some foreign opportunities as the Spanish economy has become more outward-oriented. Still, the bulk of its business comes from Renfe, and while existing supply contracts ensure the firm's viability in the medium run, its long-term survival continues to be problematic. Neither is the issue of ownership and funding resolved. The firm is now controlled by several members of the third generation since founding, who are not always in agreement, and attempts to bring in stable institutional investors have thus far failed.

The worker-owned cooperatives

As in the case of family firms, theorists of economic development have frequently argued that worker ownership is a "utopia" bound to fail because it creates the wrong kind of incentives for both workers and managers (Kerr et al. 1960: 227; Sachs 1993: 82–3). Spain may perhaps be the exception that proves the rule. Its worker-owned cooperative sector is large and internationally competitive. At the end of 2002 there were 42,191 cooperatives and other worker-owned enterprises, with a total of 385,450 employee-owners or 2.4 percent of Spain's employed population, up from 2.0 percent in 1994. The sector is growing more rapidly than GDP or the employed population. Slightly over half of the cooperatives are in the service sector (mostly distribution), 27 percent in manufacturing, 12 percent in construction and 8 percent in agriculture (CEPES 2003: 56, 82). Strikingly,

[21] *El País Negocios*, 24 August 2003.

some of the cooperatives have become multinational enterprises, including agricultural cooperatives with foreign distribution and sales offices, mostly in Europe (Agro Sevilla Aceituna, Anecoop), or even production facilities (Coren, Corporación Alimentaria Peñasanta, Feiraco).

The most famous of the cooperatives is Mondragón Corporación Cooperativa (MCC), the largest cooperative group in the world, with over 66,500 employees and €9,200 million in revenues, making it one of the ten largest companies in Spain, and among the 500 largest groups in Europe.[22] Cooperatives belonging to the group are engaged in everything from chips, appliances, automobile components, and furniture to machine tools, robotics, elevators, heavy machinery, and large construction projects. Mondragón also includes a savings bank (Caja Laboral Popular), and Spain's fifth-largest retailer (Eroski). Unbelievable as it may be, Mondragón has become a multinational enterprise with thirty-eight manufacturing plants and nearly 100 distribution operations in Western and Eastern Europe, the Americas, North Africa, and Asia. About 46 percent of employees are in the Basque Country, 42 percent in the rest of Spain, and 12 percent abroad. After a decade of intense growth in which the number of employees has more than doubled from 25,000 in 1992 to the present 66,500, only slightly over half of them are worker-owners. The manufacturing cooperatives account for slightly more than 40 percent of employees and revenues. They have established thirty-eight production plants on four continents, and acquired a dozen foreign firms, especially in Europe. Most of the foreign plants represent horizontal investments seeking to overcome trade and other types of barriers, reduce transportation costs, or supply customers' foreign-based assembly plants. Only a few of the plants are vertical investments intended to reduce costs. None of the foreign operations are incorporated as cooperatives; they are either fully or partially owned by one of the cooperatives in Spain.

The first Mondragón cooperative was founded in 1956. It was not until the 1970s that international growth became a priority. Between the early 1970s and the early 1990s Mondragón's exports

---

[22] The corporate information on MCC comes from its 2002 annual report, available from www.mcc.es.

of manufactured goods climbed from 10 to 31 percent of total production, mimicking the transformation of the overall Spanish economy. The cooperatives have learned over the years to adopt the financial, organizational, and marketing techniques used by any capitalist enterprise. As the title of an internal report of 1989 suggests unambiguously, Mondragón made the transition "From Sociological Experiment toward an Entrepreneurial Group" (Whyte and Whyte 1991: 195–211). Jesús Larrañaga, one of the founders of Fagor Electrodomésticos (the home appliance market leader in Spain with a 24 percent market share), once observed that Mondragón "uses a dual model, operating as a cooperative wherever feasible and as a capitalist company elsewhere" (*El País Vasco*, 4 May 1998). Thus Mondragón's success as a multinational enterprise has been built on the basis of its financial independence, a highly motivated workforce, a savvy policy of foreign investments, and a long-term commitment to worker training, brand development and R&D (Guillén 2001c: 88–93; Whyte and Whyte 1991: 63–7, 211–21). Thus the international success of Mondragón is fully consistent with theories of foreign growth and investment.

Family firms, cooperatives, and the process of creative destruction

The family firms discussed in this chapter have achieved considerable international success. To be sure, they appear to be limited in certain ways, and their future trajectory is far from certain. But this is true of every company, whether it is owned, controlled, and managed by the members of a family or not. As Joseph Schumpeter once put it, capitalism works through a process of "creative destruction." The market economy needs lots of entrepreneurs, a few of whom will succeed while the vast majority fail. It is the dynamic, and draconian, interplay between entrepreneurs (and their employees) and the market that drives economic growth. Innovation in terms of product, process, or organization is the only way in which entrepreneurs can possibly make a dent. Family firms in Spain – and elsewhere – contribute to innovation and job creation in crucial ways. In fact, in some cases they perform better than their non-family counterparts. Even those who doubt the prospects of family firms would admit that most of the large firms that exist in the world today started out as family firms. Thus, at the very least, every country needs a vibrant sector of family firms to foreshadow the future.

The cases reviewed unambiguously corroborate the theories of the multinational firm outlined in chapter 2. The patterns of forward vertical expansion into foreign distribution channels and of horizontal foreign expansion followed by the winemakers, the food-processing firms and the clothing companies can be accounted for by reference to their intangible assets (technology, brands, organizational know-how) and their need to neutralize the impact of uncertainty and asset specificity along the value chain. The automobile component and railway rolling stock manufacturers, which are not as dependent on locational sources of comparative advantage as the firms in the more traditional industries, also expanded abroad on the basis of their intangible assets.

The patterns observed are not specific to the industries that I have chosen to cover. Spanish family-owned firms in dairies (Leche Pascual, ILAS), fishing (Pescanova), pharmaceuticals (Ferrer Internacional, Laboratorios del Dr. Esteve, Laboratorios Almirall), eyewear (Indo), cosmetics (Antonio Puig, Myrurgia), hotels (Barceló, NH, Sol Meliá), printed media (*Hola*) and transportation (ALSA), to name but a few, have also expanded abroad in ways consistent with established theory.[23]

Spanish worker-owned cooperatives have also suffered from their small size. They learned a long time ago that in order to prosper they needed to join forces with each other in the form of associations, confederations, and other types of networks (CEPES 2003). The Mondragón experience could be interpreted as proof that cooperatives can succeed internationally only if they grow big enough. Certainly, MCC's size and diversification has enabled it to benefit from developing and sharing human, financial, marketing, and technological resources at the group level. It is important to note, however, that the eighty odd cooperatives that are part of MCC are owned separately by their respective worker-owners. Each of the cooperatives remains relatively small in size, makes many decisions autonomously and

---

[23] Many of the family-owned multinationals are from Catalonia (Fontrodona Francolí and Hernández Gascón 2001). On ALSA, perhaps the most successful Spanish firm in China, see *Información Comercial Española* 797 (February 2002): 71–6.

has direct representatives on MCC's decision-making bodies. Thus, Spanish cooperatives demonstrate that networks of relatively small economic units can become internationally competitive (Perrow 1992).

The evidence presented in this chapter indicates that the internationalization of Spanish family- and worker-owned enterprises has followed patterns predicted by established theory. Home market saturation and investments in intangible assets have been the key driving factors. In the next two chapters I will examine the patterns of international expansion of firms in a different type of industry, namely, oligopolistic or highly concentrated ones like banking, telecommunications, oil, gas, electricity, water, and air transportation. The conclusion will be similar: Spanish firms in such industries have invested abroad largely following well-entrenched theoretical predictions and prescriptions, demonstrating yet again that Spanish foreign direct investment is far from anomalous or paradoxical.

4 Deregulation, oligopolistic competition, and internationalization

> Multinational enterprises are large firms
> that typically operate in concentrated
> industries and earn both monopoly profits
> and rents to their proprietary assets.
>
> Richard Caves (1996: 97)

ROUGHLY four-fifths of the foreign direct investment undertaken by Spanish firms over the last two decades is accounted for by some of the largest firms in the country: Telefónica, Repsol-YPF, Gas Natural, BBVA, Grupo Santander, Endesa, Iberdrola, Unión-Fenosa, and Agbar. These firms operate in industries that are characterized by being highly concentrated and regulated, namely, telecommunications, oil and gas, banking, electricity, and water and waste disposal. Firms in other highly concentrated industries such as the media, security services, construction, insurance and healthcare have also become major foreign investors. After a decade of intense growth, several of these firms are among the largest in Europe, if not the world, within their respective industries. Five of them (Telefónica, Repsol-YPF, Grupo Santander, BBVA, and Endesa) are included on *Fortune* magazine's Global 500 ranking of the world's largest corporations. Only some of them started out as state-owned companies (e.g. Telefónica, Repsol-YPF, Endesa, Gas Natural).

The Spanish case thus seems to confirm what economists have observed since the 1960s, namely, that large firms in oligopolistic industries are far more likely to invest abroad than other types of firms (Caves 1996: 97). This is the case because large, oligopolistic firms tend to have stronger competitive advantages and more financial resources to invest abroad. Firms in these concentrated industries obtain *extraordinary profits* when they have the ability to individually or collectively control production, and thus affect prices. This typically takes place when competitive entry is restricted because of regulation, as in telecommunications or electricity. They can also obtain *rents* if they own some scarce asset (technology, brand, know-how, connections) that enables them to put the competition at a disadvantage, either at home or abroad. In practice, Spanish firms in these industries have obtained extraordinary profits and scarcity rents in the home market, although due to privatization and deregulation both have declined over the last few years. The resources thus generated, and the opportunity to earn additional profits and rents abroad (especially in Latin America), have been major drivers of their foreign expansion.

This chapter, however, will not only consider this classic economic explanation of the foreign expansion of large Spanish firms. Interviews and subsequent events clearly indicate that another major cause of expansion was managerial and political in nature, namely, to avoid being acquired by their bigger European rivals in the wake of Spain's entry into the European Union in 1986 and the completion of the single market at the end of 1992. During the 1990s, Spanish companies in the service sector became keenly aware of the fate of many of their counterparts in the manufacturing sector (automobile assembly and components, chemicals, electrical appliances, machinery, food-processing, and so on) and even in some service industries (insurance and distribution). Dozens of major Spanish firms were acquired by foreigners, mainly French, and the alarm went off in many quarters. Some blamed the terms under which Spain became an EU member for the debacle, citing the fact that a quick opening of the country's manufacturing sector was agreed upon in exchange for a better treatment of agriculture and several service industries, especially utilities and banking.

Mergers, restructurings, and privatization as a prelude to foreign investments

It is hard to overemphasize the importance of the fact that neither the Spanish government nor the companies themselves wished to see what they perceived as key service industries falling into the hands of foreigners. Mergers, restructurings, privatization and foreign investments were all part of an emergent strategy to grow in size and profitability so as to be in a better position to compete in a wider European economic space. What is most relevant to my analysis of foreign expansion is that, in most cases, it was preceded by mergers, restructuring and privatization.

Mergers of state-owned and/or private companies took place in the oil, gas, banking, and electricity industries, giving birth to companies such as Repsol, Gas Natural, Endesa, Iberdrola, Unión-Fenosa, BBVA, and Grupo Santander. This process started during the early years of the Socialist governments of Felipe González (1982–96) with combinations in the oil industry, which had traditionally been very fragmented. Later, the government encouraged, for a mixture of economic and political reasons, mergers in the electricity and banking industries. Corporate and strategic restructurings took place both prior to and after the mergers.

Ownership structures were overhauled, especially in the public sector. The Socialist government set the process in motion in 1985, although it did not engage in full privatizations, but rather in partial public offerings of shares, as in the cases of Endesa (1988), Repsol (1989), Argentaria (1993), Gas Natural (1996), and Telefónica (1996). Upon coming to power in 1996, the Popular Party implemented one of the largest privatization programs in Europe, eventually selling nearly fifty companies, most of which were privatized in full. Public offerings were used in thirteen of the cases. Domestic retail investors received special treatment in all but three. Initially, the state kept a "golden share," which it later sold. (At the end of 2002 the state accounted for a mere 0.5 percent of total market capitalization, compared to almost 17 percent back in 1992.) In several instances, a prominent Spanish financial institution (e.g. BBVA or a major savings bank) was given an "institutional stake" to guarantee "Spanish" control. For example, Endesa's largest shareholders presently include Caja Madrid (5 percent) and La Caixa (5 percent); Telefónica's biggest investors are BBVA (5.5 percent) and La Caixa (3.6 percent). Repsol-YPF's case is somewhat more complicated because it counts La Caixa (10.2 percent), BBVA (8.0 percent), a consortium of three savings banks (5.6 percent), Pemex (4.1 percent), Iberdrola (3.3 percent), and Endesa (3.0 percent) as its leading shareholders. Also special is the case of Iberia, privatized in 2000. Both "industrial partners" (British Airways and American Airlines) and institutional ones (BBVA, Logista, Ahorro Corporación, and El Corte Inglés) were given sizable stakes.[1] As a result of privatizations, the prices for telephone calls,

---

[1] The information on privatization comes from the *Informe de Actividades* of the Consultative Council on Privatizations for the years 1998 through

electricity and other utilities fell below the average for the EU (Trigo Portela 2004: 57–9).

In addition to orchestrating institutional stakes, the government passed a law in 1995 that enabled it to require by decree "prior administrative approval" for the privatized firm to make certain strategic decisions or for the direct or indirect acquisition of a sizable proportion of shares in previously state-owned companies. Golden shares, institutional stakes, and administrative pre-approval have proved to be effective mechanisms for monitoring and controlling previously state-owned firms. It is important to note that between 30 and 60 percent of the shares of the largest Spanish multinationals – whether previously state-owned or not – are owned by a collection of foreign institutional investors, mainly American, British, and continental European. This has enabled the firms to raise capital effectively, but has also put them at the mercy of portfolio capital fluctuations, especially in response to crises and financial meltdowns in Latin America (see chapter 6). Foreign institutional investors have flocked to Spanish privatizations, for a good reason. According to the calculations of the Consultative Council on Privatizations, the privatized firms offered stock market returns comparable to those of the Ibex-35 index or major mutual funds until 1999. In the early 2000s they actually performed up to 30 percent better.[2]

Foreign expansion – especially in Latin America – took place following an overall sequential pattern relative to mergers, restructurings, and privatizations. In most cases, foreign expansion started or accelerated *after* mergers helped the firm attain critical mass in Spain (Repsol, Endesa, Iberdrola, Unión Fenosa, BBVA, Santander). Privatization also preceded the most important steps at foreign expansion of the previously state-owned firms, with the exceptions of Telefónica and Iberia, which had already made important foreign investments during the late 1980s and/or early 1990s. The sequence is not coincidental. Spanish banking, oil, gas, and electricity companies had experienced major merger and privatization processes prior to the bulk

2002 (www.ccp.es). I have also used Ariño (2004) and Trigo Portela (2004). For a comparison with privatizations in other Western European countries see Clifton, Comín, and Díaz Fuentes (2003).

[2] See the Council's *Informe de Actividades* for 2002, p. 13. See also Villalonga (2000).

of their foreign expansion, which mainly took the form of cross-border acquisitions and mergers, frequently targeting state-owned firms in the host countries. The importance of this sequence of events should not be underestimated because it explains why Spanish firms were so eager to participate in Latin American privatizations: namely, they had learned the ropes in Spain.

Mergers, restructurings, privatizations, and foreign expansion have turned Spain's large service firms into serious contenders in the European marketplace. By 2003, several of these Spanish firms had become bigger than many of their once threatening European rivals. This chapter reviews the motivations, the process, and the outcomes of the remarkable years of foreign expansion that started in the early 1990s.

The motivations

It is important to note at the outset that most of the foreign investments undertaken by large Spanish firms in oligopolistic industries have been horizontal in nature. Only a few, though quantitatively important, examples can be found of backward vertical investments in search of raw materials (e.g. oil and gas), and also a few, much less important, instances of forward vertical expansion into marketing and distribution (financial services, oil and gas distribution). Thus large Spanish firms invested abroad in search of markets. It should be remembered that in service industries, such as banking, utilities, and telecommunications, exporting is rarely a viable option. Accordingly, foreign direct investment became a necessity rather than a choice.

The reasons for the companies' eagerness to enter new markets were three-fold. First, they were facing the prospect of deregulation in Spain and in Europe, as signaled by the Single Act of 1992 (effective 1 January 1993), and the political commitment throughout the Union to extend market freedoms into the service sector. Spanish (and European) service firms understood that, sooner or later, the regime of freedom of competition already in force for the manufacturing sector would eventually be extended into services. Deregulation foreshadowed increased competition and falling profit margins, which they sought to compensate for by entering foreign markets with better profit prospects.

The second factor in favor of foreign expansion was market saturation. Service industries in Spain and elsewhere in Western Europe had
developed relatively quickly since 1980. Growth rates in the near
future were not expected to be high, except (briefly) in the wake of
some technological innovation, as the case of mobile telephony illustrates. Hence, Spanish firms knew that foreign expansion was the best
way to ensure not only profit growth but also sales growth.

The third reason for foreign expansion was largely defensive in
nature. As of, say, 1992, Spanish service-sector firms were large on
their home turf, but small in the European context. They used a
combination of defensive and offensive tactics to fend off potential
acquirers. As Casanova (2002) has recently put it, they eventually
came to the realization that "the best defense is an attack." Their
strategic response to the threat of acquisition was to grow bigger. Size
can be an effective anti-takeover measure, especially if the expansion takes place into riskier, more volatile markets. In sum, Spanish
firms decided to cope with the competitive threat coming from their
larger European rivals by engaging in a strategy of "flight forward"
(Casanova 2002).

Finally, Spain's historical achievement of being among the first set of
countries to qualify for the launching of the euro in 1998 facilitated
and accelerated the process of foreign direct investment. Spanish
multinational firms – especially the largest ones – benefited in three
ways from the euro. First, institutional investors flocked to Spanish
blue chip stocks, helping the companies raise equity capital. As noted
above, between 30 and 60 percent of the equity of the largest Spanish
multinationals is now in the hands of foreign pension and mutual
funds. Second, thanks to the euro, Spanish firms found it easier to sell
large amounts of bonds at lower interest rates. And, third, the euro
provided a safeguard against the potential negative effects of a macroeconomic crisis in one of the Latin American countries in which
Spanish firms have major investments (see chapter 6). The example
of Repsol's acquisition of YPF provides perhaps the best example of
the importance of the euro:

YPF's bylaws mandated that any acquirer pay cash. [Repsol's] Chief
Executive Alfonso Cortina thought he would have to persuade YPF
management to change the bylaws to finance the deal. But investment banks
assured Cortina that they could quickly raise the money in the European

equity and debt markets. As a result, more than 60 percent of Repsol's revenues now come from outside Spain. "It's practically impossible to think of a Spanish company launching such a big issue and placing it with success without the euro," says Cortina (*Business Week*, 22 May 2000).

The path of least resistance leads to Latin America

Given the coincidence of deregulation, saturation and takeover threats as causal factors, it should not come as a surprise that, in terms of foreign expansion, large Spanish firms chose the path of least resistance, that led them straight to Latin America (Casanova 2002; Casilda Béjar 2002; Cátedra SCH 2003; Chislett 2003; Giráldez Pidal 2002; Toral 2001). According to the managers themselves, the reasons for this geographical focus had to do with (1) the vast opportunities for growth in the region, (2) their knowledge of how to compete in industries under deregulation, and (3) the common culture and language as a facilitating factor.[3] It is important to highlight the relevance of the growth opportunities that existed in Latin America during the 1990s, especially in public utilities, infrastructure development and financial services. These industries were largely populated by state-owned firms with weak competitive capabilities, and beset by decades of underinvestment. The main countries in the region suffered from a "lost decade" during the 1980s, a long period of economic stagnation triggered by the debt crisis of 1982. Starting in Chile in the late 1970s, shifting political coalitions and external pressure resulted in the adoption of macroeconomic policies geared towards monetary stability, and of market-oriented reforms within industries, including privatization and deregulation. Economies were also opened to trade, albeit in selective ways, and foreign portfolio and direct investment. By the early 1990s, Argentina, Peru, Colombia, and Venezuela had joined

---

[3] Francisco González, BBVA, *Diario de Sesiones del Senado: Comisión de Asuntos Iberoamericanos* 141 (7 June 2001): 15; Rodolfo Martín Villa, Endesa, *Diario de Sesiones del Senado: Comisión de Asuntos Iberoamericanos* 155 (26 June 2001): 23; Ricardo Fornesa, Agbar, *Diario de Sesiones del Senado: Comisión de Asuntos Iberoamericanos* 148 (12 June 2001): 1–11; José María Cuevas, president of the CEOE big business association, *Diario de Sesiones del Senado: Comisión de Asuntos Iberoamericanos* 155 (26 June 2001): 4.

Chile on this path of reform. The region's largest economy, Brazil, followed suit in the mid-1990s. Mexico, the second- largest economy, had been pursuing reform and integration with the United States since the mid-1980s, a process that culminated in 1993 with the creation of the North American Free Trade Agreement.

It is cardinal to note that industry-specific, market-oriented reforms took place in many Latin American countries earlier than in Europe, with only a few exceptions. The sequence and rate of reform can be more easily understood with one specific example. In telecommunications, several Latin American countries privatized the state-owned monopoly during the late 1980s or early 90s (Chile, Argentina, Mexico, and Peru, in that order). Among the large European countries, only the UK privatized earlier, in 1984. Neither France, Italy, nor Spain had pursued privatization when their state-controlled monopolies started to bid for Latin American companies. Later, in the mid- and late 1990s, several Latin American countries opened up their telecommunications markets to competition earlier than their European counterparts, except for the UK, which had done so back in 1991. A similar picture emerges from industries such as electricity, water, and transportation. Banking represents a different case because of the presence of both state-owned and privately held players across the region, and it will be analyzed in depth in the next chapter.

In sum, the sequence of market-oriented reforms in key service industries was such that, during the 1990s, Spanish firms had available to them few opportunities for growth elsewhere in Europe, but plenty throughout Latin America. Opportunities in other parts of the world like North America, Africa, the Middle East, South Asia, or East Asia were not clear at the time, and in Eastern Europe privatizations took place in ways that made it difficult for foreigners to acquire controlling stakes. Spanish firms were not alone in their quest to gain a foothold in the major Latin American countries, however. Especially during the early stages of the Latin American reforms, companies from Britain, France, Italy, Canada, the US and elsewhere also placed bids, in direct competition with the Spanish firms. Process-related factors played out in such a way that, by the early 2000s, Spanish firms had become the largest operators in telecommunications, electricity, water and financial services throughout the region. I now turn to the peculiar ways in which the process unfolded.

The process

The process by which large Spanish firms invested abroad was breath-taking. Since the mid-1990s, rare was the month without a significant investment by a Spanish firm, mainly in Latin America. This hectic rhythm of expansion was driven by the entry mode of choice – acquisitions – itself dictated by the nature of the industries being entered. These features produced a series of peculiar dynamics. First, firms had to pursue the targets of opportunity that appeared on the horizon without making elaborate calculations, because the decision-making windows were short and opened in discrete and somewhat unexpected ways depending on the contingencies faced by foreign governments or owners. Second, the stream of future cash flows to be generated by the investment depended to an unusual degree on the conditions set by the host-country government, largely because the industry being entered was only partially deregulated or still fully regulated. In fact, many Spanish firms (especially Telefónica and the electrical utilities) entered foreign markets in a monopolistic regime, meaning that their future cash flows depended on political as well as economic conditions. Third, Spanish firms in the same industry frequently found themselves in competition with each other for the limited and capricious number of targets available at any given moment of time. And, fourth, emulation took place not only among firms in the same industry, but also across industries.

The case of Telefónica exemplifies three of the dynamics extremely well. Initially, the company did not fully understand the implications of the idiosyncratic ways in which investment opportunities came up. In Chile (1987) and Mexico (1990), Telefónica failed to be the winning bidder in the privatization of CTC and Telmex, respectively. The lesson it learned was useful not just to itself but also to a number of other Spanish firms: it is better to overpay than to be left out. Moreover, a high bidding price signals commitment to the market, and tends to create goodwill with the local government (Casanova 2002).

Telefónica also illustrates the importance of political advantages. In fact, it is a company that insists on organizing itself on a country-by-country basis precisely for this reason. According to its president, "In this House we always say that we are not a multinational firm, but rather a multidomestic company, and the message conveyed to each executive is precisely this one: we are a company deeply rooted in each of the countries in which we operate."[4] Interviews with former executives or with consultants revealed that it was not easy for Telefónica to learn from scratch how to operate within the intricate web of local political connections not just in one country, but in more than fifteen different ones.

As the pioneering large Spanish firm in Latin America, Telefónica became a role model to be imitated by other firms in different industries (Casanova 2002). Several executives interviewed for this project pointed out that the company had shown them the way. Telefónica, though, is not an illustration of within-industry emulation because there is no other Spanish firm of comparable stature in telecommunications. As the next chapter will show, however, in the banking sector Spanish companies became their own fiercest competitors, a situation that also developed in gas and electricity.

The role of intangible assets

The large Spanish multinationals have expanded abroad not only on the basis of monopolistic and/or political advantages but also thanks to their intangible assets. The literature on foreign direct investment is focused on technology and brands as the key intangibles (Caves 1996). Technology, however, has not been important in the case of the large Spanish multinationals, mainly because, in industries such as financial services and utilities, technology is rarely developed in-house. Their main intangibles are the brand, marketing know-how, and project-execution capabilities (Amsden and Hikino 1994).

Brands and marketing know-how have been important components of the international strategy of large Spanish firms, as the case of banking demonstrates (see the next chapter). Project execution capabilities refer to the tacit organizational and managerial know-how pertaining to large-scale undertakings such as construction, turnkey and other kinds of infrastructural projects. Firms such as Telefónica, Repsol, Iberdrola, Endesa, Unión-Fenosa, and Agbar have demonstrated over the years a superior ability to set up and run telecommunications, energy, and water infrastructures. Their skills involve the

---

[4] César Alierta, president of Telefónica, *Diario de Sesiones del Senado: Comisión de Asuntos Iberoamericanos* 155 (26 June 2001): 21.

production, distribution, and sale of various types of services. While this knowledge is not "patentable," it is rare, difficult to imitate, and valuable, the three conditions identified in the resource-based view of the firm as characterizing a true "capability" (Barney 1986; Peteraf 1993; Markides and Williamson 1996). Thus, these non-technological proprietary intangible assets have enabled large Spanish firms to obtain scarcity rents in addition to the extraordinary profits arising from imperfect competition.

The mistakes

The facts that the large Spanish service-sector firms had well-de-fined motivations to undertake foreign investments and built their expansion on a series of proprietary intangible assets does not rule out the possibility of making mistakes. Indeed, most of them – just like any other multinational firm from every home country on Earth – have made mistakes. It is only fair to point out, however, that Spanish multinationals have invested in industries that are problematic be-cause of regulatory or institutional risk (AFI 2004). And it is import-ant to keep in mind that foreign investment always is a learning process. Firms face a "liability of foreignness," and thus are likely to make mistakes as they expand abroad. The idea is to learn from the mistakes (Aharoni 1996; Johanson and Vahlne 1977).

Spanish executives are generally candid about the mistakes they have made while expanding abroad. Perhaps the most prominent case of failure is Iberia's, the flagship airline. In this instance, the strategic vision was not the problem. Madrid could be turned into a profit-able hub for passenger and cargo traffic between Europe and South America. Its geographical location on the southwestern edge of Europe, its attractiveness as a major tourism destination, and its large domestic market made it a plausible choice. Given Iberia's dominant position at Madrid airport, it could profit disproportionately from realizing that potential. The mistake had to do with the choice of means. During the early 1990s Iberia decided to participate in the privatization processes of Aerolíneas Argentinas and Viasa, the Vene-zuelan carrier, very much following the example of Telefónica. Mul-tiple labor, operational, and political problems occurred in the bizarre relationship between privatized carriers and the still state-owned Spanish flagship airline. As subsequent company executives have realized, non-equity strategic alliances could have done the job more effectively and helped avoid the pitfalls.[5] Also problematic was the attempt to create a hub in Miami to distribute European traffic bound for Central America, the Caribbean, and the southwestern United States (home to important Hispanic populations). This project was only approved by the US authorities after Spain agreed to a bilateral open-skies treaty, which eroded Iberia's market share and profits on the North Atlantic routes. Iberia's privatization in 2000 disconnected the company from the state's budget but the state enterprise holding took over Aerolíneas Argentinas. In June of 2001 Aerolíneas suspended payments, and a few weeks after September 11 the state managed to sell it to a group of Spanish investors led by Viajes Marsans.

The electrical utilities also ran into trouble on several occasions. The most widely publicized problems were those of Endesa in Chile, a country it entered in 1999,[6] and Unión-Fenosa in the Dominican Republic. Similarly, Telefónica has had its fair share of dubious investments, losses, and post-investment troubles. In 2002 it reported a net loss of €5,600 million after writing off €16,000 million of the goodwill that resulted from acquisitions in Argentina, the US (Lycos) and the third-generation mobile telephone licenses in Europe (Chislett 2003: 57). It has also faced serious difficulties in Brazil, where it was fined several times by regulators for failing to deliver a reliable service (*Financial Times*, 29 June 1999). In the mid-1990s Repsol embarked upon an ambitious though unsuccessful plan to enter the retail gasoline business in several European countries. Industry specialists also criticized the company for acquiring YPF in the midst of an economic recession in Argentina that presaged the default and devaluation of early 2002 (*International Petroleum Finance*, 4 February 2003). The banks have been the targets of criticism, especially because of their ill-fated Internet investments in Latin America and Europe (*Wall Street Journal Europe*, 27 May 2002). Blistering evaluations of Spanish investments in Latin America proliferated in the wake of the Argentine

---

[5] Xabier de Irala, Iberia, *Diario de Sesiones del Senado: Comisión de Asuntos Iberoamericanos* 177 (4 October 2001): 6–7.

[6] Rodolfo Martín Villa, Endesa, *Diario de Sesiones del Senado: Comisión de Asuntos Iberoamericanos* 155 (26 June 2001): 26. See also *Reuters News* (22 October 1997) and *Latin American Power Watch* (1 September 1999).

crisis of 2001–2, a subject that will be analyzed in depth in chapter 6. Finally, several Spanish multinationals, or their former executives, are under investigation for allegedly paying bribes. The most prominent case involves BBVA's dealings with former Peruvian President Alberto Fujimori.

An interesting peculiarity of the Spanish firms' investments in Latin America is that, from an statistical point of view, they exhibit a distinct preference for investing in countries whose governments have a high degree of discretionary power, i.e. are not subject to checks and balances by parliament or the judiciary. The absence of such institutional constraints renders those countries riskier. Thus, between 1987 and 2000, an increase of half a standard deviation in the degree to which the host-country government enjoys discretion resulted in a 37 percent increase in investments by Spanish firms in banking, oil and gas, electricity, water, and telecommunications. This preference for discretionary governments is more marked in the case of currently or previously state-owned companies such as Endesa, Telefónica, or Repsol.[7] For firms in these regulated industries, there is a clear advantage over negotiating with governments that enjoy discretionary power. The problem, naturally, presents itself when the individual or party in power is replaced. The new executive, by definition, also enjoys discretionary powers and can easily renege on the negotiations concluded with its predecessor. This situation presented itself in Argentina and Peru after 2001.

Several of the top executives of the large Spanish multinationals are on record as stating that they prefer to negotiate with discretionary governments and to have direct access to top officials. Thus, the president of electrical utility Endesa suggested that, while emphasizing that during the operative phase of their foreign investments his company preferred governments with little discretion, the reverse was true during the time leading up to initial entry: "The other big opportunity [besides Brazil] lies in Mexico, but . . . the privatization of Mexican firms requires a constitutional amendment . . . We shall see whether during the upcoming official visit of the [Spanish] Head of Government to Mexico we receive some signals regarding this issue, although

---

[7] The empirical evidence comes from my paper with Esteban García Canal (2004), in which we analyze data on twenty-five firms between 1987 and 2000.

I do not think it will happen immediately."[8] The president of Grupo Santander – one of the world's twenty top banks and the largest within the eurozone in terms of market capitalization – asserted that a multinational firm must "collaborate with local authorities and at the same time defend its interests, those of its customers, and, above all, those of its shareholders" (Botín 2002). This bank thus understands as business-as-usual the active negotiation with politicians and regulators in order to defend its interests. Even more clearly, the president of Agbar – one of the world's largest multinational water utilities – candidly shared with senators during a hearing that "another surprise we came across in South America was that authorities are much more approachable than in Spain or Europe. I can tell you that in [Latin American] countries similar to Spain in terms of population, one finds it easier to meet with a cabinet minister; it is even easier to change the appointment time. This is not as easy in Spain, and it is likely not easy either in France or Germany."[9]

To be sure, after the firm starts operations in the host country, the same executives acknowledge that they prefer governments with little ability to change the (advantageous) conditions of entry obtained during the negotiation phase. They prefer to operate in host countries in which the executive branch of government, which regulates their activities, is subject to legislative and judicial controls, i.e. where there is "political stability," a term the executives themselves used in interviews (Ontiveros, Conthe and Nogueira, 2004: 4). For instance, in hearings at the Spanish Senate, the president of Endesa, the world's eighth-largest electrical utility and a major investor in Latin America, equated "certainty" with "the rule of law" and with an "impeccable institutional functioning." "Most of our difficulties in Latin America have had to do with regulatory uncertainty."[10] Top executives of Gas Natural and electrical utilities Iberdrola and Unión Fenosa have clearly indicated in their own writings that their companies took into

---

[8] Rodolfo Martín Villa, president of Endesa, *Diario de Sesiones del Senado: Comisión de Asuntos Iberoamericanos* 155 (26 June 2001): 32. At the time of writing, Mexico had not yet privatized electricity.

[9] Ricardo Fornesa Ribó, president and CEO of Aguas de Barcelona, *Diario de Sesiones del Senado: Comisión de Asuntos Iberoamericanos* 148 (12 June 2001): 3.

[10] Rodolfo Martín Villa, president of Endesa, *Diario de Sesiones del Senado: Comisión de Asuntos Iberoamericanos* 155 (26 June 2001): 33.

account regulatory risk when picking and choosing foreign markets in which to invest (Brufau Niubó 2002; Azagra Blázquez 2002; Prieto Iglesias 2002). The mistake lies in trying to have it both ways: doing business with a government subject to few controls during the negotiation phase, but with a government subject to such controls once operations are underway so as to prevent conditions from being "arbitrarily" changed.

In spite of the mistakes, the stock market has reacted quite favorably to many of the foreign-expansion decisions made by the largest Spanish firms. A recent research paper establishes that more than half of the greenfield investments and joint ventures undertaken by Spanish firms received a positive reaction from the market, as measured by "abnormal returns" within one or two days of the announcement. (Acquisitions of foreign firms, by contrast, have not resulted in positive abnormal returns.) As predicted by theory, firms with sizable intangible assets receive an average boost of about 0.3 percent in share price (though this is not statistically significant) in terms of abnormal stock market returns in response to all of their foreign investments, i.e. including acquisitions as well as greenfield plants and joint ventures. Share prices for firms with large cash flows increase by 0.6 percent. Investments in other OECD countries result in an average boost of 0.5 percent, compared to a statistically insignificant 0.1 percent if the investment takes place in Latin America. Only in the case of greenfield establishments do Latin American investments fare better than those in the rest of the OECD (López Duarte and García Canal 2003).

The outcomes

The foreign expansion of Spanish service-sector firms has placed them among the largest and best capitalized in all of Europe. For the first time in decades a handful of Spanish firms are uniquely positioned to be "players" in the European marketplace. This is perhaps the single most important outcome of the remarkable and accelerated process of internationalization since the early 1990s. I will use two types of data to demonstrate the growing importance of the large Spanish multinationals within the European and global contexts, namely, total revenues and market capitalization. Table 4.1 shows the largest companies in telecommunications, utilities, banking and oil – the industries in which large Spanish multinationals still hold

Table 4.1. *Selected companies from the Fortune Global 500 list, 1994 and 2002*

Industry/ Company	Country	2002 Industry Rank	2002 Global Rank	2002 Revenues ($bn)	1994 Industry Rank	1994 Global Rank	1994 Revenues ($bn)	Real Revenue growth, 1994 = 100
Telecommunications								
NTT	JP	1	16	89.6	2	16	70.8	110
Verizon	US	2	24	67.6	9	237	13.8	425
Deutsche Telekom	DE	3	55	50.8	3	40	41.1	107
Vodafone	GB	4	60	47	–	–	–	–
AT&T	US	5	61	46.7	1	15	75.1	54
France Télécom	FR	6	71	44.1	5	95	25.7	149
SBC	US	7	76	43.1	15	307	11.6	323
Olivetti	IT	8	127	29.7	–	–	–	–
BT	GB	9	130	29.3	6	120	21.6	118
Sprint	US	10	149	27.2	12	271	12.7	186
Telefónica	ES	11	152	26.9	14	301	11.8	198
Royal KPN	NL	22	428	11.9	18	384	10.1	102
Utilities								
EDF	FR	1	65	45.7	2	59	33.5	118
Tokyo Electric Power	JP	2	85	40.4	1	32	50.4	70
Enel	IT	3	138	28.3	4	117	21.8	113

Company	Country							
Centrica	GB	4	201	21.5	6	215	14.9	125
Kansai Electric Power	JP	5	202	21.5	3	96	25.6	73
Chubu Electric Power	JP	6	259	17.9	5	131	20.5	76
Korea Electric Power	KR	7	279	17.1	9	343	11	135
Endesa	ES	8	305	15.8	–	–	–	–
Oil								
Exxon Mobil	US	1	3	182.5	1	8	101.5	156
Royal Dutch	GB/NL	2	4	179.4	2	10	94.9	164
BP	GB	3	5	178.7	4	31	50.7	306
Total	FR	4	14	96.9	12	98	24.6	342
Chevron Texaco	US	5	15	92	8	68	31.1	257
Conoco Phillips	US	6	36	58.4	22	280	12.4	409
ENI	IT	7	63	46.3	7	63	32.6	123
China National Petroleum Corporation	CN	8	69	44.9	–	–	–	–
Sinopec	CN	9	70	44.5	–	–	–	–
SK	KR	10	108	34.7	–	–	–	–
Repsol-YPF	ES	11	110	34.5	16	163	17.7	169
Petrobras	BR	16	185	22.6	17	169	17.4	113
Banking								
Citigroup	US	1	13	100.8	2	66	31.6	277

Table 4.1. (continued)

Industry/Company	Country	2002 Industry Rank	2002 Global Rank	2002 Revenues ($bn)	1994 Industry Rank	1994 Global Rank	1994 Revenues ($bn)	Real Revenue growth, 1994 = 100
Deutsche Bank	DE	2	47	52.1	1	60	33.1	137
Crédit Suisse	CH	3	48	52.1	18	137	20	226
BNP Paribas	FR	4	54	51.1	19	145	19.3	230
Bank of America	US	5	64	45.7	23	181	16.5	240
Fortis	BE/NL	6	73	43.6	–	–	–	–
J. P. Morgan Chase	US	7	75	43.4	35	296	11.9	317
UBS	CH	8	79	42.3	26	219	14.7	250
HSBC	GB	9	89	39.7	15	126	21.1	163
Crédit Agricole	FR	10	98	36.7	8	85	27.8	115
HypoVereinsbank	DE	11	99	36.4	27	220	14.6	216
Royal Bank of Scotland	GB	12	102	36.0	–	–	–	–
ABN AMRO	NL	13	109	34.6	13	121	21.5	140
HBOS	GB	14	125	29.9	–	–	–	–
Sumitomo Mitsui	JP	15	131	28.8	6	76	29.6	84
Wells Fargo	US	16	134	28.5	–	–	–	–

Mizuho Financial Group	JP	17	142	28.2	–	–	–	–
Barclays	GB	18	157	26.6	16	133	20.2	114
Santander	ES	19	160	26.3	51	394	9.6	238
DZ Bank	DE	20	164	25.6	21	170	17.3	128
Société Générale	FR	21	173	24.2	–	–	–	–
Wachovia Corp.	US	22	177	23.6	–	–	–	–
Mitsubishi Tokyo Financial	JP	23	187	22.8	40	326	11.3	175
Lloyds TSB Group	GB	24	195	22.4	45	357	10.5	185
Bank One Corp.	US	25	198	22.2	59	498	7.9	244
BBVA	ES	26	213	20.8	53	436	9	201
Commerzbank	DE	29	231	19.8	28	229	14.1	122
Credit Lyonnais	FR	33	251	18.2	10	92	26.4	60
Banca Intesa	IT	35	268	17.6	52	401	9.6	159
San Paolo IMI	IT	50	410	12.4	29	247	13.5	80
Central Hispano	ES	–	–	–	55	467	8.4	–

Note: A dash (–) denotes that the company was not ranked within the *Fortune* Global 500. If two or more ranked companies in 1994 had merged by 2002, the data for 1994 are for the largest of the merged companies.
Sources: Fortune, Hoover's.

their sway. I use the *Fortune* magazine rankings of the 500 largest companies in the world in terms of revenue, which started to include service as well as manufacturing firms as of 1994. I report in the table real revenue growth between 1994 and 2002 for companies ranked in both years, calculated using the implicit deflator of GDP. The five Spanish firms among the Global 500 (Telefónica, Endesa, Santander, BBVA, and Repsol-YPF), have all improved their positions since 1994, thanks to both domestic mergers (e.g. Santander, BBVA) and foreign acquisitions and growth. Thus, Telefónica has gone up three positions, Repsol-YPF five, BBVA twenty-seven, and Santander a whopping thirty-two. What is important to note is that over the eight-year period between 1994 and 2002 Spanish firms have grown faster than many of their key European competitors.

More impressive, and perhaps consequential in terms of future mergers and acquisitions, are the rankings in terms of market capitalization. As of the end of 2003, six Spanish firms were among those included on the Dow Jones Euro Stoxx indexes of the largest European and eurozone listed companies. As reported in Table 4.2, Telefónica and Santander are the firms with the largest market capitalization in the eurozone within their respective industries, ahead of their French, German, and Italian counterparts and behind only some of their British or Swiss competitors. The second-largest Spanish bank, BBVA, is only surpassed by BNP and Deutsche Bank within the eurozone. In utilities, Endesa and Iberdrola, while only half the market capitalization of Germany's E.ON, are roughly at the same level as Suez, ENEL, and RWE. Repsol-YPF is the smallest of the top European or Eurozone oil companies in terms of market capitalization, at about one-third the level of the next largest, ENI of Italy. Telefónica, Santander, and BBVA have done better in the stock market than most of their eurozone counterparts since 1998, when the euro was introduced (see table 4.2). It is important to note, however, that some European giants like Deutsche Telekom, France Télécom or Electricité de France (EdF) have the potential to overcome their Spanish rivals once a larger proportion of their shares is floated on the stock market.

After a decade of mergers, restructurings, privatizations, and foreign investments, the large Spanish multinationals have become prominent actors in the European corporate landscape. They now are "players" in the sense that they are in a position to participate in European mergers and acquisitions in their own right. As a result, Spain has joined the

Table 4.2. Companies on the Euro Stoxx indices (including total and eurozone), 1998 and 2003

Industry/Company	Country	Float 31-Dec-2003	Market capitalization (€1,000 million) 31-Dec-2003	15-Jun-1998
Telecommunications				
Vodafone Group	GB	1.00	133.9	–
Telefónica	ES	0.94	54.5	40.9
Deutsche Telekom	DE	0.57	34.9	64.1
France Télécom	FR	0.45	24.8	56.9
BT Group plc	GB	1.00	23.2	62.7
Telecom Italia	IT	0.83	20.0	34.7
Telecom Italia Mobile (TIM)	IT	0.44	16.0	–
Royal KPN	NL	–	–	25.0
Portugal Telecom	PT	–	–	9.1
Utilities				
E.On	DE	0.94	33.8	–
Suez	FR	0.93	14.9	–
Endesa	ES	0.90	14.5	20.3
ENEL	IT	0.39	12.8	–
RWE	DE	0.77	12.7	15.9
Iberdrola	ES	0.86	12.2	–
Banking				
HSBC	GB	1.00	136.4	–
Royal Bank of Scotland	GB	0.95	65.7	–
UBS	CH	0.92	58.9	32.0
Barclays	GB	1.00	46.5	–
Santander	ES	1.00	44.8	–
BNP Paribas	FR	0.94	42.4	14.2
HBOS	GB	1.00	39.5	–
Deutsche Bank	DE	1.00	38.2	39.7
Lloyds TSB Group	GB	1.00	35.5	69.3
BBVA	ES	1.00	35.0	28.7
Crédit Suisse Group	CH	1.00	34.5	52.7
ING Groep	NL	0.88	33.4	48.8
Groupe Société Générale	FR	1.00	30.6	16.2

Table 4.2. (*continued*)

Industry/Company	Country	Float 31-Dec- 2003	Market capitalization (€1,000 million)	
			31-Dec- 2003	15-Jun- 1998
ABN AMRO	NL	1.00	30.3	29.6
Unicredito Italiano	IT	0.76	20.6	14.1
Fortis	NL	0.93	19.3	9.1
San Paolo IMI	IT	0.74	11.1	–
Oil				
BP plc	GB	1.00	142.1	74.1
Total	FR	1.00	95.5	32.8
Royal Dutch Petroleum	NL	1.00	87.8	106.0
Shell Transport and Trading	GB	1.00	57.0	–
ENI	IT	0.64	38.4	48.4
Repsol YPF	ES	0.79	14.9	15.0

Note: A dash (–) denotes that the company was not ranked.
Source: www.stoxx.com.

exclusive club of European countries with large listed companies, of which only Britain, France, Germany, Italy, the Netherlands, and Switzerland are members. (Finland has one large company, Nokia.) Let us analyze the situation within each industry in more detail.

The largest Spanish multinationals

In telecommunications, Telefónica's real revenues have almost doubled in eight years, a growth rate much faster than that of European rivals Deutsche Telekom, France Télécom, BT, and Royal KPN. The Spanish firm – now fully privatized – has widened its lead over its Dutch competitor and matched BT and Telecom Italia (now owner of Olivetti) in size, both of which were twice as big back in 1994. Telefónica has expanded internationally much more rapidly than its French, German, Dutch, and Portuguese counterparts, a fact that explains why its total revenues have grown relative to theirs. Among the world's largest companies, only Britain's Vodafone and US telecommunications giants Verizon and SBC have grown faster. Telefónica is not yet a global company because its presence is limited to Europe and Latin America, although its bigger size and market capitalization gives it more leverage in terms of further acquisitions and possible mergers in Europe.

A recent arrival to *Fortune*'s Global 500 list is Endesa, the combination of formerly state-owned regional electrical utilities, now partially privatized. While only a small relative of Japanese companies and French state-owned EdF, it is large among European listed utilities. Its closest Spanish rival, Iberdrola, is also big in terms of market capitalization. In 2001 they were poised to merge, but the competition authority and the government imposed strict conditions in order to prevent too much concentration of market power. Another missed opportunity was the hostile takeover of Iberdrola by Gas Natural, opposed by the industry's regulatory authority, which could have created a large Spanish gas and electricity group. Spanish utilities are set to benefit from the creation of the Iberian market for electricity, an agreement signed in 2004 between Spain and Portugal that allows consumers to choose supplier. In electricity, Spain is proving to be much more dynamic and visionary than France or Germany, the two largest markets in Europe.

Banking is perhaps the industry in which Spanish companies have made greater progress on the European scorecard. Santander and BBVA are major players in Europe not just in terms of size but also because of their strategic stakes and cross-shareholding arrangements throughout the continent. In addition, Santander has acquired major market positions in consumer finance in both Germany and Eastern Europe (see the next chapter). The two largest Spanish banks are among the fastest growing in the world (table 4.1). In Europe, Santander's revenues are now greater than those of several of its once formidable French, German, and Italian counterparts (DZ Bank, Société Générale, Commerzbank, Crédit Lyonnais, San Paolo IMI). BBVA has also surpassed the latter three. As noted above, Santander and BBVA have climbed even more positions in the European ranking in terms of market capitalization (table 4.2). Unlike a decade ago, the two largest Spanish banks are now recognized as potential acquirers. As in the cases of Telefónica and the electrical utilities, this has been possible through a combination of domestic mergers and international expansion. As BBVA president Francisco González noted in 2001, "the Latin American investments of Spanish firms make them more powerful in negotiations with their European counterparts."[11] Other top executives interviewed for this book made similar remarks as early as 1998. It is important to note that in the mid-1990s European bankers, especially German ones, were open about their intentions to acquire Spanish banks. Just a few years later, the situation has been reversed (see chapter 5).

While the prospects for the large Spanish multinationals in telecommunications, electricity, and banking appear to be bright, the predicament of Spain's Repsol-YPF is much more fragile. In spite of its acquisition of YPF in Argentina and its international expansion throughout Latin America (both upstream and downstream) and in selected African, Middle Eastern, and South Asian locations (upstream), the company is dwarfed by its global and European rivals in terms of both revenue and market capitalization (see tables 4.1 and 4.2). Many in the financial and consulting communities believe that Repsol-YPF is definitely the most likely of all large Spanish multinationals to fall prey to a bigger rival. Gas Natural (in which Repsol owns a quarter of the equity and La Caixa an additional 32 percent), although an even smaller company that has expanded downstream into several Latin American residential gas markets, may be in better shape because gas distribution is a more fragmented industry than oil.

Other large Spanish multinationals

Though not as big as the Spanish firms included on *Fortune*'s Global 500 and the Dow Jones Euro Stoxx indexes, there are several other large companies that have made headlines because of their international expansion. They are active in the areas of water, sanitation, construction, infrastructure maintenance, health insurance, media, and security services. Like telecommunications, electricity, and banking, these are oligopolistic industries in which company-specific competitive advantages have to do not with patentable technology but with managerial and organizational skills and with project-execution

---

[11] *Diario de Sesiones del Senado: Comisión de Asuntos Iberoamericanos* 141 (7 June, 2001): 16–17.

capabilities. Brands also play a role, especially in health insurance, the mass media, and security services.

The most international of Spanish water utilities is Aguas de Barcelona (Agbar), which is active in water, sanitation, waste disposal, and health insurance. Its water customers number nearly 25 million across Argentina, Brazil, Colombia, Cuba, Chile, Uruguay, Portugal, Morocco, and the United States. Agbar generates almost half of its revenues and more than 60 percent of its profits from abroad. Although still small by European standards, it has used its strength in the water business to diversify into related areas, with only one major act of unrelated diversification (health insurance through its acquisition of Adeslas). Like the large Spanish multinationals, it has expanded abroad via acquisitions and administrative concessions, frequently in conjunction with international and local partners. For instance, its most important US concession is the state of Washington's vehicle inspection program. Also active in health insurance is Mapfre, a full-line insurer, which generates half its revenue from abroad, mostly Latin America, and which is now shifting its focus towards Europe. Insurance, however, is not an industry in which Spanish firms have excelled, with many of them being acquired by their larger European rivals.

The major Spanish construction firms have catapulted themselves through domestic mergers and international expansion and acquisitions into the group of leading European companies in the infrastructure construction and management business: Acciona, ACS-Dragados, FCC, Ferrovial, and OHL. These firms have diversified into a wide array of services including waste treatment and disposal, street cleaning, park preservation and maintenance, facilities maintenance, parking operation and maintenance, toll highway operation and maintenance, airport operation, and telecommunications, among others. Their traditional construction and civil engineering business accounts for no more than two-thirds of total revenue, and in some cases for only half. Another distinguishing feature is that they have relied on Latin America for growth to a much lesser extent than the other large Spanish multinationals. Thus Spanish construction firms are active in a wide range of infrastructure-related service activities in countries as diverse as Canada, Poland, Australia, Egypt, Morocco, Argentina, Chile, Brazil, the United States, and the United Kingdom. Typically, Latin America represents no more than two-thirds of their international business, in Ferrovial's case less than a quarter. Although all of them have a long history of international construction activities in as many as seventy different countries, they differ in the proportion of revenues coming from abroad: approximately 30 percent for Ferrovial, 25 percent for Dragados (before its acquisition by ACS), 20 percent for Acciona, 15 percent for ACS, 15 percent for FCC, and 10 percent for OHL. The fact that Spain has witnessed a huge infrastructure boom during the 1990s and early 2000s has had a major effect on their operations. International activities, however, account for slightly higher proportions of operating profits than sales, clearly indicating that higher margins abroad will continue to fuel their international expansion. Construction and infrastructure service firms are perhaps the Spanish firms best positioned to expand into the new Eastern members of the EU, where a major investment boom is likely to unfold.

In 2000 Ferrovial acquired Poland's biggest builder, Budimex. According to its CEO, Rafael del Pino, "Budimex showed how we were able to enter a different kinf of market, with an entirely different language, and teach them our strategy. Poland is very much in position for take off especially with EU funds" (*Financial Times*, 15 June 2004).

In the mass media sector, Prisa (the publisher of the daily *El País*) has expanded its international newspaper, publishing, printing and radio broadcasting operations, especially since the late 1990s. In 2000 it acquired Santillana, a Spanish textbook publishing company with forty years of experience in Latin America. This and other purchases of Latin American publishers has turned Prisa into the largest textbook publisher in the region, which represents two-thirds of Santillana's revenues and profits, and about 20 percent of Prisa's overall. Although not as product-diversified as Prisa, other Spanish publishers have long had an important presence in Latin America, especially Planeta.

The last major oligopolistic industry in which Spanish firms are making a mark internationally is security, surveillance, and cash transport services. Prosegur, founded in 1976, is among the largest in the world, although dwarfed by market leader Securitas, which generates seven times as much revenue. Prosegur's first international step was an acquisition in Portugal in 1990. Since 1995 it has undertaken major acquisitions in Argentina, Chile, Brazil, Peru, Uruguay, Paraguay, Italy, Switzerland, and France. With nearly 60,000 employees worldwide, it obtains approximately 30 percent of its revenues from Latin America and 20 percent from Europe.

The large Spanish multinationals share some of the distinguishing features of their foreign competitors. They operate in oligopolistic and somewhat regulated service industries, in which keeping up with rivals and getting along with governments are critical to success. They are not technology leaders in the traditional sense of the term. Rather, they have expanded internationally on the basis of marketing knowledge, organizational skills, and project-execution capabilities. Domestic mergers and foreign acquisitions (mostly in Latin America and Europe) have enabled them to enter the ranks of the largest and best-positioned competitors. The peculiarity of the Spanish case has to do with two aspects. First, few large multinationals have emerged from oligopolistic manufacturing industries (e.g. Acerinox in steel and Repsol in oil and petrochemicals). Second, much of the expansion of the oligopolistic service multinationals has taken place in Latin America, at least to date.

Looking towards the future: will Europe be next?

Spanish firms in oligopolistic industries such as telecommunications, electricity, water, oil, gas, banking, insurance, construction, infrastructure services, the mass media, and security services have undergone massive change and international expansion over the last decade. They have grown in size domestically (through mergers) and internationally (mainly through acquisitions, joint ventures, and administrative concessions). They have encountered many of the problems that beset multinationals in these industries, no matter what their country of origin, namely, managing relationships with local governments and joint-venture partners, developing appropriate command and control mechanisms, hiring and motivating expatriate managers, integrating acquisitions, and weathering macroeconomic storms in emerging economies, to name but a few. They have become bigger in size and hence more prominent and competitive within the European marketplace.

Still, it would not be unfair to say that the easy part has been done. Being a multinational firm is not simple, especially in oligopolistic industries in which mistakes are expensive and hard to reverse. Executives, consultants, analysts, and government officials interviewed for this book differed as to what the next steps should be for the large Spanish multinational firms to take. While some think that the next mountain to climb should be North America, Asia, or the Pacific, others highlighted the importance of consolidating their positions in Western Europe, entering Eastern Europe, and participating in possible cross-border mergers with other European firms.

Only a few of the companies discussed in this chapter already have a strong position in Europe outside Spain (Ferrovial, Prosegur). Many others are stepping up their presence. During late 2003 and early 2004 several Spanish firms took visible steps to expand in both Western and Eastern Europe. For instance, Santander has made acquisitions in the consumer finance business in both Germany and Poland, Gas Natural hopes to enlist 1.5 million customers (20 percent of its total) in Italy and Greece after making acquisitions, and Endesa is raising its stake in SNET, France's third-largest electricity generator. Other companies are ready to make acquisitions in Europe, but they are facing, in the words of Mapfre's president José Manuel Martínez, "nationalist sentiments." "We are under the impression," he explains, "that the large European companies do not like a Spanish firm to be the acquirer . . . It is hard for them to come to terms with the idea of a little Spaniard buying a German, French or Italian company" (*Expansión*, 26 February 2004). As former Bank of Spain governor Luis Angel Rojo has argued (*Cinco Días*, 17 November 2003), Spain has liberalized its oligopolistic industries more rapidly than most continental European countries, and its companies and banks have encountered political difficulties when attempting to play in Europe. He specifically argues that "Spanish banks are very competitive in the retail market. They realized they were in a position to enter other countries but were not allowed to do so; and that is one reason they turned to Latin America."[12] The next chapter will analyze in more depth the prospects for European growth and acquisitions in the case of the banking sector.

Virtually every interviewee agreed that, no matter what happens next, the accelerated international expansion of the large Spanish firms has changed the face of the country, both domestically and internationally, and turned them into competitors that other European firms need to take seriously into account. At long last, Spanish firms have become relevant international competitors in their own right.

---

[12] The press has touted the possibility of cross-border European mergers and acquisitions in the banking sector (*El País*, 11 November 2003, 25 November 2003, 5 January 2004 and 12 January 2004; *Cinco Días*, 17 November 2003; *Financial Times*, 22 January 2004, 3 May 2004).

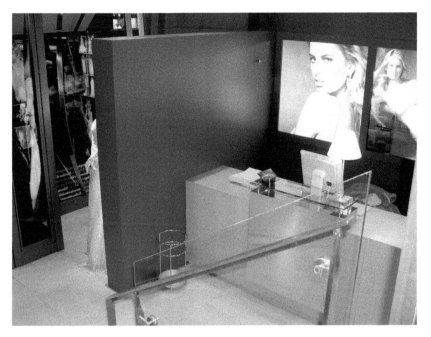

1. The world's largest maker and seller of bridal wear is Barcelona-based Pronovias, with a 5 percent global market share. The picture shows its Paris store (see chapter 3). Photo courtesy of Pronovias.

2. Inditex's Zara is perhaps the best-known Spanish brand around the world (see chapters 3 and 8). The firm designs, makes, and sells 11,000 different clothing items each year. The picture shows one of more than 700 Zara stores outside Spain, in Miami, Florida (see chapter 3). Photo courtesy of Inditex.

3. Alsa, now the largest Spanish bus transportation company, has been active in China since 1984, through a joint venture with the Tianjin Taxi Company, where it serves over sixty routes on a regular basis. Its international operations extend into all of Europe, Morocco, Argentina, Chile, and the United States. Photo courtesy of Alsa.

4. Talgo trains serve the Seattle–Portland and Seattle–Vancouver corridors. The firm's most important weakness is that it only designs and manufactures the passenger cars, and not the locomotives (see chapter 3). Photo courtesy of Patentes Talgo.

5. Grupo Antolín, the world's largest maker of interior liners for automobiles, has a manufacturing presence on four continents. The picture shows the company's technical and commercial office in Weyhausen, Germany (see chapter 3). Photo courtesy of Grupo Antolín.

6. Ficosa International has established manufacturing plants in seventeen countries in Europe, the Americas, and Asia (see chapter 3). It operates design centers in Barcelona and Troy, Michigan (in the picture). Photo courtesy of Ficosa International.

7. Aguas de Barcelona (Agbar) is the spanish utility company with the widest international spread. It is active in water, sanitation, waste disposal, and health insurance. Its water customers number nearly 25 million across Argentina, Brazil, Colombia, Cuba, Chile, Uruguay, Portugal, Morocco, and the United States (see chapter 4). The photo shows the water treatment plant of subsidiary Aguas Andinas at Farfana, Chile. Photo courtesy of Agbar.

8. In spite of its resounding success in Spain, El Corte Inglés, the country's largest retailer, has rarely ventured abroad. Its new Lisbon store occupies an entire block in one of city's busiest centers. AP Photo/ Steven Governo.

9. President Emilio Botín has turned Grupo Santander into one of the world's largest financial companies. A long-time banker, Botín easily qualifies as one of the country's most astute and skillful managers. Photo by Rafael Martín, courtesy of Expansion.

10. Foreign investment has awarded Spanish companies more visibility within the global financial community. BBVA chairman Francisco González, center, New York Stock Exchange co-president Catherine Kinney and the Spanish bank's vice-chairman Jesús Cainzos, right, applaud the NYSE opening bell, 2 October 2002. AP Photo/Richard Drew.

11. Many of the large Spanish multinationals operate in highly regulated industries in which politics play a prominent role. Spanish magistrate Baltasar Garzón, left, talks to Peruvian President Alejandro Toledo at the Government Palace in Lima, 19 April 2002. Garzón was investigating allegations that Spanish companies paid bribes to former Peruvian President Alberto Fujimori. AP Photo/Oscar Paredes-Presidencia.

12. Spanish Prime Minister José María Aznar, left, listens as President Bush speaks to reporters, the Azores, 16 March 2003. Contrary to Spanish public opinion, Aznar was a staunch supporter of US-led armed intervention in Iraq, a policy that some attribute, at least in part, to Spain's growing economic and financial interests in Latin America, the US's "backyard" (see chapter 7). AP Photo/EFE Sergio Barrenchea.

13. A recently laidoff Telefónica del Perú worker hits a metal bowl as police guard the government palace in Lima, 22 July 2002. Her poster reads: "No more layoffs." Protesters were demonstrating against some 500 job cuts. However, the company has managed its labor relations remarkably well, encountering relatively few labor problems abroad (see chapter 9). AP Photo/Silvia Izquierdo.

14. Perhaps the worst string of international mistakes were those made by Iberia, the national airline (see chapter 4). A demonstrator runs through burning tires outside the company's Buenos Aires main office, Friday, 8 June 2001, during a twenty-four-hour general strike called by opposition labor unions to protest the government's economic policies and the critical situation faced by Aerolíneas Argentinas, the formerly state-run airline then controlled by Iberia. AP Photo/Diego Giudice.

15. Ferrovial is the Spanish construction and services company with the widest international spread. In 1999 it led the consortium that was awarded the financing, construction, maintenance, and management of the 108-kilometer highway 407 ETR in Toronto, an investment worth €2,400 million. It was Canada's largest privatization to date, and the first toll highway in the world with a fully electronic payment system and freedom to set rates.

5 | *The Spanish banks go global*[1]

> The Latin American investments of Spanish firms make them more powerful in negotiations with their European counterparts.
>
> Francisco González,
> President of BBVA (2001)[2]

T HE two banks that are now in the forefront of Spanish financial globalization – Banco Bilbao Vizcaya Argentaria (BBVA) and Grupo Santander – are relative latecomers to internationalization. Spain lost most of its colonies early in the nineteenth century and so did not develop banks like the UK's Barclays (Dominion, Colonial and Overseas), France's Banque de l'Indochine, the Netherlands' Nederlands Handel-Maatschappij, or Portugal's Banco Nacional Ultramarino. At the end of the nineteenth Century, banking in Spain's remaining major colonies – Cuba, the Philippines, and Puerto Rico – was in the hands of leading local banks such as the Banco Español de la Isla de Cuba, Bank of the Philippines, and Banco Español de Puerto Rico.[3] The Spanish–American War then cost Spain these colonies too. The banks that today carry Spain's flag in Europe and the New World were domestic banks that grew into their international roles mostly via acquisition.

Until the late 1980s, Spanish banking was highly cartelized, leading the banks to focus on the easy profits available at home. They did not really venture abroad; their primary destinations were financial

---

[1] This chapter was originally written by Adrian E. Tschoegl, based on several articles we have co-authored on the internationalization of the Spanish banks. I am grateful to him for agreeing to include a revised version in this book.

[2] *Diario de Sesiones del Senado: Comisión de Asuntos Iberoamericanos* 141 (7 June 2001):16–17.

[3] Banco Español de la Isla de Cuba was established in 1854 as the Caja Real de Descuentos, and failed in 1926. Bank of the Philippine Islands was established in 1851 and is still functioning. Banco Español de Puerto Rico was established in 1888 and was absorbed by Banco Popular de Puerto Rico in 1936.

centers, both international and national when they followed trade, though they engaged in a little cross-border investment in France. However, deregulation in the mid- and late 1980s caused the cartel to break down, giving rise to rivalry among a shrinking number of increasingly large banks. In the late 1980s and early 1990s Banco Santander started off a rush to Latin America in which its domestic rivals, Banco Bilbao Vizcaya (later merged with Argentaria to form BBVA) and Banco Central Hispano (subsequently merged with Santander), followed its acquisition of banks throughout the continent. By the turn of the century, BBVA and Santander had become the largest financial institutions in Latin America, among the top five in the eurozone and in the top twenty-five in the world (see chapter 4).

International banking: modes and motives

Banks are peculiar multinational enterprises because of the characteristics of dealing in finance as a business. To provide some conceptual background, this section deals with motives for and modes of internationalization of banking services. Motives are the reasons that bring foreign banks to the host countries. Modes involve the legal form of the banks' presence. The issue of the mode of foreign direct investment is not just a matter of legal minutiae. Rather, the mode of a bank's presence in a country reflects and conditions its strategy; therefore, an understanding of modes is essential to an understanding of the strategy.

Motives for internationalization

In his pioneering article on foreign direct investment in banking, Grubel (1977) distinguished three markets: the wholesale, the corporate, and the retail. The intention to operate in the wholesale foreign exchange and money markets leads banks to the major world financial centers such as London, New York, Tokyo, and Hong Kong (Tschoegl 2000). The intention to serve corporate clients – domestic clients moving abroad or host country firms either seeking or open to dealing with foreign banks – leads banks to locate in regional and national financial centers such as Miami or Buenos Aires, Manila or Santiago.

Until recently, foreign banks have generally avoided the retail banking sector abroad. Where retail banking is well developed and competitive there is no reason to expect foreign banks in general to be better than local banks (Tschoegl 1987). Thus, Demirgüç-Kunt and Huizinga (1999) and Claessens et al. (2000) found that foreign banks tend to have lower margins and profits than domestic banks in industrial countries. However, the opposite holds true in developing countries. Similarly, Dopico and Wilcox (2002) showed that foreign retail banks have a smaller presence in mature markets but a greater share in under-banked markets. These studies imply that, first, one should not expect much in the way of cross-border mergers in commercial banking within developed regions such as Europe, but, second, one could see foreign banks going into developing countries that have opened their once protected banking systems to foreign entry.

There are two exceptions to the argument why foreign banks should avoid developed retail banking markets. The first involves ethnic banking, whereby banks follow migration patterns; this can often lead banks to neighboring countries. The second exception arises when a bank can no longer grow at home. At that time it may come to possess what Kindleberger (1969) has called "surplus managerial resources." It may then decide to grow abroad when it sees an opportunity arising out of combining these surplus resources with what Berger et al. (2000) call a global advantage: they argue that some US banks succeed in the competition with local banks elsewhere in the world simply by being better managed. More generally, the literature on productivity (Bartlelsman and Doms 2000) clearly shows that firms differ in their productivity and that this difference may persist for years. However, US banks are not the only well-managed banks in the world. The intense rivalry of the late 1980s and the 1990s made the Spanish banks highly efficient too (Pastor et al. 2000). History further shows that foreign banks eager to apply their management skills to the retail sector in the host country frequently believe that it is more cost-effective to improve a larger, local acquisition than to build up an operation entirely from scratch.

A third factor that has emerged in the literature as being of some importance to understanding banking FDI in particular cases is strategic interaction between firms. This approach has its origins in the literature on oligopolistic reaction (Hymer 1976; Knickerbocker 1973) or "follow-the-leader" behavior (see chapter 2). The broader phenomenon, of which oligopolistic reaction is simply one outcome, is that firms' FDI strategy depends not only on their own capabilities, but also on the behavior of their chief competitors. Oligopolistic reaction has characterized the international expansion of banks from Germany, Scandinavia (Boldt-Christmas et al., 2001; Engwall and Wallenstäl 1988; Jacobsen and Tschoegl 1999), Singapore (Tschoegl 2002), and Spain (Guillén and Tschoegl 2000).

Modes of operation

The most common forms of legal presence for a bank are representative (rep) offices, agencies, branches, affiliates, and subsidiaries, though their availability to foreign banks varies by country. That is, some countries permit foreign banks to operate via a branch but not a subsidiary, or vice versa. Legal form is not an arbitrary formality but is intimately tied to both the banks' strategies and to the regulatory environment.

A rep office performs liaison activities for the parent but cannot make loans or take deposits. Banks may use rep offices to source loans or deposits that the bank then books in an agency or branch elsewhere. By contrast, agencies and branches have their own books. An agency may make loans but it does not take deposits.

A branch may make loans or take deposits; generally it provides a full range of banking services. Abroad, banks prefer to use foreign branches (or agencies if necessary) for wholesale and corporate banking activities, including foreign-exchange and money market trading because a branch lends, borrows, and trades on the basis of its parent's full capital base. (Although some host-country authorities require an agency or branch to maintain a capital account, this has little meaning except as a device for limiting the branch's activities.) Thus the branch can lend more to any one borrower than could a subsidiary of similar size and, in borrowing and trading, the branch shares the parent's credit rating. Because it is part of the parent bank, an agency or a branch requires careful supervision by home-country authorities, as mistakes could bankrupt the parent. However, activities such as trading or lending to local subsidiaries of home-country firms are ones that the bank must necessarily manage centrally.

An affiliate or associate is an independent legal entity (i.e. locally incorporated) in which the foreign bank has less than majority ownership. Generally, foreign banks prefer not to put their name on affiliates, as that would suggest full responsibility for an entity over which they do not exercise full control. Furthermore, if through a combination of share ownership and management contract the foreign bank does exercise control, then it will wish eventually to assume full control to capture more of the return from its management without having to dispute transfer pricing decisions with minority shareholders. Still, in some cases foreign banks continue to maintain affiliates rather than subsidiaries, perhaps in order to limit the parent's responsibility.

A subsidiary, like an affiliate, is a separate legal entity incorporated in the host country, but one in which the foreign parent has majority or full ownership. A subsidiary may fail even though the parent is solvent. Conversely, a subsidiary may be solvent even though the parent has failed. The subsidiary lends based on its own capitalization rather than that of the parent, something that can prove to be a major constraint. Certainly, a subsidiary can refer to its parent a loan that exceeds its allowable lending limits but, in that case, the bank could lend from a branch in the first place. Thus a subsidiary provides a less capable platform from which to conduct corporate lending or trading activities (Heinkel and Levi 1992). Also, a branch tends to cost less to establish than a subsidiary as there are no costs of incorporation, no need to report annually or quarterly to local registrars of companies, no need for a board of directors, and so forth. However, when a bank has sufficient assets at risk and where the risk is specific to a particular host country, it becomes sensible to incorporate locally.

A foreign bank with a number of branches in a country thousands of kilometers from home, branches whose profitability depends on a local economy about which the parent knows little, may decide to incorporate locally to enlist the governance services of the local central bank, and of local depositors when there is no deposit insurance. These parties are more likely to sense and react to problems of which headquarters, dependent on reports from its managers, might be unaware. Thus, when the assets at stake are large enough and the local regulatory authorities are competent, the foreign parent may decide that the costs of incorporation are an acceptable cost for assistance with governance.

The Basle Concordat of 1975 (amended in 1983) established that home-country supervisory authorities are responsible for solvency supervision of the parent's agencies and branches abroad. This is logical as it is the home-country authorities that have legal access to the parent's books, and because a branch fails when its parent fails.

Host and home-country supervisory authorities are jointly responsible for solvency supervision of subsidiaries, with the host country having primary responsibility. Again this is logical as the subsidiary is a legal entity in the host country and so the local authorities have access to its books. Also, a subsidiary can fail even when the parent is solvent. However, the home-country authorities are responsible for supervision on a consolidated basis as subsidiaries affect the parent's solvency and the parent cannot disclaim all responsibility for its subsidiaries.

The recent Basle II capital Accord will take effect in 2006. It expands on the Basle I capital Accord of 1988 by imposing new methods for calculating capital adequacy, new measures for managing operational risk, and increased transparency and reporting both to regulators and the marketplace. Spanish capital adequacy regulations are already more stringent than Basle I and the European Union's regulations now in force. Therefore the Spanish banks are not greatly concerned about their ability to comply with Basle II. Still, the new rules will require significant reform in bank management, and compliance will require that the banks make significant investments in information technologies, and accounting and control.

As one would expect from the preceding arguments, the Spanish banks generally used rep offices, agencies, and branches when they established themselves in international and national financial centers. When the banks engaged in retail banking – whether in France, Portugal, Argentina, Chile, or Puerto Rico – they acquired local banks that they kept as locally incorporated subsidiaries.

The Spanish banks come of age

The Spanish financial system has undergone substantial change since 1975, culminating in 1998 when Spain helped found the Economic and Monetary Union (EMU). The Banco de España (est. 1782) received the monopoly on note issuance in 1874; until then commercial banks such as Banco Santander and Banco de Bilbao (see below) issued their own notes. The Banco de España became a real central bank with the Banking Act of 1921; however, the government did not nationalize it until 1946. From the 1960s on, central bankers tried to reform financial markets and the government's deficit-financing practices so that inflation could be curbed, a goal that proved elusive until the mid-1980s. In 1994 the Law of Autonomy gave the central bank a large measure of independence to free it to fight inflation. The central bank's supervision of the banking system was a classic example of the exercise of "moral suasion," which Breton and Wintrobe (1978) argue involves an exchange of favors: the central bank polices a banking cartel in return for the banks acceding to its wishes.

Banking in Spain has always been covered by a shroud of secrecy. Critics traditionally grouped the banks with the Church and the military under the rubric of *poderes fácticos* – the powers that be. The banking law of 1940 made it almost impossible for banks to grow domestically other than by acquisition. In 1962 a new law allowed commercial banks to become universal banks and to acquire shares in industrial companies. Spain's banks labored under an interventionist state bureaucracy. Tight regulations during the 1950s resulted in high costs and profits. The chairmen of the then so-called "Big Seven" – Banco Español de Crédito (Banesto), Banco Central, Banco Hispano-Americano, Banco de Vizcaya, Banco de Bilbao, Banco Santander, and Banco Popular – began to meet once a month for lunch so as to exchange information, organize the market, and lobby the government. The banks succeeded in influencing key reforms: restructuring of deficit financing in the early 1980s, membership in the EU in 1986, and liberalization of the stock market in 1988. Until the mid-1980s, Spain's banking sector was one of the most protected and regulated in the world, a situation that Pérez (1997) has referred to as "banking on privilege."

Starting in 1990, the competitive environment in the Spanish banking market changed. Earlier, Barclays and other foreign banks had offered interest on current accounts without triggering much response from the majors. This changed when Santander set off a war among the large banks by offering high interest rates on a checking account, and by revolutionizing the mortgage loan market. BBV and the other leading banks responded in kind. The war abated by the end of the year, but the chairmen discontinued their monthly luncheons.

The banks' influence caused the government to be ambivalent about the entry of foreign banks. Although it welcomed them for the pressure they brought to bear on the big banks, its nationalist instincts were obvious in the seven-year protection period that it negotiated for the banking sector in Spain's European Union accession treaty. Until 1992, the government continued to limit foreign bank entry on a discretionary basis and to maintain existing limitations on foreign banks already operating in Spain. However, in 1992, the Spanish authorities lost the right to block the entry of any European bank, leading them to liberalize entry more broadly. So far, Citibank, Barclays, Deutsche, and other European banks have pursued niche growth strategies or acquired smaller Spanish banks.

The most momentous recent changes in the Spanish banking system have involved mergers among the Big Seven. After several abortive attempts at hostile takeovers, even some that the Socialist government of Felipe González had encouraged, the Big Seven became the Big Four. In 1988 Bilbao and Vizcaya merged. Then in 1991 Banco Central and Hispano-Americano combined to form Banco Central Hispano (BCH). Simultaneously, the government reorganized the state-owned banks to create the megabank Argentaria. In 1994 Santander beat out BBV and BCH to acquire 48 per cent of Banesto in an auction that the central bank organized after having rescued the bank from near bankruptcy. This catapulted Santander into first place among Spanish banks. Then in 2000, Santander and BCH merged to form Banco Santander Central Hispano (BSCH), recently renamed as Grupo Santander, whose key brands include Banesto and Santander Central Hispano. Immediately thereafter, BBV merged with Argentaria to form BBVA.

In addition to the commercial banks, the savings banks (*cajas de ahorro*) are also an important banking institution. These are mutually owned and therefore impervious to hostile takeovers or mergers. Because the *cajas* are the depositories for a large part of the Spanish people's savings, they have been regulated even more stringently and conservatively than the banks. The government has gradually allowed the *cajas* – originally restricted to their provinces of origin – to expand nationally and has encouraged mergers among them. Over the last decade the *cajas* have eroded the banks' market share by more than 10 percentage points. The *cajas* have managed to surpass the banks in total deposits and to nearly overtake them in loans.

The various pedigrees of Spanish banks

Banco Santander was founded in 1857. Its current chairman is Emilio Botín (b. 1934), whose family has controlled the bank since the 1950s. Although Santander initially specialized in the Spanish-American trade flowing through the northern port city of Santander, the bank did not venture abroad until the 1950s when it opened its first representative offices in Mexico City and London. In the 1970s it expanded its network of offices in Latin America and elsewhere.

Santander started its current expansion abroad in the late 1980s with several small acquisitions, including Portugal's Banco de Comércio e Indústria in 1990. Santander initially built its position in Latin America around Santander Investment, its investment-banking arm, and many of its acquisitions are banks with a strong local investment banking franchise. The head of Santander Investment was Ana Patricia Botín, the chairman's daughter and heir apparent, who left Santander after the merger with BCH but has since returned as CEO of Banesto. Santander has generally bought majority stakes in its acquisitions and has put its brand name on them.

Banco Central Hispano (BCH), the third-largest bank in Spain during the 1990s, was the result of the merger between Banco Central, founded in 1919, and financially troubled Banco Hispano-Americano. Wealthy landowners, and others with money that they had suddenly to withdraw from Cuba and Puerto Rico in the wake of the US–Spanish War, founded Banco Hispano-Americano in Madrid in 1901 (Tortella 1995).[4] Despite its overseas connections, the bank became primarily a domestic institution (García Ruiz 2000). BCH inherited a number of investments that Central and Hispano-Americano had made in the 1960s, but disposed of or reorganized most of these. BCH was therefore a latecomer in the recent Spanish drive into Latin America. It was also the only bank that accomplished its entry through joint-venture arrangements with local partners.

Banco Bilbao Vizcaya Argentaria (BBVA) is the second-largest bank in Spain. Its origins go back to 1857, when the Board of Trade of the port city of Bilbao backed the creation of Banco de Bilbao as an issuing house and discount bank. In the following decades the bank became a key financier for the development of steel-making in the Basque region. Banco de Bilbao opened its first foreign office in 1902, in Paris, but remained focused on the domestic market. Banco de Vizcaya started in 1901, also in Bilbao. Both banks grew via domestic acquisitions but

---

[4] Banco Santander, under the direction of Emilio Botín, the grandfather of the chairman of Santander at the time of the 1999 merger, was in 1919 one of the founding shareholders of Banco Central (Ruiz 2000).

Vizcaya always had a stronger foreign orientation. In the late 1920s it founded the Banque Français et Espagnol in Paris. From the early 1970s it opened branches in New York, Amsterdam, London, Paris, and San Francisco and rep offices in Mexico, Frankfurt, Tokyo, and Rio de Janeiro. Banco de Bilbao and Banco de Vizcaya merged in 1988 to form BBV. During the 1990s, BBV followed Santander into Latin America. It originally tended to buy minority stakes, providing the project was large enough and BBV had management control. Over time the bank gained confidence and knowledge, and when the price was acceptable, it increased its stake to a majority position. In 1999 Banco Bilbao Vizcaya acquired Argentaria to become BBVA.

Argentaria was a government-owned amalgam of various banks with a preexisting presence in Latin America through its subsidiary, Banco Exterior de España (BEX). The government founded BEX in 1929 to support foreign trade, seek new markets for national products and assist Spanish companies with importing and exporting. BEX also maintained retail operations in Panama and Paraguay.

Other Spanish banks have been more timid in terms of international expansion, preferring instead to focus on the home market. Banco Popular Español, established in 1926 and now the third-largest bank in Spain, has subsidiaries in France and Portugal. It also has rep offices in Belgium, Chile, Germany, Hong Kong, Venezuela, Morocco, the Netherlands, Switzerland (Geneva and Zürich), and the UK.

The fourth-largest bank, Banco Sabadell commenced operations in 1881, when a group of businessmen and traders from Sabadell (Barcelona) founded the bank to finance the local textile industry. However, it opened its first overseas branch in London only in 1978. In 1994 it formed Banco del Bajío in León, Mexico. It also has operations in Cuba and a subsidiary in Andorra. In 2003 Sabadell bought Banco Atlántico from the Arab Banking Corporation. Banco Atlántico's origins go back to 1901, when two brothers who had been running an exchange bureau in Cuba since 1885 transferred their business to Barcelona. They joined with some local merchants to open a bank that concentrated on receiving transfers of Catalan funds from Cuba for investment in securities. By 2000 the bank had a branch in London and subsidiaries in the Bahamas, Gibraltar, Monaco, Panama, and Switzerland which specialized in private banking.

Lastly, the *cajas* have rarely expanded outside Spain. Barcelona-based La Caixa, the country's largest, has an international presence in the form of shareholdings, including a 3.6 percent stake in Deutsche Bank and a 1.5 percent stake in Suez, in addition to even larger interests in a wide array of Spanish firms with foreign investments (Acesa, Agbar, Gas Natural, Repsol-YPF, Endesa, and Telefónica). Several other *cajas* have a few representative offices, branches, joint-ventures, and subsidiaries abroad.

The international presence of the Spanish banks

As analyzed in chapter 4, the Spanish banks have pursued foreign opportunities for many of the same reasons that prompted other firms in oligopolistic industries such as electricity, water, telecommunications, oil, and gas to undertake investments beyond the country's borders: (1) saturation of the home market; (2) takeover threats from their once larger European rivals; and (3) the need to keep up with each other in the quest for foreign opportunities (Guillén and Tschoegl 2000). The 1990s have changed the face and operating structure of the Spanish banks, and the perception that the global financial community has of them. Latin America has been the most important destination for Spanish banks, but they also have a presence in other parts of the world, especially Europe, North America, and North Africa. The analysis below shows that the Spanish banks have a long-standing international vocation and that their attempts to develop a foreign presence have been complex and mixed in terms of results.

Going next door: France, Portugal, Gibraltar, Morocco, and Andorra
France was for several Spanish banks the first foreign country in which they invested. Banco de Bilbao opened a branch in Paris in 1902, becoming the first Spanish bank to do so. Towards the end of the 1930s, Banco de Vizcaya participated in founding the Banque Française et Espagnol. Santander has a branch in Paris that dates back to the 1960s. Central Hispano had a network of some ten branches but it had cut this back to one (in Paris) prior to the merger with Santander. Banco Popular Español established a representative office in Paris in 1968 that it soon upgraded to a branch. This, in turn, grew to some fourteen banking offices in Paris, its environs, and elsewhere in France. In 1991 Popular incorporated this network as a joint-venture subsidiary with Banco Comercial Portugués (BCP), under the name Banco Popular Comercial. In 2001 the partners split with Popular

taking full control of now Banco Popular France. The bank now has twenty-eight branches that target Spaniards resident in France and individuals and companies with links to Spain.

When it took power in 1975, Portugal's revolutionary government nationalized the domestic banks, but permitted the four foreign banks, none of which was Spanish, to continue to operate. BBV was the first Spanish bank to invest when in 1991 it bought Lloyds Bank's retail network. (Lloyds had been operating in Portugal for 128 years.) In 2000 BBVA also bought Crédit Lyonnais' retail banking interests. Lastly, the merger with Argentaria brought BBV the branches that in 1994 Banco Exterior had acquired in return for the sale of its subsidiary Banco Simeón to Portugal's largest savings bank, the Caixa Geral de Depôsitos.

Banesto sidestepped Portuguese law and bought 50 percent of Banco Totta e Açores in a privatization. In 1995 it sold the bank to Antonio Champalimaud, Portugal's richest individual. BCH had an alliance with BCP from 1993 to 1999, when the merger with Santander brought about a conflict of interest. The alliance included an agreement not to compete in each other's market, but Santander had a subsidiary in Portugal that it was unwilling to divest. Santander therefore sold its 14 percent stake in BCP.

Santander entered Portugal in 1993, establishing its own bank, Banco Santander Portugal (BSP). In 1999 Santander attempted to establish an alliance with Champalimaud, who agreed to sell his family's 40 percent stake in the insurance company Mundial Confiança, which in turn controlled a financial group comprising, inter alia, various Portuguese banks. The European Commission cleared the sale, but the Portuguese government nevertheless blocked it on the grounds that the deal violated insurance regulations. The final settlement gave Champalimaud a 4 percent stake in Santander in return for his 52 percent share of the financial group. Caixa Geral then bought the group from Santander, but immediately sold back two banks belonging to the group, Banco Totta e Açores and Crédito Predial. In 2003 Santander bought Royal Bank of Scotland's 13 percent stake in Banco Santander Portugal, bringing its stake up to 98 percent. Santander now owns three banks, Banco Totta e Açores (universal bank), Crédito Predial (mortgage lending) and BSP (high net worth and urban customers), as well as an investment banking arm, Banco Santander de Negocios. In 2002 SCH made Portuguese one of its two official languages. Through its ownership of Banco Totta, Santander has a representative office in Johannesburg, a branch in Luanda, and subsidiaries in São Tomé and Principe and Mozambique.

Banco Popular started establishing branches in Portugal in 2000, but then in 2002 acquired Banco Nacional de Credito Immobiliare (BNCI; established 1991). BP then transferred its branches to BNCI. Earlier, BP had briefly owned shares in Banco Comercial Portugués (BCP). In addition, Caja Madrid has a branch in Lisbon.

Politics have ensured that Gibraltar figured late in the Spanish banks' expansion, despite its physical proximity. In 1987 Banco de Bilbao and Banco Central established the first operations in Gibraltar by Spanish banks. Banesto followed. Mergers in Spain both reduced the number of Spanish banks and rearranged ownership. Banco de Bilbao (Gibraltar) became BBVA Privanza International (Gibraltar). Santander and Royal Bank of Scotland have set up a joint-venture, Royal Bank of Scotland (Gibraltar). Through its acquisition of BSCH, SCH also owns 50 percent of HispanoCommerzbank Gibraltar. Lastly, Banco Atlántico, now a subsidiary of Banco Sabadell, also has a subsidiary. All focus on private banking.

Morocco started to liberalize in 1983 but did not really permit new foreign entry until 1991. The banking system had a strong French presence. Currently, both Santander and BBVA have affiliates in Morocco. Through its merger with BCH, Santander apparently acquired a 20 percent share in Banque Commerciale du Maroc (BCM; est. 1911), commonly known as the bank of the royal family, and the second-largest bank in the country. BCM has branches in Paris and Brussels, and rep offices in Madrid, Barcelona, and Milan. SCH and BCM co-own the offshore bank Attijari International in Tangiers, which BCH helped establish in 1994. SCH also owns 10 percent of Banque d'Affaires de Tunisie and 4 percent of Egypt's Misr International Bank.

At one point, Banco Exterior had a branch in Morocco. BBVA established BBVA-Marruecos for the purpose of providing financial services to the Spanish companies operating there, which it sold in 2001 to the Moroccan-owned Wafabank for cash and additional shares. As a result of the deal, BBVA's position in Wafabank rose to 10 percent. However, in late 2003, BCM announced that it would merge with Wafabank, and that it had bought BBVA's shares. The merger is to be completed by late 2004. It is not yet clear if and how the merger will affect the two Spanish banks.

In 1999 the government of Andorra, a small country between Spain and France, authorized Banco Sabadell to establish BancSabadell Andorra, which began operating in 2000. BBVA owns a major share of the Banc International-Banca Mora group, which is the result of the merger of Banca Mora and Banc Internacional d'Andorra, in which BBVA owns 51 percent. The Barcelona-based savings bank, La Caixa, has a 33 percent stake in Credit Andorra and fully owns CaixaBank.

Europe: using alliances, clubs, and acquisitions
In spite of the Maastricht Treaty and Monetary and Economic Union, there has been little cross-border merger activity in banking in Europe (Buch and Delong 2003; Tschoegl 2003a). National markets are mature, with well-entrenched competitors, and despite "European passport" legislation entitling banks in one European country to operate in any other member country, the major banks have limited their cross-border presence. Other reasons for the lack of enthusiasm for cross-border acquisitions include differences in legal and tax regimes, as well as cultural barriers.

Because of the role of London as the world's premier banking center, the Spanish banks established branches there relatively early. Santander and BBVA have branches in Frankfurt, Milan, and Paris as well as London. But the most important way in which Spanish banks have a presence in Europe is by means of alliances with European banks. From 1986 to 1998, BBV was a member of the Inter-Alpha Group of banks. Founded in 1972, the alliance now comprises one bank from each of thirteen countries. Inter-Alpha was a response to the then forthcoming formation of the European Free Trade Area, and many internationally inexperienced European banks felt that the way forward was to club together. It set up joint representative offices in the US, Latin America, Tokyo, Hong Kong, Singapore, Tehran, and most recently Moscow. Today, only the last two survive; in the other markets, member banks were able to generate sufficient business to establish their own operations. When BBV resigned from the group in 1998, Santander took up the "Spanish seat."[5]

---

[5] The thirteen members are: AIB Group of Ireland, Banco Santader of Spain, Banco Espirito Santo of Portugal, BHF of Germany, Crédit Commercial de France, ING of the Netherlands, Instituto Bancario San Paolo

Banco Sabadell is also a member of the Mediterranean Bank Network (MBN). This club comprises banks from ten countries that border the Mediterranean and has as its objective to establish a 'strategic alliance' to promote inter-regional commercial and business relationships.[6] Each member can veto the admission to the club of any other bank from its home country.

Although none of them specifies this as an objective, the clubs may function as mutual non-aggression pacts. They are simply a more formal grouping than what the empirical evidence suggests are similar implicit pacts among the largest European banks (Choi et al. 1986, 1996, 2003). Inter-Alpha, in particular, is the sole survivor of a number of clubs from the 1960s and 1970s (Ross 2002).

Both Santander and BBVA pursued a strategy of acquiring small stakes in several European banks. The furthest developed of Santander's alliances is that with Royal Bank of Scotland (RBS), which the two banks established in 1989. One of the first fruits of the alliance came that same year, when the banks established Royal Bank of Scotland (Gibraltar) as a joint-venture. In January 2000 Santander's holding in RBS peaked at about 10 percent. Later, Santander's support was critical to the success of RBS's bid for National Westminster, completed in March 2000. Santander also has or has had positions in Société Générale (5 percent), San Paolo-IMI (7 percent), and Commerzbank (5 percent). Thus, in 2000 the five partners (Santander, RBS, Société Générale, San Paolo-IMI and Commerzbank) announced a plan to launch an e-marketplace for treasury and capital markets products. More recently Santander has sold its stake in Société Générale and may be reconsidering its other equity alliances. Santander's boldest move came in the summer of 2004, when it announced the acquisition of Abbey National, a British bank with 18 million

---

di Torino of Italy, Kredietbank of Belgium, Merita Bank of Finland, National Bank of Greece, Nordbanken of Sweden, Royal Bank of Scotland, and Unibank of Denmark. Williams and Glyn's Bank, which RBS subsumed, was one of the five founding banks.

[6] The current members are: Bank of Valletta (Malta), Türkiye Garanti Bankasi (Turkey), Nova Ljubljanska Banka (Slovenia), and Banque Internationale Arabe de Tunisie (Tunisia), Israel Discount Bank (Israel), Banco Sabadell (Spain), Lyonnaise de Banque (France), Bank of Jordan (Jordan), Zagrebacka Banca, and Banco Popolare di Verona e Novaro.

customers, for $15,000 million. When completed, the deal would catapult Santander into the world's ten largest financial groups.

Similarly BBVA has or has had small equity stakes in Banca Nazionale del Lavoro (BNL), Crédit Lyonnais, and Fortis. The alliance with BNL, for one, is ongoing. However, after Crédit Agricole acquired Crédit Lyonnais, BBVA sold the shares in Agricole that it had received in return for its shares in Lyonnais. La Caixa has small stakes in Deutsche Bank and Fortis.

The motives behind these shareholdings are rarely made explicit. One may suspect that they function to preempt one set of possible acquirers and to acquire allies for any fight to ward off other acquirers. However, this strategy of alliances does not mean that the Spanish banks eschewed all acquisition in Europe. In 1987 Santander bought the Bankhaus Centrale Credit (CC Bank) in Germany, with its thirty-one branches, from Bank of America, which was in the process of restructuring and reducing its overseas presence. CC Bank specializes in consumer credit, especially for automobiles, and has since established subsidiaries in Austria, the Czech Republic, Hungary, Italy, and Poland. From 1988 to 1996 Santander shared ownership of CC Bank with Royal Bank of Scotland. In 2001 Santander acquired AKB-Bank in Germany, which specialized in financing automobile purchases. Combining AKB-Bank with CC Bank will result in a finance company with a market share of 68 percent of Europe's largest automobile financing market. In 2003 Santander bought PTF, Poland's largest auto finance company. By contrast, BBVA closed its Frankfurt branch in 1992. Another market in which the Spaniards have established subsidiaries is Belgium. In 1988, Santander acquired the former Belgian subsidiary of France's Crédit du Nord, and named it CC-Banque Bélgica; later Santander sold the bank. In 1989 BCH established Central Hispano Benelux with Cob Banque d'Epargne owning a 25 percent stake which it sold in 1993 to BCH. After the merger between BCH and Santander, this became Santander Central Hispano Benelux.

The United States
The Spanish banks have expressed little interest in American retail banking but have established themselves in the financial centers of New York and Miami. Banco de Bilbao was the first to open an office in New York (1965), which it closed within the year. Between 1975

and 1978 several Spanish banks arrived: Bilbao, Urquijo, Hispano Americano, Central, Santander, and Catalana. Generally, they entered with representative offices or agencies that they later upgraded to branches. Banesto established a branch in 1984 and Banco Exterior established one in 1995, after entering with a representative office in 1991.

The state of Florida opened to foreign banks in 1978, leading Exterior, Santander, Bilbao, Vizcaya, and Central to open agencies within the next two years. Miami has since emerged as a financial and business center for Latin America, acting as a node for flows of trade and investment between the United States, South America, and Europe (Ó hUallacháin 1994). In the 1980s, several more Spanish banks opened agencies, primarily to serve Latin American clients. In 1993, Banco Sabadell opened its Miami agency to serve clients primarily in the Dominican Republic, Guatemala, Mexico, and Venezuela. In 2001 Sabadell converted the agency to a branch. The following year Banco Pastor, Caja Madrid, and Caixanova established agencies too, bringing the number of Spanish banks with offices in Miami to about ten. Caixanova, a mutual savings bank from Galicia, opened its regional office in Miami as part of an effort to reach the 600,000 Galicians that live in South America. In 2003 Santander bought Coutts International's Latin American private banking division from RBS, which had acquired it with its acquisition of National Westminster Bank, so roughly doubling its assets in Miami.

As far as subsidiaries are concerned, in 1980 Banco Central bought United Americas Bank and renamed it Banco Central of New York. The subsidiary operated until 2001, when Santander liquidated it. Banco Exterior created Extebank in 1980 by acquiring and combining Century National Bank and Suffolk County Bank. In 1995 Banco Exterior sold Extebank's eight branches to North Fork Bancorporation of Long Island and Suffolk County, but transferred the international assets to the branch it had just opened. Neither of these operations appears to have had any compelling logic behind it such as tapping Hispanic populations or strategic justification.

The most visible US investment was Santander's purchase in 1991 of a 13 percent stake in First Fidelity Bank in New Jersey, after a search lasting some nine months that considered eighty targets. Santander picked First Fidelity because its focus on consumer banking and services to small and medium-size enterprises was similar to its own and because the US mid-Atlantic region offered the best economic potential. Santander took the view that the US market was so large and so competitive that a strategic alliance made more sense than an independent retail presence. The strategy, therefore, was similar to the one it pursued in Europe.

In the following four years Santander built up its stake in First Fidelity to 30 percent, while First Fidelity proceeded to buy several smaller banks, including Bank of Baltimore in 1994. Then, in 1995, North Carolina's First Union Bank made a bid on First Fidelity, a merger that Emilio Botín and Santander enthusiastically backed. The merger converted Santander's stake in First Fidelity, which had cost it about $650 million to acquire, into an 11 percent stake in First Union. When asked whether he would retain the stake in First Union, Emilio Botín reportedly said, "While our initial investment, made in 1991 in First Fidelity Bancorp, was a strategic move for us, our current investment in First Union is not strategic in nature." Santander sold its stake in 1996 in a secondary offering for an amount in excess of $2,000 million, which it used to amortize the goodwill in its acquisitions of banks in Argentina, Chile, Colombia, Mexico, Puerto Rico, and Venezuela (see below).

In 2004 BBVA took the first few steps of what some see as an emerging strategy for the United States market by acquiring California's Valley Bank for $16.7 million and Texas's Laredo National Bancshares for $850 million. The idea is to gain a foothold across the border from Mexico – where it controls Bancomer – so as to participate in the lucrative $13,000 million a year remittance business. BBVA plans to organize a US banking division once these acquisitions are completed. An interesting new product consists of enabling Mexican immigrants in the US to pay for a mortgage on homes in Mexico, a possibility first introduced by Mexico's Hipotecaria Nacional, which BBVA acquired in September 2004 for $375 million (New York Times, 22 September 2004).

Early on the Spanish banks were drawn to Puerto Rico, a US possession, which became one of the first places in the Western hemisphere where they entered into retail banking. In 1976 Santander purchased First National Bank of Puerto Rico, which it renamed Banco Santander de Puerto Rico. Two years later it acquired Banco Crédito y Ahorro Ponceño with its thirteen branches in Puerto Rico and one branch in New York. In 1989, Santander acquired Bayamón

Federal Savings Bank from the FDIC and changed the name to Santander National Bank. The next year Santander acquired Caguas Central Federal Savings Bank from the Resolution Trust Corporation. The acquisition made Santander the second-largest bank in Puerto Rico. In 1994 Santander merged Santander National Bank into Banco Santander de Puerto Rico and two years later it added in BCH's subsidiary as well.

BBV followed Santander into Puerto Rico. In 1979 Banco Occidental, a small Spanish bank, bought Banco Comercial de Mayagüez. Banco Vizcaya bought Occidental in 1982 when the latter failed. In the 1990s BBV started to expand its operations with the purchase in 1993 of Royal Bank of Canada's subsidiary, Royal Bank of Puerto Rico. Two more acquisitions, both in 1998, followed: Banco Ponce and Chase Manhattan Bank's retail assets and liabilities. Santander and BBVA now rank second and third in size after Puerto Rico's own Banco Popular.

Latin America

Until the 1990s the Spanish banks' involvement in Latin America was essentially limited to corporate banking. In 1950 Santander created its Latin American Department, and over the next decade or so established rep offices in Mexico, Argentina, Venezuela, and Cuba. In the late 1960s Exterior, Bilbao, and Vizcaya opened offices or established subsidiaries as circumstances warranted.

During the 1980s and 1990s many Latin American countries moved towards financial liberalization, in part in response to the urgings of the IMF and the World Bank, and in part in response to domestic financial crises. This financial liberalization has taken the form of a reduced role, primarily via privatization, for government ownership of banks, and an increased role for foreign banks, which have been allowed to acquire domestic banks. It also has involved dismantling regulations restricting lending or deposit rates and affecting the allocation of credit. Simultaneously, and perhaps paradoxically, crises have led to a strengthening of the regulatory agencies and the laws governing the financial sector with the goal of undermining and dismantling too cozy relationships between the regulators and their charges. The privatization of many government banks and the consolidation of private domestic banking have accompanied and facilitated the entry of foreign banks.

Latin America attracted the Spanish banks for several reasons (Guillén and Tschoegl 2000). First, unlike in Western Europe, Latin American banking markets have high growth potential. In the mid-1990s, between just 30 and 50 percent of the adult population, depending on the country, had a bank account, and no more than 20 percent a credit card. Second, the countries were undergoing a process of liberalization and deregulation similar to Spain's a decade earlier (Mas 1995; Molano 1997). Thus, the Spanish banks were comfortable with liberalization and were ready to apply their newly acquired knowledge elsewhere. Third, although riskier, Latin America offered much higher margins than Europe. Between 1990 and 1994 net interest margins as a percentage of total assets ranged between a low of 5 percent in Mexico and a high of 9 percent in Argentina compared to 1–4 percent in Europe or the US (Goldstein and Turner 1996).

It is also important to note that relatively few banks from other countries were in a position to take advantage of the Latin American opportunity when it presented itself (Guillén and Tschoegl 2000). American banks were somewhat discouraged by their devastating experience in the region during the early 1980s, and were turning inward, focusing on the consolidation taking place at home. Japanese banks were only beginning to come to terms with their country's financial bubble. Similarly, French and Italian banks were reeling from financial problems. Though solid, German banks were focused on Eastern Europe and keen on abandoning retail for investment banking. Only HSBC and some Canadian banks had an appetite for Latin America at the time. Despite the limited interest in Latin America by other banks, a two-way race between Santander and BBV drove acquisition prices up, as predicted by oligopolistic theories of foreign direct investment. Between 1997 and 2002, BBVA made thirty-four major acquisitions in Latin America, spending $7,800 million; Santander spent $12,300 million to buy twenty-seven banks (Bátiz-Lazo et al. 2003). By the turn of the century, the Spanish banks had come to account for slightly more than half of all foreign bank assets in the region, and had become the largest financial institutions. They are the market leaders in pension plans and at the end of 2003 accounted for some 38 percent of assets under management in Latin America with BBVA holding 26 percent, Citibank 25 percent, and Santander 13 percent (*Expansión*, 26 April 2004). The following paragraphs provide an overview of the arduous process by which the Spanish banks became the leading financial institutions in the region.

As the pioneer in liberalization and deregulation, Chile attracted the interest of the Spanish banks early on. Santander entered the country in 1978 with one branch and initially established its subsidiary in 1982, when it acquired insolvent Banco Español Chile, which in 1989 became Banco Santander Chile. In 1993 Santander acquired Fincard, then Chile's largest issuer of credit cards, and in 1995 it acquired Financiera Fusa, a consumer finance company targeting lower-income customers. In 1996 it acquired Banco Osorno y La Unión to become the second-largest commercial bank in Chile. Also in 1996 BCH formed a 50–50 holding company (O'Higgins Central Hispano – OHCH) with the Lúksic group which already owned Banco O'Higgins. OHCH then bought Banco Santiago from the central bank, which had acquired the shares in a rescue, and merged O'Higgins into it. BCH transferred to OHCH its former subsidiaries in Argentina, Uruguay, Paraguay, and Peru. When Santander and BCH merged, Santander bought out the Lúksic group's shares, giving it control of both Santander Chile and Banco Santiago. This led to regulatory concerns about concentration in the banking sector that now are moot. In 2002 the Bank of Chile exercised a put option, selling 35 percent of Santiago to SCH, which already held 44 percent; Santander then merged its two subsidiaries. For many years, BBV only had a representative office in Santiago. In 1998 BBV bought Banco Hipotecario de Fomento (BHIF) from the Said family, to form what is now BBVA Banco BHIF. At the present time, the Spanish banks have about a 23 percent share of the Chilean banking market.

While Santander took the lead in Chile, BBV was the first mover in Mexico's retail banking sector, a much larger market. The domestic investor group that had bought Probursa in the 1980s from the Mexican government quickly realized the skill deficit they were facing. BBV took an initial 2 percent stake that it built up to 70 percent as the government eased entry regulations. BBV Probursa also acquired the assets, deposits, and branches of Banco Oriente and Banco Cremi. Then in 2000 it acquired Bancomer, which it merged with BBV Probursa to form BBVA Bancomer, now Mexico's second-largest bank. In early 2004 BBVA acquired the rest of Bancomer it did not already own, in a move that was well received by analysts. BBVA has been signaling that Mexico is its most important subsidiary in Latin

America, and one that it intends to use as a springboard into the US Hispanic market (*ABC*, 31 March 2004). BCH became the second entrant when it took an 8 percent stake in Grupo Financiero Bital (Banco Internacional de México) in 1992; its affiliate Banco Comercial Portugués took a similar stake. Bital had also acquired Banco Atlántico from the government. After the merger with BCH, Santander sold its shares in Bital.

Initially, Santander took small steps in Mexico, in large part because that was all that Mexican law permitted. Santander established a representative office in 1951, an investment banking operation in 1989, and an affiliate in 1994. The push into retail banking came in 1997 when Santander acquired 60 percent of InverMéxico, which included brokerage and insurance companies as well as Banco Mexicano. Santander merged Banco Mexicano with its affiliate to create Banco Santander Mexicano. In 1997 Hongkong and Shanghai Banking Corporation (HSBC) acquired 20 percent of Banco Serfin, Mexico's third-largest bank. However, in 1999 Santander beat HSBC in a bid to acquire the remaining shares of Banco Serfin in a government auction. At that time HSBC sold its 20 percent to Santander. The latter then merged its holdings to create Banco Santander Serfin, the third-largest bank in Mexico. Presently, BBVA and Santander are the second- and third-largest banks in Mexico, respectively, behind Citibank, which acquired Banamex in 2001 and then merged it with its earlier acquisition. Together Santander and BBVA account for about 42 percent of the assets in the Mexican banking system.

Argentina was the third major country that the Spanish banks entered. The difficulty here was that the only possible acquisition targets were banks owned by local business people, because neither the federal nor the provincial governments were willing to privatize their large banks. In 1996 Santander acquired Argentina's Banco Río de la Plata, one of the most profitable and best-capitalized banks in the country. It also established a strong position through acquisitions and joint-ventures in pension fund management. At the same time, BCH acquired 50 percent of Banco Tornquist and 10 percent of Banco de Galicia y Buenos Aires. When Santander and BCH merged, they acquired the remaining shares in Tornquist, which it merged into Banco Río. Also in 1996, BBV entered the country by acquiring Banco Francés, another well-run bank with a compatible culture, together with its foreign operations, including an Uruguayan subsidiary acquired from Banesto. The next year, Francés acquired Banco de Crédito Argentino. This was a troubled bank that BBV then merged into Francés. Lastly, in 1999 BBV acquired Corp Banca. Although the Spanish banks acquired the largest non-government-owned Argentine banks, the federal government and some of the provinces own banks that are larger still.

The Spanish banks made acquisitions in Colombia and Venezuela at the same time as in Argentina. In 1996 BBV bought a minority stake in Banco Ganadero, which it later upgraded to majority and full ownership. The next year Santander bought 55 percent of Banco Comercial Antioqueno (Bancoquia) under an agreement that had Bancoquia sell its stakes in investment banking, warehousing, and Colsabank first, but also buying Invercredito, a Colombia consumer lending company. Today Santander fully owns its subsidiary in Colombia. Together, BVA and Santander account for about 11 percent of banking system assets.

In 1997 BBV acquired 55 percent of Banco Provincial in Venezuela, which had itself just acquired large minority positions in Banco de Lara and Banco de Occidente. In 1999, Banco Provincial merged with Banco de Occidente and Banco Popular y de los Andes, and in 2000 BBVA merged with Banco de Lara. In 1997 Santander acquired Banco de Venezuela. In 2000 Banco de Venezuela acquired Banco de Caracas, and fully absorbed it in 2002. Together, BBVA and Santander account for about 30 percent of the assets in the banking system.

Due to its belated adoption of privatization and deregulation, the Spanish banks entered Brazil relatively late. This country is, however, Latin America's largest, accounting for two-fifths of regional GDP. Santander was the first to enter when it bought Banco Geral do Comercio in 1997. The next year Santander acquired Banco Noreste from the Cochrane Simonsen family. Finally, in 2000, it purchased Banco do Estado de São Paulo (Banespa) a relatively large and profitable bank, in a privatization. BBVA has not been lucky in Brazil. It had bought Banco Excel-Economico in 1998 for one real, but sold it in 2003 to Bradesco because it realized that it would be too expensive to achieve a profitable scale. As part of the sale price, BBVA received a small equity stake in Bradesco.

The Spanish banks also have positions in other Latin American banking markets, including Peru, Uruguay, Paraguay, Bolivia, and

Panama. Some of these date back to Banco Exterior, and some were acquired in the late 1990s. In 2002 Santander sold its Peruvian subsidiary to a local bank.

Lastly, several Spanish banks currently have operations in Cuba. The first to enter was Banco Exterior de España, which established a representative office in 1995. In the same year Banco Sabadell also established a rep office in Havana, and a 50–50 joint-venture – Financiera Iberoamericana – with Cuba's Grupo Nueva Banca. Caja Madrid did not enter until 1998. However, in addition to opening a rep office it formed a majority joint-venture with Cuba's state-owned Banco Popular de Ahorro to offer corporate financing services primarily to Spanish companies looking to invest on the island.

Asia-Pacific

Spanish banks have a minimal presence in the Asia-Pacific region. Although Santander and BBVA operate in financial centers such as Hong Kong, Beijing, Sydney, Singapore, and Tokyo, they do not have a retail presence. In 1995 Santander established a subsidiary in the Philippines, after failing to obtain authorization from the government to establish a branch. In 2003 it sold its Philippine operations to a local bank.

The predicament of the Spanish banks

Through domestic mergers and foreign acquisitions, the leading Spanish banks have climbed in global rankings and captured the imagination of observers of international financial markets. Their internationalization proceeded in three distinct phases. The first, which stretched from the end of colonial times to the late 1980s, was one of cautious and limited international banking as the banks followed trade, established themselves in major global financial centers, and set up small retail banking operations here and there. During the 1980s, the banks' strategic attention focused almost entirely on Spain as deregulation unleashed a spate of mergers and then a rivalry among the survivors. This rivalry gave rise to the second phase as the Spanish banks established alliances in Europe, rushed to acquire banks throughout Latin America, and engaged in a number of experimental forays into retail banking elsewhere in the world, ranging from neighboring countries in Europe and North Africa to the United

States and the Philippines (Cardone-Riportella and Cazoria-Papas 2001). This process involved dozens of acquisitions and mergers, with all the difficulties usually attached to them. The Latin American expansion enabled the banks to generate profits and to increase their size with a view to further acquisitions and mergers.

The merger of Santander and BCH into Grupo Santander, and of BBV and Argentaria to form BBVA started a third phase, one of consolidation. Both big banks have started to withdraw from tangential markets to concentrate on core ones. For instance, they are seeking to limit their exposure to Latin America by exiting countries (e.g. BBVA from Brazil and Santander from Peru) or scaling back operations. They have also disposed of some of their European shareholdings while making new acquisitions in consumer finance.

In expanding internationally, the Spanish banks have displayed several capabilities. First, they possess the excess managerial resources required to evaluate, undertake, and integrate foreign acquisitions. Initially, the banks relied on managerial personnel brought in from the home country. A team of several dozen managers would run acquired banks during the first few months, gradually shifting to local staff. Second, they have well-organized back-office operations, which they have replicated in each of the acquired banks. These operations include information technologies, risk assessment and human resource training (Guillén and Tschoegl 2000). Third, they are capable of transferring brands and marketing skills between countries. In many instances, they have introduced banking products first developed in Spain. The best example is the lottery-linked deposit account, a product that appeals to people of limited means who are reluctant about taking their money to a bank. In Latin America this kind of initiative has worked well because it tends to expand the size of the market in a part of the world in which few people have faith in the financial system (Guillén and Tschoegl 2002).

In the longer run, we may see a fourth phase in which several scenarios are possible. The Spanish banks might sell some of their retail operations in Latin America to the degree that economic reforms succeed, competition intensifies, and margins fall (Tschoegl 2003b). Or they might find a way to offer higher value-added banking services, thus escaping from the profit squeeze. A third possibility is that they use their newly acquired size to engage in acquisitions or mergers in Western and/or Eastern Europe in a variety of banking segments, including consumer finance and investment banking (see also chapters 4 and 10).

The next chapter will show that, although damaged by the crisis in Argentina during 2001 and 2002, the two large Spanish banks have weathered the storm quite well and remain among the largest, best capitalized, and most profitable banks in Europe. They are not yet truly global institutions like Citibank, but they are generally regarded as successful competitors who know the retail business extremely well.

PART II

The consequences

6 | Spain's new financial role in the global economy

> The contagion [from the Argentine default of January 2002] will be slow because direct investments move much more slowly than other financial assets, but it is likely to spread. Spanish banks and utilities that are hurt in Argentina are likely to retrench in other emerging markets, especially if the stock market penalizes them for their overseas exposure.
>
> George Soros (2002: 144)

T HE rise of the Spanish multinational firm has transformed the country's stature in the world. In this chapter I define and document the implications of the increased presence of Spanish business abroad by examining the economic, financial, and regulatory implications. I will use the Argentine default and devaluation of early 2002 as a case study to illustrate the new role that Spain has come to play in global economic and financial affairs as a result of FDI. In subsequent chapters I analyze the diplomatic repercussions, the impact on Spain's image in the world, and the social implications.

From an economic and financial point of view, Spain's enhanced stature as a foreign direct investor carries with it both benefits and costs. The benefits derive from two possible sources: (a) the economic profits and rents that can be obtained, directly or indirectly, from the foreign investments; and (b) the potential of having a greater say in international organizations, forums and negotiations in which important economic and financial decisions are made. The costs accrue from the exposure to events in other parts of the world which may negatively affect the performance of the Spanish economy or the stability of its financial system.

The benefits of Spain's enhanced financial stature

The economic benefits from the international expansion of Spanish firms are straightforward to define. They include (a) the increased profits from operating in markets in which business margins are greater, and (b) scarcity rents obtained from exploiting intangible assets in multiple markets as opposed to just the home market. Judging from the stock market reaction, Spanish companies – and their foreign and domestic shareholders – have benefited from their international expansion. The stock market value of Spanish firms has increased relative to many of their European rivals (see chapters 4 and 5). As will be analyzed below, the largest Spanish multinationals came to generate between 25 and 50 percent of their profits in Latin America. Some specific investments have been more profitable than others. For instance, in 2001 Santander acquired Banespa in Brazil for about $6,000 million, reporting profits of $524 million in 2001, nearly $800 in 2002, and $807 in 2003. Banespa now has 21,700 employees, 900 more than when it was acquired. In other cases, Spanish firms have lost money with their foreign operations, as discussed in chapters 3 and 4.

The enhanced stature of the Spanish stock exchanges

The increase in FDI might also offer an important economic benefit in terms of the enhanced stature of the four Spanish stock exchanges, now linked through a common trading system. There are two aspects to this phenomenon. First, foreign investors can buy stock in Spanish companies in order to get exposure to Latin America, and they can do so in euros, thus minimizing transaction costs, although they are indirectly subject to currency fluctuations insofar as Spanish firms doing business in the region are subject to them. It is difficult to assess the extent to which the greater profile of the Spanish stock markets has diverted portfolio investment from Latin American exchanges. What is certainly true is that Spanish acquisitions in the region have reduced the number of listed companies and the liquidity of Latin American exchanges.

A second aspect of the enhanced visibility has to do with Spain's attempt to serve as a financial bridge between Europe and Latin America through the creation of the Latibex. Created in December 1999 by the Spanish government, it is the only international market for Latin American securities. According to its own website,

the Latibex is an ideal way to channel European investment efficiently towards Latin America. European investors can buy and sell shares and securities in leading Latin American companies through a single market, with a single operating system for trading and settlement and a single currency, the euro. The market is based on the trading and settlement platform of the Spanish stock market, in such a way that the Latin American securities listed on Latibex are traded and settled like any other Spanish security. Meanwhile, Latibex gives Latin American companies easy and efficient access to the European capital market. In short, it brings European investors close to one of the world's most economically attractive regions, streamlining the operational and legal complexity and reducing risks.[1]

The Latibex project has done reasonably well given the turmoil in stock markets around the world since 1999, and Latin America's deep economic troubles. Although fewer than thirty companies are presently listed, this is sharply up from the original five back in December 1999. Some regional heavyweights are now traded: Bradesco, Banco de Chile, Eletrobras, Endesa Chile, Grupo Modelo, Petrobras, and Telmex. The index has additional visibility because the FTSE tracks its performance with the FTSE Latibex All-Share index, and, since February 2004, with the FTSE Latibex Top index of the fifteen most liquid stocks. The international financial media were skeptical at first about Latibex's prospects (e.g. *Wall Street Journal*, 26 November 1999; *Wall Street Journal Europe*, 2 December 1999; *Financial Times*, 2 December 1999). The *Wall Street Journal* reported that,

The Madrid project is a high-stakes gamble. But if it is successful, the new market could provide Latin American companies with access to Europe's rapidly growing capital markets . . . Nobody expects the Latibex market to start with a bang. For one, it will have formidable competition from the New York Stock Exchange, whose 106 Latin stock listings include the region's biggest banks, utilities, retailers and industrial companies. In contrast to New York or Paris's market for European depositary receipts, Madrid has

[1] www.latibex.com.

invited the members of the half-dozen participating Latin American exchanges to become members of the new electronic market. Rather than trade in American depositary receipts, or ADRs, Latin American companies will trade directly in euros in Madrid (*Wall Street Journal Europe*, 26 November 1999; *Wall Street Journal*, 29 November 1999).

Growth of the Latibex was initially hindered by the decision by several Spanish multinationals to buy out several of their Latin American subsidiaries. Experts remain unsure whether the Latibex will be able to displace the New York Stock Exchange – where about ninety Latin American companies are presently listed using the American Depository Receipt system – as the main exchange for Latin American equities located outside the region (*Financial Times*, 28 March 2001). A good sign is that the FTSE decided in late 2002 to open its fourth European office in Madrid so as to manage indexing activities in Portugal and Italy as well as Spain (*Financial Times*, 26 September 2002).

Economic diplomacy

A separate category of potential benefits has to do with the possibility that a large FDI position might enhance Spain's stature in international economic organizations, forums, and negotiations in which important economic decisions are made. Interviews at the Ministries of the Economy and Foreign Affairs and at the central bank revealed that this is a topic that greatly preoccupies officials. In some areas, Spain has been able to acquire a new presence, as for instance in the Basel Committee on Banking Supervision, in which there has been a Spanish permanent representative since early 2001. However, Spain still lacks a permanent executive director at the IMF, where smaller countries from the point of view of GDP or FDI like Australia, Belgium, the Netherlands, Switzerland, or Saudi Arabia have more voting power. There are few Spaniards in key positions of power at any of the international organizations with an economic or financial mission, except for the Inter-American Development Bank and the IMF. And Spain is not a member of the G7, where many important decisions are made. As the next chapter will document, Spain has not yet managed to translate its new financial weight and influence into decision-making power in multilateral or bilateral forums, especially at times when its interests are threatened.

The costs of Spain's new financial role

Virtually every business executive, government official, or expert interviewed for this book pointed out that the rise in Spanish foreign direct investment has brought about a major change in terms of the exposure of the Spanish economy and financial system to external events or "shocks." (I will use the term "exogenous shock" in reference to the effect on a certain country caused by a dramatic turning point in macroeconomic and/or financial variables in another part of the world. Truly exogenous shocks are causally unrelated to the affected country's own macroeconomic or financial variables.) In particular, Spanish FDI in Latin America, a more volatile region than Europe, potentially exposes the GDP growth rate, the interest rate, the balance of trade, the financial system, and the Madrid stock exchange to events in that region. The potential impact on Spain of a crisis in Latin America is certainly constrained by the relatively large size of the Spanish economy compared to those of most Latin American countries (only Brazil's is larger), the adoption of the euro as the legal currency, and the fact that less than 6 percent of Spanish exports are destined for the region. As this chapter will show, however, the potential impact operating through the financial channel is considerably larger.

The many edges of the Argentine crisis

The signs of crisis and financial meltdown in Latin America became unmistakable towards the late 1990s, especially after the Russian default of 1998 and the Brazilian devaluation of January 1999, which sent Argentina into a severe, four-year recession. During the second half of 2001 the international financial press started to warn about the impact that a major Latin American crisis would have on the Spanish economy and financial system (e.g. *Financial Times*, 16 October 2001, 22 December 2001; *Wall Street Journal*, 20 July 2001). Financial gurus like George Soros added their influential voices to a growing chorus of doom-mongers (Soros 2002: 144). These warnings were hard to dismiss given the large exposure of Spanish firms to the region and the fact that at the time more than half of the equity of many of the largest firms and the entire listed equity in Spanish stock markets was owned by foreigners (see chapter 4).

The Argentine default and devaluation of January 2002 confirmed what many had feared. By the end of 2003, however, it had become apparent that neither the Spanish economy nor the financial system had suffered substantially. The reasons for this relatively happy turn of events are complex. First, as noted above, Spain's exposure to Latin America is asymmetric in that it operates mostly through certain financial channels and not so much through commercial channels. Second, Spain's membership in the European Monetary Union provided a safety net that shielded the Spanish economy and financial system from the likely devastating effects of a major currency devaluation and the increase in sovereign risks and interest rates. And, third, the regulatory authorities adopted rather effective preemptive measures and the foreign-investing firms and banks themselves took appropriate accounting and strategic measures. With this information in mind, let us review the nature and the consequences of the Argentine crisis.

The Argentine roller-coaster
Argentina is one of the most unstable countries in the world. In the sixty years between 1943 and 2003 the country had twenty-three presidents (nine generals among them) and fifty-three economy ministers. Moreover, macroeconomic and foreign investment policies were shifted from relatively liberal to staunchly populist and interventionist ones, or vice versa, in 1946, 1953, 1962, 1966, 1970, 1976, 1981, 1986, 1990, and 2001 (Guillén 2001c). The last cycle before the arrival of Spanish investors started in 1989 with food riots and an episode of hyperinflation which peaked in March of that year at an annualized rate of 20,000 percent. After decades of emergency economic programs, visionary currency stabilization plans, and economic and social hardship, in mid-1989 Argentine voters elected Carlos Menem, a member of the Peronist Party. He ran for office on an intriguingly ambiguous platform. Upon assuming office several months ahead of schedule given the gravity of the situation, he surprised virtually everyone by appointing to his cabinet and staff several liberal economists from one of the leading business groups in the country, the legendary Bunge and Born, and some noted anti-Peronists. Menem perceived the need to force changes onto state finances and labor negotiations as well as to fix the perennial problem of currency instability. After several failed attempts to curb inflation,

the newly appointed Economy Minister Domingo Cavallo implemented the dollar–peso convertibility plan of February 1991, which eventually achieved monetary stability.

During the early 1990s, Menem's reforms affected virtually every aspect of the economy, including money and banking, the state budget, state-owned enterprises, trade, and regulation (Toulan and Guillén 1997). Of especial relevance to the future was the Mercosur customs union negotiated with Brazil, Uruguay, and Paraguay. At first sight, Menem's reforms yielded spectacular results: inflation below 5 percent within two years of convertibility and close to zero thereafter, annual GDP growth rates ranging between 5 and 10 percent, and rising inward foreign investment signaling a renewed confidence in the Argentine economy, which proved resilient to the largely undeserved side-effects of the Mexican crisis of 1994–5.

Spanish firms would be the leading participants in the process of privatization and deregulation initiated by Menem. Over sixty state-owned firms totaling $60,000 million worth of assets were privatized, including such flagships as the oil firm YPF, the telephone company ENTel, and the flag carrier Aerolíneas. Many other firms held by private investors and families were also sold to foreign investors. Argentina was, overall, the most important destination of Spanish FDI until the late 1990s, when investments in Brazil took the lead (Fernández-Otheo Ruiz 2003: 76). Moreover, Spain became the largest foreign direct investor in Argentina, accounting for just over half of all inward FDI during the 1990s. Virtually every major Spanish firm made major investments, totaling €26,000 million.

The unfolding of the crisis

The first signs of palpable trouble appeared after the Brazilian devaluation of January 1999. Its impact was immediate given the situation of free trade between the two countries in most product categories and Argentina's commitment to maintaining parity with the dollar. At the time Brazil accounted for a quarter of Argentine exports. In 1999 Argentine GDP fell by almost 4 percent. Although it recovered slightly during 2000, it fell again by 5 percent in 2001. In December 2000 the country secured an IMF loan worth $40,000 million, one of the largest ever made by the multilateral organization. In early 2001 the governing coalition started to unravel. Later that year Cavallo joined the cabinet as Economy Minister and on 1 December 2001 he introduced the infamous and unpopular *corralito* or freeze on cash withdrawals from bank accounts, a desperate attempt to avoid a run on financial institutions and save the convertibility scheme. Later that month President Fernando de la Rúa and his cabinet were forced to resign after rioting resulted in sixteen deaths.

In early 2002 Interim President Adolfo Rodríguez Saá, who remained in power for only seven busy days, announced that Argentina would suspend payments on its debt. A few days later, President Eduardo Duhalde, who had been newly appointed by Congress, announced the end of currency convertibility. Within weeks, the peso lost two-thirds of its value. Argentina had just broken the world record for a sovereign default: $155,000 million. It did not enter into an agreement with the IMF until almost two years later. In April 2003 Argentinians elected as their new President Peronist Néstor Kirchner, who adopted a defiant and populist posture towards foreign investors and multilateral organizations, which he toned down slightly after official visits to Washington and Madrid. After hitting bottom in early 2003, the Argentine economy grew at an annualized rate of nearly 10 percent later that year, and inflation came down to less than 3 percent. The crisis had resulted in a reduction of economic activity by one-third and a doubling of the proportion of the population living in poverty to nearly 60 percent. Unemployment rose to 22 percent before dropping to 18 percent.[2]

While the Argentine economy is growing again, there are three pending problems that continue to affect Spanish companies. First, the September 2003 agreement with the IMF was only a partial one, which did not achieve a restructuring of the country's foreign debt. Second, the abandonment of dollar convertibility and the subsequent loss in the value of the peso made it necessary to revise upwards the prices for privatized services like energy and telecommunications. The government, however, refused to do this until early 2004, and then only partially. And, third, banks have been affected by the forced conversion of debts and deposits into pesos at a level well below the going market rate, and by the freeze on bank withdrawals, which was not abandoned until March 2003.

[2] World Bank (2003: 2, 4, 11).

The impact on Spanish firms

The Argentine crisis immediately put Spanish firms in the spotlight because they had become the country's largest suppliers of gasoline, gas, electricity, water, and telecommunications: essential goods and services that even an economy in crisis needs. They found themselves in a most delicate position. Utility companies were inescapably dependent on political decisions as to regulated prices. Banks became subject to a series of emergency regulations that prevented them from doing business as usual while becoming the targets of criticism of irate depositors wishing to withdraw their money at dollar parity. Argentina's largest oil company, Repsol-YPF, was torn between the political necessity of not raising prices domestically and the imposition of a new tax on exports that made foreign sales less profitable. Spanish firms became the target of criticism for making some scattered statements about the uncertainties of the situation (*Clarín*, 22 December 2001; *La Nación*, 4 January 2002, 2 October 2002; *El País*, 18 May 2002). The fact that most Spanish multinationals seemed to support the losing candidate in the May 2003 election, former President Carlos Menem, did not help matters (*La Nación*, 6 May 2003), prompting one of them, Telefónica, to change the top management of its Argentine subsidiary (*El País*, 7 June 2003).

While the most immediate victims of the crisis were the Argentinians themselves, the recession, default and devaluation had a series of ripple effects on Spanish companies, including reduced revenues, profits, and asset values. In turn, these problems negatively affected share prices and corporate debt ratings. In response, Spanish firms suspended investment plans and made accounting provisions to cover operating and asset losses (see table 6.1). However, unlike their counterparts from other countries, rare was the Spanish firm that decided to pack up and leave Argentina. The single most important complaint on their part was the uncertainty as to what might happen in the future, especially in industries in which the government holds the key to how prices and other regulations might evolve. In the following paragraphs I review briefly the impact company by company, drawing on Argentine and Spanish newspapers and on the companies' 2002 annual reports to shareholders, which were dominated by Latin American developments.[3]

---

[3] See also the report by CESLA (2002).

Table 6.1. *The impact of the Argentine crisis on the largest Spanish multinationals, 2000–2*

Company	Main Argentine subsidiaries	EBITDA (% of total)	Effects of the crisis on the subsidiary	Provisions
Repsol-YPF	YPF	2000: 56.9% 2001: 47.3% 2002: 42.8%	Indirect tax hikes Freeze on regulated prices Tax on exports	2001: €2738 million 2002: €27 million
Gas Natural	Gas Natural BAN	2000: n.a. 2001: 10.7% 2002: 3.1%	Reduction in sales due to falling incomes Freeze on regulated prices Increase in unpaid bills	2001: n.a. 2002: n.a.
BBVA	BBVA-Banco Francés Consolidar	2000: 9.8% 2001: 8.7% 2002: 5.8%	Freeze on deposits Unpaid loans and mortgages. Conversion of assets and liabilities into pesos. Public's lack of trust.	2001: €1354 million 2002: 100% of Banco Francés continues provisioned.
Santander	Banco Río de la Plata	2000: n.a. 2001: 1.9% 2002: n.a.	Freeze on deposits. Unpaid loans mortgages. Conversion of assets and liabilities into pesos. Public's lack of trust.	2001: €1287 million 2002: 100% of Banco Río continues provisioned

Telefónica	Telefónica de Argentina	2000: n.a.	Reduction in sales due to falling incomes.	2001: €1424 million
	Telefónica Móviles Cablevisión Atlántica de Comunicaciones Azul TV	2001: 11.3% 2002: 3.3%	Freeze on regulated prices. Increase in unpaid bills.	2002: n.a.
Aguas de Barcelona	Aguas de Argentina	2000: n.a.	Reduction in sales due to falling incomes.	2001: n.a.
	Aguas Provinciales de Santa Fe	2001: n.a.	Freeze on regulated prices.	2002: €67 million
	Aguas Cordobesas	2002: n.a.	Increase in unpaid bills.	
Endesa	Edesur	2000: n.a.	Reduction in sales due to falling incomes.	2001: n.a.
		2001: 2.5% 2002: 1.7%	Freeze on regulated prices. Increase in unpaid bills.	2002: €356 million 2003: €36 million

EBITDA = Earnings before interest, taxes, depreciation, and amortization

Repsol-YPF has by far the largest exposure in Argentina: about 40 percent of its profits and assets prior to the 2002 default and devaluation. It is also the only company whose interests were explicitly addressed in the September 2003 agreement with the IMF, when the government committed to a reduction of export taxes for oil products and the updating of gas prices. Although Repsol had to allocate €2,738 million to provisions, it has announced new investments worth nearly €4,900 million (*El País*, 14 November 2003). Part of the reason why Repsol-YPF has done relatively well in Argentina is due to the fact that, unlike other Spanish firms, it did not support the candidacy of Menem in the 2003 presidential elections. The outcome may have helped the company because most of its oil production is in the Province of Santa Cruz, in Patagonia, Kirchner's home turf (*El País*, 20 April 2003).

Telefónica reported an impact of nearly €1,400 million, including goodwill, financial, and asset losses. Prior to the crisis the company generated 13 percent of its profits in Argentina. During 2002, the effect of Latin American troubles resulted in a 8.4 percent reduction in annual profits. The number of Telefónica employees in Argentina, however, dropped by less than 7 percent (*El País*, 28 September 2003). Telefónica's response to the crisis has been to weather the storm, just the opposite of the shareholders of its main competitor, Telecom Argentina. In 1999 two of them – J. P. Morgan and Pérez Companc – sold their stakes to the leading investors, France Télécom and Telecom Italia. In September 2003 the French company decided to bail out, citing a strategic refocusing towards Europe (*La Nación*, 9 September 2003). In 2003, Telefónica, in part as a gesture towards the government, announced a series of staggered investments amounting to nearly €500 million (*El País*, 22 September 2003).

BBVA and Santander were affected both by the crisis itself and by the desperate measures adopted by the government in December 2001 to avoid a run on deposits. They own Argentina's second- and third-largest banks, respectively, as well as a number of other financial companies, especially in the pensions business. Unlike Crédit Lyonnais and Bank of Nova Scotia – who sold their smaller Argentine banks in May and September 2002, respectively – the Spanish banks decided in 2001 to make provisions covering 100 percent of their investments rather than leaving the country, a move welcomed by the financial media (*Financial Times*, 9 May 2002). The bill amounted to about

€1,300 million each. They made additional, smaller provisions during 2002 in order to cope with the deteriorating value of the peso. It is important to keep in mind that BBVA also suffered indirect losses through its holdings in Telefónica and Repsol-YPF.

Endesa is perhaps the company that managed the crisis less adeptly. Its southern cone operations, coordinated through its Chilean unit, Enersis, were already under stress before the Argentine collapse. At the time about 10 percent of its profits came from Argentina. The firm suffered from the freezing of regulated electricity prices and decided to reduce investments. On 17 October 2003 a black-out affecting 390,000 homes in the Buenos Aires area serviced by Endesa made the headlines. Many in Argentina, including the President, suggested it might have been a premeditated move to apply pressure and obtain rate hikes. The company was ultimately able to prove it had been the result of a series of thefts that caused three electricity towers to collapse (*Wall Street Journal*, 12 May 2003, 13 August 2003). Endesa's predicament continues to be problematic, given the government's refusal to fully update electricity rates for the end consumer. A similar problem affected Agbar with an interruption in water service in the northern Buenos Aires area.

Among construction firms, Dragados (later acquired by ACS) and OHL were the most affected because of their toll highway concessions. Mapfre, NH Hoteles, and Prosegur also reported significant losses. Each of these companies made provisions for amounts ranging from €30 to 65 million. Media companies such as Recoletos and Prisa were affected to a much lesser extent.

It is important to highlight that many Spanish-owned operations in Argentina returned to profitability in 2003, including Telefónica and Gas Natural, though others like Endesa (Edesur) and Repsol-YPF (Metrogas) did not (*El País Negocios*, 21 March 2004). The banks continue to face a difficult situation.

The impact on company valuations and on the stock market
One of the most important changes witnessed by the Spanish economy over the last decade has been the increasing importance of the stock market. In the ten years to the end of 2003, the number of listed companies grew more than five-fold from 376 to 2,016, and market capitalization more than four-fold to €547,800 million, with 47 percent of the listed equity owned by foreigners (down from 53 percent in

Table 6.2. The Latin American exposure of the leading Spanish companies

Company	Latin American investments as a % of market valuation	Latin American profits as a % of total profits
Telecoms/media/internet		
Prisa	20	15
Telefónica	40	50
TPI	20	15
Telefónica Móviles	30	35
Terra-Lycos	25	25
Banking		
BBVA	28	31
Santander	35	52
Oil and gas		
Repsol-YPF	60	55
Gas Natural	15	18
Utilities		
Endesa	31	25
Iberdrola	12	7

Source: Wall Street Journal Europe, 2001, June 18, p. 11.

2000). The rise in outward FDI by Spanish listed firms has exposed the stock market to the vagaries of the global economy, especially Latin America. As noted above, the increasing importance of the Spanish multinationals and their foreign investments has brought about many benefits. But the costs are also obvious.

In June 2001, at the time Argentina's troubles intensified, the *Wall Street Journal Europe* warned its readers about the potential impact of a default and devaluation on the valuation of Spanish companies. Drawing on data from Santander's equity research organization,[4] the *WSJE* published the information reported in table 6.2, which highlighted the Latin American exposure of eleven large Spanish firms in terms of two variables: the ratio of their investments in the region

---

[4] See an updated version of the data in "Trading Places: A Comprehensive Guide to Trading Opportunities." Santander Central Hispano-European Equity Research, 12 May 2003.

relative to their market valuation, and the proportion of profits coming from their Latin American operations. At the time, the eleven companies represented 78 percent of the market capitalization of the Ibex-35 index of blue chip stocks, and about 40 percent of total stock market capitalization. Thus a significant portion of the valuations on the Madrid stock exchange have become dependent, in part, on the performance of the Latin American economies. In some cases, more than half of the profits and perhaps of the valuations now depend on that rather volatile part of the world. As an analyst at ING Barings in Madrid pointed out, the Spanish stock market "is perceived increasingly as a risk market," and added: "A devaluation [of the Argentine peso] would be very negative. But that's not the scenario we're working with" (*Wall Street Journal*, 18 June 2001). Fortunately, the Bank of Spain and the companies themselves were.

While Spanish stock exchanges may have differentiated themselves from other European markets in terms of industry mix and global exposure, they have done so in a very peculiar way, i.e. with a strong concentration in industries subject to regulation and political interference, and in a region of the world known for its volatility. Table 6.3 compares the change in share price for the six largest Spanish multinationals compared to their European peers. In the twelve months after Argentina's default and devaluation, the stock prices of some of the leading Spanish companies dropped more than those of their European industry peers (e.g. BBVA, Telefónica, and, especially, Endesa), although in some cases the reverse was true (Iberdrola, Telefónica Móviles), and in others the difference was negligible (Santander and Repsol-YPF). During 2003, as the news from Latin America turned positive, Santander, Telefónica, Telefónica Móviles, Endesa, Iberdrola, and especially Repsol-YPF, surged ahead of their European peers, outperforming them handsomely. Thus Spanish multinationals recoverd swiftly from the Latin American crises of the turn of the century.

Quantifying the macroeconomic impact of the Argentine crisis

While the Argentine crisis did not have the dire effects anticipated by some, it did have noticeable consequences, especially for Spanish firms. It was a serious exogenous shock, although its consequences were mitigated by the strength of Spanish economic and financial institutions as well as preemptive actions undertaken by both

Table 6.3. Share price performance of major Spanish companies relative to their European peers, during 2002 and 2003

	% Change on the Madrid stock exchange	% Change in the Dow Jones Euro Stoxx 600 industry-specific index
2002		
BBVA	−34.4	−26.2
Santander	−30.5	−26.2
Telefónica	−43.2	−38.4
Telefónica Móviles	−24.0	−38.4
Endesa	−36.5	−26.5
Iberdrola	−8.7	−26.5
Repsol-YPF	−23.1	−19.6
2003		
BBVA	+20.1	+20.6
Santander	+43.6	+20.6
Telefónica	+36.5	+18.2
Telefónica Móviles	+33.6	+18.2
Endesa	+36.8	+9.5
Iberdrola	+17.4	+9.5
Repsol-YPF	+22.7	+1.0

Note: The following Dow Jones Euro Stoxx 600 indices were used for the industry comparisons: DJSBANKP (banks), DJSENGYP (energy/oil), DJSESTLSP (telecommunications), and DJSESUTIP (utilities).
Source: Bolsa de Madrid; www.stoxx.com; Wharton Research Data Services.

companies and the central bank. According to the calculations by Blázquez and Sebastián (2003), during the five-year period starting in 1998 and ending in 2002 Spanish GDP could have grown by 14.5 percent instead of the actual 13.7 percent. They reach this estimate by considering several channels of contagion (see Table 6.4). First, they note that lost exports because of the Argentine crisis probably reduced the GDP growth rate over the entire five-year period by 0.2 percentage points, an amount that would have been much greater if Spanish exports to Argentina were not as small as they were (barely more than 1 percent of total Spanish exports). Thus the contagion effect through the trade channel was rather small. Second, the effect operating through the business channel was more significant because of the large

Table 6.4. The impact of the Argentine crisis on the rate of growth of Spain's GDP, 1998–2002

Channel of contagion	Effect on the rate of growth of GDP
Trade	−0.2
Finance	
Holdings of Argentine public debt	0.0
Default impact on spread	0.0
Stock market	−0.6
Immigration	+0.3
Companies	−0.3
Total	−0.8

Source: Blázquez and Sebastián (2003:369).

investments of Spanish firms. Spanish firms lost potential profits to an amount that is difficult to calculate. Using a variety of methods, Blázquez and Sebastián (2003) conclude that Spanish GDP would have grown at a rate 0.3 percentage points greater because of the contagion effect through the company channel. For instance, during 2002 Spanish companies with operations in Argentina made provisions reaching almost €10,000 million in order to eliminate from their annual accounts the negative effect of the crisis. Third, the Argentine crisis contributed to an increase in the number of people migrating to Spain: about 110,000 during 2002 alone. Given that this group is as well-qualified as the average Spaniard, its contribution to GDP probably amounted to an additional 0.3 percentage points.

The impact of the crisis through the financial channel differed depending on the specific mechanism. In terms of the potential increase in public debt volatility and interest rate spreads, the crisis did not exert an important effect, especially because Spain had already adopted the euro. While between October 1997 and December 2001 the Argentine spread increased from 461 to 1,684 basis points, the corresponding figures for Spain shifted from 27 to 31. Moreover, while the Argentine and Spanish spreads were highly correlated prior to the adoption of the euro, the contagion virtually disappeared thereafter (Blázquez and Sebastián 2003). Similarly insignificant was the contagion due to the loss in value of Argentine public debt because

Spanish holdings were barely 0.2 percent of the total. The most important impact operating through the financial channel had to do with the adverse effect of the Argentine crisis on company valuations, as noted above. According to Blázquez and Sebastián (2003), this effect reduced GDP growth over the five-year period by 0.6 percentage points because of the reduction in consumption caused by the fall in the financial wealth of Spanish households.

The regulatory response

Severe as the Argentine and other Latin American crises were, their impact could have been much worse had it not been for the efficient ways in which most of the affected companies handled the situation. An important contributor to this success was the Bank of Spain, which is in charge of overseeing the stability of the financial system. Anticipating the potential difficulties lying ahead, it quietly embarked on a number of actions that minimized the impact of the crisis on the Spanish economy and financial system.

The key role of the Bank of Spain

Spain's central bank has played a central role in the containment of the fallout from the various Latin American crises, including Argentina's. The Bank of Spain is both the country's monetary authority and the regulatory authority overseeing deposit and credit institutions, meaning that it must safeguard the solvency of the financial system in addition to fighting inflation and helping the economy expand along a sustainable path of growth. Traditionally, it has been an "enclave of excellence" within the state bureaucracy, attracting some of the country's finest economists and financial experts (Pérez 1997). In 1994 it was granted a relatively large degree of autonomy or independence from political power as a way of freeing it from the pressures of special interest groups and helping it focus on the goal of fighting inflation. It has been part of the European System of Central Banks since January 1999, when Spain adopted the euro as its currency.

In the mid-1990s the Bank of Spain became keenly aware of the possible implications of the boom in FDI by Spanish banks and non-financial companies. It then allocated human and material resources to assess and monitor the risks arising from a concentration of foreign investments in the relatively volatile Latin American economies. According to interviewees, over the years the Bank of Spain developed a very good sense of the direct exposure of Spanish banks to Latin America by virtue of their operations throughout the region, although they are still scrambling to understand and quantify the second-order effects coming from the exposure of non-financial companies such as Telefónica, Repsol or Endesa, in which the banks own stock. In its annual reports on financial stability, the Bank of Spain has taken FDI into account, noting the importance of the banks' Latin American exposure.[5] In addition, the central bank required banks to beef up their levels of provisioning in an anticipatory way, rather than waiting until an actual crisis occurred to take action. The governor of the Bank of Spain declared that the two large banks "were managing the impact of the crisis appropriately. We have asked them to manage the risks and to make suitable provisions, and that is exactly what they are doing" (*Expansión*, 22 January 2002). Instead of detailing the specific measures adopted by the Bank of Spain, it is more telling to describe the International Monetary Fund's assessment of Spain's proactive approach to the increased threat of an exogenous shock on its financial system due to FDI, especially in the banking sector.

The praise of the International Monetary Fund

If there is one actor which has gone out of its way to praise the Spanish regulatory authorities and the Spanish banks in their response to the challenges of Spain's newly acquired international financial stature, it is the International Monetary Fund (IMF). Already in early 1999, as the jitters from the Brazilian devaluation were starting to be felt throughout the region, and especially in Argentina, the IMF pointed out that "the crisis in Latin America will impose costs on some banks, but the *prudent provisioning* undertaken over the past years should enable them to face these without much difficulty."[6] A year later, the IMF persisted in its praise, even pointing out that Spain could benefit

---

[5] *Informe de Estabilidad Financiera*, November 2002 and November 2003.

[6] IMF, *Spain: 1999 Article IV Consultation Mission*, 30 March 1999. http://www.imf.org/external/np/ms/1999/033099.htm. Emphasis added.

from its exposure to Latin America by becoming a financial "bridge" with the rest of Europe:

Spanish banks are *well-capitalized and profitable*, and have taken a leading position in global markets, particularly in Latin America. . . [T]he creation of the *Latibex* is further evidence of the potentially very profitable niche that Spain has created as a bridge for capital flows between Europe and Latin America. Existing regulatory mechanisms, which involve the Bank of Spain, the Comisión Nacional de Mercado de Valores [the equivalent of the Securities and Exchange Commission] and the Dirección General de Seguros [the Insurance Regulatory Directorate], are functioning well, although of course regulators will need to continue to respond flexibly to new demands as markets evolve. . . In banking supervision, the recent move by the Bank of Spain to increase provisioning requirements is *path-breaking and well-timed*: it will prepare now for the inevitable day when nonperforming loans rise in response to an eventual economic slowdown.[7]

By late 2001, the eventual economic slowdown in Latin America had already materialized, and the fears of an Argentine default and devaluation acquired new currency. The IMF continued to praise the foresight of Spanish regulators and banks:

The banking sector in Spain has undergone a profitable expansion, including in international markets. Supervisors had already, in 2000, introduced a *forward-looking, and path-breaking, provisioning system* to ensure a more adequate building of bank reserves over the business cycle. They are continuing to pay particular attention to the risks associated with the development of bank investments in Latin America, given the uncertainties concerning economic developments in that region. They have ensured a *conservative accounting treatment* of investments, forged working links with overseas supervisors, and strengthened their own capacity for monitoring risk. . . Overall, levels of capital in the financial system are high.[8]

While the Argentine financial meltdown of January 2002 had an important impact on Spanish equities, the IMF correctly assessed the risk of a systematic impact on the Spanish economy and financial

---

[7] IMF, *Spain: 2000 Article IV Consultation Mission*, 20 July 2000. http://www.imf.org/external/np/ms/2000/072000.htm. Emphasis added.

[8] IMF, *Spain: 2001 Article IV Consultation Mission*, 22 October 2001. http://www.imf.org/external/np/ms/2001/102201.htm. Emphasis added.

system as remote. In spite of the potential "fall-out from the difficulties in some Latin American countries. . . there are, on current prospects, grounds for reasonable confidence that the likelihood of adverse developments with significant economic repercussions for Spain *remains low.*" And it added that

in the banking sector, the salient feature is the *resilience* it has shown during an undoubtedly difficult period. Despite developments in Argentina that have in several respects been more severe than anticipated, notably as regards the adoption of measures affecting the banking system (such as the *pesificación asimétrica* [or asymmetric conversion of dollar assets and debts into pesos]), the banks concerned have been able to endure and indeed fully absorb the effects of the crisis, with complete provisioning of both credit risks and investments. And this has been done through a reduction in profits – the banks' first line of defense – with profit growth nonetheless remaining positive and in line with the banks' timely reassessment of prospects for the year. This outcome reflects *the banking sector's strong starting position in terms of capitalization, provisioning, efficiency, and profitability, based on a vibrant domestic franchise, but is also the result of the Bank of Spain's proactive role in promoting conservative risk management practices.*[9]

In late 2003, with the worst of the Argentine crisis over, the IMF summarized the events as follows, suggesting that Spain's handling of the crisis was a model for other countries to imitate when facing similar situations:

The *resilience* shown by the Spanish banking system to the difficulties in Latin America *deserves to be highlighted.* Indeed, the speed and extent of the turnaround in 2003 has been pronounced, with major banks' results surpassing market expectations. The Spanish banking system continues to show *high levels of solvency, profitability, and efficiency,* supported by a firm and *proactive supervisory stance of the Bank of Spain.* In this light, we believe that *both Spain and the international community could derive useful indications from the conduct of a Financial Sector Assessment Program* (FSAP).[10]

---

[9] IMF, *Spain: 2002 Article IV Consultation Mission*, 11 November 2002. http://www.imf.org/external/np/ms/2002/111102.htm. Emphasis added.
[10] IMF, *Spain: 2003 Article IV Consultation Mission*, 17 November 2003. http://www.imf.org/external/np/ms/2003/111803.htm. Emphasis added.

Conclusion

The rise in foreign direct investment by Spanish companies has un-deniably exposed the economy and the financial system to a high level of risk, especially because of its concentration in Latin America. However, an equally unquestionable statement is that Spain and its firms have managed the turbulent waters of the global economy skill-fully, to the point that a major crisis in Latin America has barely affected the stability of the financial system or the economic well-being of the Spanish population. Rather than being lucky, however, Spain and its companies planned for the difficulties, thus avoiding a debacle. While Soros (2002: 144) was right in predicting that the stock market would penalize Spanish banks and utilities, they weathered the storm without retrenching or withdrawing. Their cred-ibility as companies committed to an international presence has thus been enhanced.

7 | *Foreign policy and international stature*

> When in 1995 Secretary of State Warren
> Christopher defined Telefónica as the main
> instrument of Spanish foreign policy in
> Latin America, he was implicitly arguing
> that it was a company rather than the
> government which was furthering Spanish
> interests in the region.
>
> Fernando Delage (2003:569)

M ULTINATIONAL corporations have grown so big that
their foreign activities often have implications for the stature of the home country in global affairs and for the conduct of foreign policy. The reverse is also possible: the activities of
multinational firms can be affected by the foreign policy of the home
country. The government can also use the multinationals as tools to
achieve diplomatic goals. As outlined in chapter 2, there is no agreement in the international relations literature about the connection
between a country's foreign stature and policy, on the one hand, and
its multinational firms, on the other. The realist perspective considers
multinationals to be instruments in the hands of their home states. The
pluralist approach, however, sees a more complex interaction between
multinationals and their home governments. Finally, the constructivist
perspective downplays the importance of interest-driven action by
states or multinationals, emphasizing instead the role of shared or
negotiated norms of appropriate behavior in the international arena.
The evidence to be presented in this chapter indicates that the increased presence of Spanish firms abroad has shaped foreign policy
more than the reverse. There is very little evidence indicating that
firms have been used by the government in its pursuit of foreign-policy
goals, although it is true that the government has benefited from the
enhanced stature generated by foreign investment. This conclusion
seems counterintuitive given that government-controlled firms have
always accounted for a large portion of all Spanish investment abroad

(see chapter 4). Thus the pluralist perspective seems to fit the Spanish pattern better than the realist approach. There is also some evidence that the Spanish government and its firms follow shared norms.

Spain has become one of the world's ten largest foreign investors. While its economic and financial interests lie primarily in Latin America and Europe, the country's foreign-policy interests also include North Africa (the Maghrib) and the United States. This chapter will chart the evolution of Spanish foreign policy over the last twenty-five years, pointing out its main contradictions, and suggesting how it can be made compatible with the country's enhanced role in global economic affairs. The shifts in foreign policy from Felipe González to José María Aznar and José Luis Rodríguez Zapatero will be analyzed in the context of a country that lacks sufficient clout to pursue anything other than a pragmatic foreign policy based on alliances with other countries.

Spanish foreign policy and the multinationals

Spain is a small though geopolitically and linguistically important country (Méndez and Marcu 2003), which is only now coming out of two hundred years of isolation from global affairs. In fact, between 1500 and 1815 Spain participated in all of the major armed conflicts that took place in the western hemisphere, but during the nineteenth and twentieth centuries it did not take part in *any* of them (Alvarez Junco 2001:501). It was also the first European power to lose the better part of its colonies in the early nineteenth century, in the wake of the Napoleonic invasion of the metropole. Spain was forced to withdraw from its Caribbean and East Asian possessions during the US–Spanish war of 1898, the last armed conflict with a foreign power. The Civil War of 1936–9 further debilitated the country's international stature both in terms of the process – driven by the intervention of Germany, Italy, and the Soviet Union – and the outcome, which relegated Spain to pariah status because of General Franco's support of the Rome–Berlin Axis during the initial years of World War II. Though formally allied with the United States since the early 1950s, the country remained diplomatically isolated and pusillanimous, with little legitimacy and meager resources to pursue a meaningful and active foreign policy. The last remnants of its once vast empire were abandoned in the early 1970s as Franco's life was coming to an end. The anachronism of being the last dictatorial regime left in Western Europe and the gross mishandling of the crisis with Morocco over the decolonization of the Western Sahara territory wreaked havoc on Spain's stature in global affairs (Tusell 2000; Gillespie and Youngs 2000).

Starting in the 1960s, and more forcefully since the transition to democracy in the late 1970s, Spanish diplomatic efforts became dominated by the overarching goal of joining the European Union(EU) (Marks 1995). Other historically important parts of the world for Spain – notably Latin America, and Morocco and Algeria in the Maghrib – took a back seat, except for a facade of cultural cooperation and friendship. Meanwhile, relationships with the United States remained cordial but distant, with public opinion strongly opposed to the presence of US troops on Spanish soil and to American policies in Latin America. In a surprise move opposed by a majority of Spaniards, the centrist government of Leopoldo Calvo-Sotelo made Spain a member of NATO in 1981, though without integrating Spanish armed forces into the alliance's command structure. The Socialist governments presided over by Felipe González (1982–96) continued to put Europe at the core of Spain's foreign policy. During the election campaign, González committed the government to calling a referendum on NATO membership, managing to win just enough popular support by linking the issue to EU membership and to a reduction in the number of American troops and bases. The outcome of the vote was eagerly awaited by Germany, which had been Spain's most ardent supporter in its quest for EU membership and which looked forward to Spain's continued presence in the military alliance (Balfour and Preston 1999). In January 1986, after two decades of failed attempts, Spain became a member of the EU.

The preeminence of the EU as the main area of Spanish foreign-policy activity can be justified in a number of ways. Spain is, despite the clichés and Alexandre Dumas' confused notion about the location of the Pyrenees, a European country, historically and culturally (Díez Medrano 2003). Moreover, the EU is Spain's most important economic partner, accounting for more than two-thirds of imports, exports, and inward investment, and about 40 percent of outward investment. Not surprisingly, two-thirds of the official visits by the King, the Crown Prince, or the Prime Minister are directed towards other European countries. Spain's accession to the EU, however, unfolded in ways that seriously compromised the country's foreign policy towards other parts of the world, especially Latin America. Unlike Great Britain and France, Spain did not succeed in having the rest of the EU recognize its historical ties to its former colonies (Freres and Sanz Trillo 2000). Moreover, after the deepening of the EU's terms of membership with the Maastricht Treaty and the single market of 1992, the country could no longer use trade policy as a foreign-policy instrument. Thus, during the 1980s and early 1990s, Spanish policy towards Latin America focused on other issues – human rights, the promotion of democracy, cultural cooperation, and a rather romantic push to resurrect the idea of an Iberian-American community of nations – which put it on a collision course with US interests and policy, especially in Central America during the closing years of the cold war.

Foreign policy meets new economic realities

While the EU continues to be the country's most important economic partner, Spanish foreign relations have witnessed somewhat of a revolution over the last decade, mainly for three separate economic reasons. The first is immigration. After decades of being a net migration country, Spain has become a magnet not just for European retirees yearning for a pleasant climate but also for hundreds of thousands of South Americans and North and Sub-Saharan Africans seeking a better life. At the end of 2002, more than 1.3 million foreigners were legally resident in Spain, most of them recent arrivals, and two-thirds of them employed and making contributions to the social security system (MIR 2003; Vilar and Vilar 2003). Immigrants without papers number up to an additional half a million. These immigration flows are quite large for a country with just over 40 million people and no recent experience of massive immigration. The economic bonanza of the late 1990s, however, made it easier to absorb them.

The second major change has been the growing dependence on natural gas supplies from Algeria, which presently account for nearly 60 percent of the country's gas consumption and about 9 percent of total consumption from all energy sources (Mineco 2003:99–114). Not only is Algeria a politically troubled country, but 40 percent of the gas flows to Spain using a pipeline that travels through the perhaps less shaky but still unstable kingdom of Morocco, with which Spain has major disputes over fishing rights, the decolonization of the

Western Sahara, immigration and the two North African cities and various islets that Spain still holds.

And the third, and perhaps most important, category of economic changes affecting Spanish foreign policy and international stature over the last decade is the wave of investments by Spanish firms in Europe and Latin America, especially in those countries in which they now hold leading market positions, namely, Portugal, Argentina, and Chile. These investments – mainly in politically sensitive sectors such as banking, construction, highways, utilities, and telecommunications – have suddenly become a major item on Spain's foreign-policy agenda. In Portugal, Spanish diplomats have had to confront a backlash against the Spanish "economic invasion," at the same time as the two Iberian countries were trying to join forces to reassert the importance of the western edge of the EU as it welcomed ten new member countries from Eastern Europe with relatively well-educated populations eager to work for lower salaries. In Argentina, the interests of Spanish companies affected by default and devaluation have become a major issue in the bilateral relationship. In Chile, the 1998–9 episode over the extradition of former President Pinochet to face civil-rights charges in Spain strained relations at a time when Spanish firms were consolidating their positions in leading sectors of the economy. The most prominent firms – Telefónica, Endesa, and the banks – were the targets of criticism and even violence by pro Pinochet groups. During the months-long crisis, the Spanish government studiously avoided taking sides in the judicial process while maintaining a low profile and engaging in backstage actions to reassure the Chilean government (Fazio Vengoa 2000:73). In Peru the accusations of human-rights violations by the Fujimori administration gave Spanish diplomats and the government itself some headaches during 1998 as they tried to strike a delicate balance between criticizing the Peruvian President and supporting the presence of Spanish firms in highly regulated industries like telecommunications and banking (Fazio Vengoa 2000:73).

FDI, the United States, and foreign policy towards Latin America

Students of Spanish foreign policy have noticed that the recent wave of FDI in Latin America represents a key change that fits a long-term pattern of evolution in the transatlantic relationship, though without producing an in-depth analysis of the consequences.[1] Spanish foreign policy toward Latin America has evolved from a misplaced, unfeasible and unwelcome emphasis on Spain's cultural leadership in the region during the 1960s and 1970s, to an effort to promote human rights, peace, and democratization during the 1980s, and to issues of economic development, trade, investment, and migration during the 1990s and 2000s (Grugel 1995; Youngs 2001). As Baklanoff (1996) aptly put it, a shift from "lyrical" to "practical" *hispanismo* has occurred. Spanish foreign policy towards the region has been traditionally weak because of the lack of a vision, the meager resources allocated to it, the little interest displayed by the public, and the greater importance attached to the relationships with Europe and the US (Freres and Sanz Trillo 2000; Fernando Delage 2003). In the wake of EU membership, Latin America has become an insignificant trading partner, accounting for less than 5 percent of total Spanish trade. The relationship between Spain and Latin America only acquired real substance or content during the 1990s with the rise in Spanish foreign investment and international aid toward Latin America and with migration flows in the opposite direction.

The crisis over the extradition to Spain of former Chilean President and dictator Augusto Pinochet in 1998–9 to face human-rights charges and the Argentine default of 2002 have brought to the surface the foreign-policy tensions associated with the massive foreign investments undertaken by Spanish businesses. It is not a coincidence that the strains reached worrisome levels in the two countries in which Spanish FDI has the greatest relative impact. While extensive in absolute terms, Spanish investments in Brazil and Mexico are but a drop in the ocean in the two largest economies in Latin America. Tiny Chile and midsized Argentina present a different outlook. Spanish firms

---

[1] A number of books and edited volumes make reference in passing to the growing relevance of outward FDI in Latin America for Spanish foreign policy. Unfortunately, no more than a few sentences are deemed necessary to address this issue (Tusell 2000:27; Freres and Sanz Trillo 2000:569–70; Fernández Navarrete 2003:148; García Pérez 2003:548). Some recent books or chapters in books do not even refer to Spanish FDI (Balfour and Preston 1999; Ferré 2000; Gillespie and Youngs 2000; Pérez Herrero 2003).

have invested aggressively in highly visible and politicized industries such as banking, telecommunications, electricity, water, oil, gas, and construction. They account for important shares of the domestic market. It is precisely in the wake of the growing problems faced by Spanish firms in some of the region's economies, and by their intention to be long-term players in Latin America, that a major debate emerged over the best way to tackle the situation. During the early 2000s, the discussion became polarized between those who defended a policy of joint action with the US so as to pursue, among other things, Spanish economic interests abroad, and the critics of that option.

A closer relationship with the US as the solution

One approach to defend the new Spanish economic and financial interests in Latin America, and to a lesser extent Morocco, is to strengthen relations with the country that calls the shots in many parts of the world, namely the United States, the country that exerts the strongest influence over multilateral economic and financial organizations like the World Bank and IMF. This is the option that José María Aznar implemented during his years in office (1996–2004). As Del Arenal (2003) points out, Aznar's rapprochement with the US and distancing himself from France and Germany date back to his early months in office. The first step took place in 1996, when the government integrated Spanish armed forces within the military command of NATO. That same year policy towards Cuba was aligned with the US position, except for the trade embargo. In 1998 Aznar defended American and British bombing of Iraqi targets. In 2001 Spain and the US initiated a series of regular annual bilateral summits. Later that year, Aznar backed Bush in his decision to abandon the Antiballistic Missile Treaty. In early 2002 the government agreed to expand the facilities of the US naval and air force base at Rota in southern Spain and to facilitate using Spain as a springboard for military operations in the Middle East. In April 2002 Spain joined the US in paying a diplomatic visit to the self-proclaimed President of Venezuela shortly before sitting President Hugo Chávez regained control.

Aznar's decision to staunchly support the US and the UK in their invasion of Iraq in March 2003, without an explicit UN resolution and against Spanish public opinion, represented the dramatic culmination of the policy of closer ties across the North Atlantic. The Spanish government had been among those reacting most strongly to the

11 September 2001 terrorist attacks. Some interviewees speculated that Aznar's decision owed much to his psychological mindset after having narrowly escaped a terrorist bomb when he was the opposition leader in the mid-1990s.

Some foreign-policy experts see the rapprochement with the US as a perfectly sensible and well thought-out option for Spain. Chief among the supporters of the US option is Eduardo Serra, a former Defense Minister and president of the foreign-policy think tank Real Instituto Elcano. As its director has repeatedly pointed out, Aznar's decision to side with the US on Iraq – even at the risk of dividing Europe and of losing electoral support for his party and government – is "neither as radical nor as novel as many would have it and is, moreover, quite comprehensible seen in context" (Lamo de Espinosa 2003). Undoubtedly, Aznar's foreign-policy gamble helped him make headlines around the world, repositioned Spain away from the Paris–Berlin axis,[2] and enhanced his political stature abroad, though hurting it at home. Fortune would have it that Spain was about to serve a two-year term as an elected, non-permanent member of the UN Security Council starting in January 2003, which made Aznar's position more momentous and internationally visible.

According to Lamo de Espinosa, there are five main reasons for a Spanish foreign policy more closely tied to the US, of which only one has been made explicit, namely, American backing of Spain's efforts to eradicate the Basque terrorist group ETA and its political supporters, which Washington has recently placed on its list of terrorist organizations. The other four reasons were never officially articulated by the government, but seem to make sense, for Spain can perhaps benefit from a closer relationship with the US and its "special" European

---

[2] The Aznar government's distancing of France and Germany manifested itself not just in terms of foreign policy but also economic policy. In a lecture on 12 January 2004, Economy Minister Rodrigo Rato went out of his way to highlight that Spain should abandon – and had already started to abandon – the long-standing practice of servile imitation of France and Germany. He explained that Spain's remarkable economic successes – zero deficit, tax reductions, four million new jobs, and membership in the euro – made it possible for the country to have an independent voice in European affairs and to stand tall next to the Union's larger powers. He strongly argued for a Spain that influences rather than merely follows Europe.

allies (the UK and Portugal) in terms of gaining additional leverage to counterbalance the EU's expansion to the East, defending its cities and territories in North Africa (see Aznar 2004:168), exercising cultural influence over the expanding Hispanic population in the US, and protecting the investments of Spanish firms in Latin America.

The latter motive ranks perhaps as the second strongest after terrorism. Lamo de Espinosa (2003) argues that the US is still the dominant political and economic power in Latin America, a region that has been gradually pulling away from Europe. First, Mexico entered into a free-trade agreement with the US effective from January 1994. Ten years later Chile followed suit. Colombia's government has become dependent on anti-terrorist funding from the US. Brazil and Argentina are as distrustful of Europe as they are of the US. In the meantime, trade disputes have proliferated between the EU and various Latin American countries. Finally, the United States is the largest shareholder in the IMF, an institution that plays an important role in Latin America.

Writing from Madrid, *Wall Street Journal* correspondents seemed to agree with this interpretation of events. In their view, there is "good reason" for Spain to cement its relationship with the US:

In just over a decade, Spanish companies have invested more than $90 billion to expand in Latin America, and have increasingly spoken of using Mexico as a platform to enter the US market. In December [2002], for instance, Bank of America Corp. agreed to pay $1.6 billion to Spain's Banco Santander Central Hispano SA for a 25 percent stake in Grupo Financiero Santander Serfin SA, one of Mexico's biggest banks. Both Santander and Bank of America hope the deal will enable them to cash in on the growing Latino market for remittances, while providing Santander with a stepping stone into the US.

And then they refer to yet another quite tangible benefit of US-Spanish rapprochement:

When Argentina hit a snag this month during negotiations with the International Monetary Fund over a debt-refinancing package, Spain and the US teamed up to help broker a deal vital to the interests of Spanish and US companies in Argentina (*Wall Street Journal* 16 September 2003, p. A15).

In interviews with journalists, politicians, and business leaders, I have been able to confirm that there was some connection, however tenuous, between Spanish investments in Latin America and Aznar's shift in foreign policy towards the US. One key aspect, however, seems clear, namely, that Spanish businesses did *not* lobby the Spanish government to back the US in its global anti-terrorist policies in exchange for having more of a free hand in Latin America and helping out during times of financial turbulence. At most, US tolerance of and even support for Spanish economic and financial interests in the region were an unintended by-product of the foreign-policy shift. Another intriguing fact is that when Argentina's newly elected President Nestor Kirchner met President Bush in Washington on 23 July 2003, a few weeks after the "official" end of the Iraqi campaign, more than half of the conversation had to do with Spanish interests in Argentina. Reportedly, the US President, whom Aznar had visited two weeks earlier, asked Kirchner to "treat well his friends the Spaniards."[3]

Some Aznar government officials argued in interviews that the origins of the policy of rapprochement with the US was not interest-driven but ideas-driven. In their view, Aznar's most important success was to project an image of a "serious," "capable," "confident," and "normal" country that can play the game of the global economy and of international affairs on a par with other midsized powers. Thus Aznar systematically sought to eradicate the centuries-old image of a country regarded by foreigners as "exotic" and "backward" (see the next chapter). His strategy was to turn Spain into an economically dynamic, fiscally responsible, and internationally engaged country. In his mind, the US and the UK were the role models to imitate because of their faith in individual freedoms, their long institutional continuity, and their ability to defend themselves against external threats; the "sclerotic" Europe exemplified by France and Germany, the model to avoid (Aznar 2004:160). Aznar pursued free-market policies and tax reductions like no other Spanish head of government, and his inspiration owes much to the Anglo-Saxon model. These officials recognized, though, that Spanish economic and financial interests have come to play a role in foreign policy-making, albeit mostly

[3] Spain contributed 1,300 soldiers to the Iraqi pacification effort (0.83 percent of the total, 5.1 percent of troops other than American). Only the UK, Italy, Poland, and the Ukraine have sent more troops. In part as a reward for its support of the US, Spain was selected to host the Iraq donors meeting (*International Herald Tribune*, 23 October 2003; *New York Times*, 25 October 2003).

during Aznar's second term in office, when the most important fiscal, economic, and regulatory reforms were already well under way.

The critics

During the Aznar period, critics charged that the policy of alignment with the US did not make any sense at all given Spain's other foreign interests, and that, even if the policy made sense, the instruments to implement it effectively do not exist. This group included foreign-policy experts, business executive and journalists as well as opposition leaders, who in March 2004 regained control of Congress and the government. The first part of their argument is that the policy of closer ties to the US has made Spain's traditional policy towards Latin America, Europe, the Mediterranean, and the Middle East more complicated. The critics were right in that the largest Latin American countries did not support the invasion of Iraq, and tensions grew in February 2003 when Aznar and his Foreign Minister tried to persuade Chile and Mexico, two other non-permanent Security Council members at the time, to go along with it. (Interestingly, Chile was able to get away with its opposition to the invasion of Iraq and conclude a free trade agreement with the US in late 2003.) It is also true that relations with France and Germany worsened. These two countries are Spain's most important trading partners (over 30 percent of total trade), and Germany is a major contributor to the EU's cohesion funds, from which Spain has benefited handsomely. Spain's traditional role in the Middle East as a mediator – though often more critical of Israel than not – was altered as well. In interviews, the executives of some large firms with investments in Latin America and/or the Arab world expressed their reservations and apprehensions about Aznar's foreign policy, although they pointed out that their interests had not been hurt. Smaller multinationals have been much more critical.

Another important component of the criticism is that the US is not the right partner for Spain to defend its economic and financial interests. While the US is the world's dominant financial power, US firms and banks have their own agenda in Latin America. Moreover, the US does not have a comprehensive policy towards the region as a whole, other than the pursuit of free trade, which is often at odds with the EU (Del Arenal 2003; Palacio and Rodrigo 2003). Thus Spain's position and interests in Latin America are not that compatible with those of the US.

Some critics also pointed out that, even if closer ties to the US were the best way to defend Spanish foreign economic interests, there are almost no instruments and structures in place to implement the policy in practice. Among these critics were Fernando Delage and José Luis Gómez Navarro, both affiliated with Estudios de Política Exterior SA, a Madrid-based research and publishing organization. Their argument is, in essence, one of lack of embeddedness: that is, the idea that government policy of any kind can only work if the relevant social actors are involved in it. As sociologist Peter Evans (1995) has argued, communication and action channels between the government and relevant social actors are needed to implement policies successfully. The critics blamed not only the Aznar government for failing to establish and nurture such channels, but also the largest firms. There was, for instance, an attempt in the late 1990s – before diplomatic problems erupted in Chile and Argentina – to organize a foreign-policy lobbying group comprised of the largest firms with foreign investments. Reportedly the effort failed because of disagreements about priorities and preexisting rivalries among firms.[4]

The most blistering criticisms, however, were reserved for the con-servative government. Aznar, his detractors charge, initiated a revolu-tion in Spanish foreign policy almost single-handedly, without taking into account the perspectives and knowledge of the diplomatic corps and the foreign-policy expert community, and against the will of a majority of the population. While a new policy has been formulated and executed on prominent occasions like the crisis over Iraq, no instruments or structures exist to make sure that whatever new capital or influence accrues from a special relationship with the US can be used to advance Spain's interests around the world. Specifically, the critics charged that there was, and continues to be, a complete lack of coordination among foreign policy-making officials, the Spanish rep-resentatives at international agencies such as the IMF, and the officials in charge of development aid. Two cases are invoked by the critics to illustrate the implementation problem: the difficulties of Spanish firms

---

[4] It is important to note that some company executives interviewed for this book denied any such attempt to create a lobby, pointing out that it would be unnecessary given that the presidents and CEOs of Spain's six or eight largest multinationals know each other very well and are in touch regularly without any need for a formal lobby.

operating in Peru, an important recipient of Spanish development aid, and the accord between Argentina and the IMF of September 2003, perceived by many as contrary to the interests of Spanish firms. Let us discuss the latter in more detail.

The accord between Argentina and the IMF concluded in September 2003 did not include any firm commitments to compensate banks and utility companies for the adverse effects of the abandonment of peso–dollar convertibility discussed in chapter 6. It is important to note that the deal was struck after both the invasion of Iraq and the July visit by Kirchner to Washington, developments that should have helped Spanish interests. The international financial press could not be more explicit in its denunciation of the deal, pointing out the lack of commitment on Argentina's side to compensate foreign banks and utilities, most of them Spanish-owned. The media called the accord "one of the softer bargains the IMF has struck in recent years" (*Financial Times*, 14 September 2003), and "the speediest and kindest the IMF has ever agreed to" (*The Economist*, 13 September 2003). The *International Herald Tribune* (owned by The *New York Times*) headlined that Argentina did not make "any major concessions" (12 September 2003), while *Corporate Argentina* reported "Creditors outraged by IMF pact" (12 September 2003). In its *Press Releases and Documents*, however, the Voice of America's headline stated, "Bush Praises Argentina for New IMF Accord" (12 September 2003; see also *Cinco Días*, 13 September 2003; *Clarín*, 13 September 2003).

It is certainly true that the letter of intent signed by Argentina did not include any specific timetable to compensate the banks for the conversion of deposits and debts into devalued pesos or to raise the regulated utility rates that had been set in terms of convertible pesos worth one US dollar. All the press reported were vague verbal promises made by President Kirchner to IMF managing director Horst Koehler: "The [Argentine] government accepted, there has to be a law passed, even by the end of this year, that sets a framework for adjustment for utility prices" (*Dow Jones International News*, 12 September 2003; see also *Cinco Días*, 13 September 2003, *El País*, 12 September 2003 and *Expansión*, 16 September 2003).

It is not clear, however, why an accord between the IMF and a sovereign country ought to include any clauses protecting the specific interests of multinational firms from a foreign country. In the language of IMF-borrower agreements, country commitments to reach certain targets or to implement institutional reforms are called "conditionality terms." During the 1990s, the average IMF program included three times as many terms as during the previous decade. The record was set in the agreement with Indonesia, which contained 140 conditionality terms (Goldstein 2001:39). The IMF justifies conditionality terms on the grounds that they help countries signal credibility to the international financial community and "securing this depends not only on short-run macroeconomic management given an existing set of institutions, but also on the quality of the institutions themselves." These could include "budgetary institutions . . . the central bank (covering independence, competence, etc.), the regulatory regime governing banks and financial markets, and so on" (Khan and Sharma 2001:20–1). Not only leftist critics of the IMF but also mainstream economists such as Jagdish Bhagwati, Martin Feldstein, Paul Krugman, Jeffrey Sachs, and Joseph Stiglitz, among others, have blamed the IMF for seeking to shape domestic policy agendas and institutions (Guillén 2001c:194; Stiglitz 2002).

Although I do not consider it appropriate for the IMF to meddle with a troubled country's internal affairs in ways that are not directly related to the funding program under negotiation, it is fair to ask why the emerging "special" relationship between the United States and Spain promoted by Aznar failed to produce an IMF accord more favorable to Spanish business interests. One of two things may have produced this less-than-ideal outcome for Spanish firms in Argentina, according to the critics of Aznar's foreign policy. First, the US could have ignored or downplayed Spanish interests during the negotiations because they were different than its own. Second, Spain could have forgotten to ask the US to further Spanish economic and financial interests during the negotiations and/or to inform the US representative at the IMF that Spain wished the issue of compensation for the banks and the utilities to be on the accord. There is evidence that the US was at the time pushing issues on its own bilateral agenda with Argentina which were not very important to Spain (for example, trade negotiations), although it did insist on the need to address the problem of utility rates (*Clarín*, 13 September 2003; *La Nación*, 13 September 2003).

Some of the foreign-policy analysts I have interviewed believed the second possibility to be closer to the reality of what happened than the first. They argue that Aznar – and perhaps also the Spanish firms – were somewhat naïve in thinking that support for the US in Iraq and elsewhere would automatically translate into US support for Spanish interests the first time that such a backing was needed. As a result of the lack of well-established lobbying mechanisms, information exchange, and coordination among foreign-policy agencies, Spain lost an opportunity to advance its interests. In interviews, Aznar government officials addressed this criticism by arguing that if Spain had not intervened, Argentina and the IMF might not have concluded an agreement at all. Proof of this may be that Argentine Presidents Duhalde and Kirchner have publicly applauded Spanish efforts to make an IMF deal possible.[5] It also seems to be the case that Spanish firms preferred a "soft" IMF deal with Argentina to no deal at all. For instance, executives such as Santander's Emilio Botín and Francisco Luzón expressed some guarded optimism about the accord, adding that they expected their interests to be addressed in the following months (*Cinco Días*, 12 and 13 September 2003). The Argentine government, however, continued to ignore their demands until early 2004, when it committed itself to increasing prices for regulated utilities in 2005.

The Maghrib

Another area in which, according to the supporters of Aznar's foreign policy, better relations with the US could make a difference is the Maghrib, especially Morocco and Algeria. Arguably the EU could not help resolve the largely symbolic crisis over the islet of Perejil in summer 2002, in part because France has its own interests in the area. However, the US did (Lamo de Espinosa 2003). If Spain were to face a major security problem – terrorism or a Moroccan attack on the Spanish-held cities in North Africa – Europe would likely be unable and perhaps even unwilling to act. Protection of the Straits of Gibraltar, the most important waterway in the world with a daily traffic of 220 large vessels, is basically guaranteed by the US naval and air forces stationed at Rota, in southern Spain, a base that the Spanish government agreed to expand in 2002 (Méndez and Marcu 2003).

[5] Interestingly, former President González also traveled to Argentina to defend the interests of Spanish firms (*Clarín*, 22 December 2001; *El País*, 9 January 2002). The effectiveness of this top-level lobbying, however, remains the subject of much discussion (see also chapter 6).

It is certainly true that Spain has sizable economic interests in the Maghrib, especially in terms of immigration control and natural gas. Investments by Spanish companies are much smaller than in Latin America or Europe, though still significant. Spanish diplomats face a difficult task because of the conflict between Morocco and Algeria over the Western Sahara. Spain entertains different policy goals towards each country, namely, fishing, migration and territorial disputes with the former, and gas supplies with the latter. Spanish investments in manufacturing are important in both cases. Spanish foreign policy in the area thus involves a hard balancing act, and playing off one country against the other would be too risky a strategy (Martínez Carreras 2003).

The critics of Aznar's policy pointed out in interviews that many of the more than 200 Spanish firms with operations in Morocco are fuming about Aznar's confrontation with Rabat over immigration and territorial disputes. They would prefer a smooth relationship in which Spanish diplomacy made it easier for firms to stay away from major controversies. Critics noted that the increased presence of Spanish businesses and the use of development aid should give foreign policy-makers more leverage when trying to lessen the enormous economic disparity between Spain and the Maghrib, which, in per capita income terms, presently stands at 6:1 (the ratio between the US and Mexico is 4:1).

The relationship with Portugal and the rest of the EU

While Spanish firms have invested nearly as much in Europe as they have in Latin America, it is only in Portugal that FDI has had a major impact in terms of Spain's foreign relationships. The reasons are clear: Portugal is a small economy (about one-fifth of the size of Spain's), and Spanish firms have invested aggressively in highly visible and politicized sectors such as banking and construction. In financial services, Spanish-owned or -controlled companies account for 15 percent of the Portuguese market, and in construction for about 30 percent (Chislett 2004; *El País Negocios*, 28 December 2003). Still, Spain is only the fifth-largest foreign investor in Portugal. As in the Maghrib, Spanish diplomacy faces a delicate task in Portugal because the two Iberian countries need each other in order to counterbalance the EU's expansion to the East and to develop the infrastructure projects in the energy and transportation sectors that will help articulate a truly unified Iberian economic space.

The tensions over Spanish investment in Portugal first emerged in 2002, when a group of forty prominent businesspeople and intellectuals sent the Portuguese Prime Minister and President a document showing their concern over the "invasion of foreign capital." This document became known as the "Patriots' Manifesto" (*ABC*, 5 November 2003; *El País*, 8 November 2003; *El País Domingo*, 25 April 2004). "Throughout history," declared Vitor Bento, one of the signatories, "Portugal has managed to remain free from Spanish influence by belonging to different international alliances. This is the first time we have been part of the same ones. People tend to see national sovereignty from a narrow, political point of view. We are trying to point out that in an era of market globalization, the economy too is vital to a country's autonomy" (quoted in *The Economist*, 23 January 2003, and *Financial Times*, 3 June 2003). Two of the forty signatories, however, have recently sold their companies to Spanish interests.

Headlines such as "Portugal, capital Madrid" have hailed Spanish takeovers of Portuguese companies. What angers the Portuguese is not so much that Spanish firms invest in Portugal but that when their own firms wish to do so in Spain, they are stonewalled. The two most widely cited examples are Caixa Geral de Depósitos' bid for Spain's Banco Atlántico, which ended up being acquired by Banco Sabadell in late 2003, and Electricidade de Portugal's unsuccessful attempts to exercise its voting rights as the owner of 40 percent of Hidrocantábrico, a midsized Spanish electrical utility.

During 2003 the backlash against Spanish investments became unmistakable. *Focus* magazine editorialized: "We shop at El Corte Inglés, dress at Zara, have a coffee at Il Caffe di Roma, eat at Pizza Hut, arrange for our vacations at Halcón, buy glasses at Multiópticas" (*El Mundo*, 30 December 2003). In February 2003, even the President of Portugal, Jorge Sampaio, commented that "without centers of decision-making, there is no nation," in a clear reference to Spanish corporate takeovers (*El País Domingo*, 25 April 2004). And in November 2003 he declared at a dinner with Spanish politicians and businesspeople in Madrid that Spain protects its economic interests while Portugal lets Spaniards invest freely, and justified Portuguese apprehensions as understandable (*ABC*, 5 November 2003). Spanish and Portuguese diplomats had to start working fast in order to contain the damage before the upcoming Spanish–Portuguese summit in December, which was to approve the framework for the creation of the common Iberian energy market and several high-speed railway links.

Spanish investments in Portugal – and the indigenous reaction to them – have created a conundrum for diplomats because both countries face enormous challenges in the EU. The Aznar government was bitterly unhappy about France and Germany's attempt to revisit the Nice Summit accords of 2000 over the distribution of voting power in the expanded, twenty-five-member Union. Spain and Portugal are united in their apprehension about the EU's "shift towards the East," and are both critical of France and Germany for their assumption that the Paris–Berlin axis ought to define European foreign policy. Spain is also one of the most ardent supporters of the Stability and Growth Pact, which France and Germany have violated with their excessive budget deficits.

The future of Spanish foreign policy

The general election of 14 March 2004 returned the Socialist Party to power after eight years of conservative rule. The programmatic differences between the two dominant parties are multifaceted, extending well beyond foreign-policy issues. The latter, however, were crucial in determining the outcome of the election, taking place as it did in the wake of the horrible terrorist attacks of 11 March, which resulted in 191 deaths and 1,400 wounded, and were attributed to an Al Qaeda cell. For months, Socialist candidate José Luis Rodríguez Zapatero had promised the return of the 1,300-odd Spanish troops stationed in Iraq. Within thirty-six hours of being sworn in as the new head of the government, he ordered an immediate recall. He also announced a renewed effort to approve a European Constitution, and pointed to France and Germany as Spain's key allies. He clearly intends to reverse Aznar's foreign policies and thus return to the trajectory established during the initial years of the transition to democracy.

The chain of events that unfolded in early 2004 has two kinds of repercussions for Spanish foreign policy-making. First, although the new government will most likely pursue a set of foreign-policy goals and means supported by a majority of the population and the political parties, it will need to wrestle with the international perception that Spain is a country that changes its foreign posture every decade or so.

And, second, a renewed European emphasis will surely help some of the Spanish companies with strong interests in the EU, though it may hurt others with their eyes set on the United States or parts of the world in which the US is influential, at least in the short term.

Any government needs to face up to the complexities of foreign policy-making, observing its political, economic, cultural and social dimensions. Foreign policy is crucial because it projects the country's intended role in the world as well as its identity, and it only works when the population supports it. Unlike domestic policies, there are serious limitations as to how much a country can achieve in foreign affairs. A certain system of alliances with other countries has to be defined, and implementation must take place in conjunction with both foreign partners and domestic actors. Finally, the consequences of using the various foreign-policy tools are harder to calculate and anticipate than in the case of domestic policy-making.

Spanish foreign policy-making is further complicated by the country's problematic relationships with its neighbors and with the United States. The country is dependent on the EU marketplace, on Germany for EU funding, on France for collaboration against the ETA terrorist band, on Algeria for natural gas exports, on Morocco for protection against unregulated migration flows from all of Africa, and on the United States regarding defense, security, and certain financial issues. This is a remarkably complex set of multilateral relationships. On the positive side, Spain is endowed with two cardinal foreign-policy assets, namely, its geopolitical location and the vibrancy of Spanish as the world's third most widely spoken language. These assets, however, bring with them risks as well as opportunities. Spanish foreign policy is necessarily constrained by the contradictions of a country historically, economically, and culturally at the crossroads of Europe, the Mediterranean, and the Americas, even though the strongest affinity is with Europe. It is in this complicated context that Spain has become, in addition, a major foreign investor, which represents yet another opportunity and challenge for the future.

Foreign investment and Spain's quest for diplomatic stature

Spanish foreign policy has made remarkable progress over the last quarter-century, although the country remains a third-tier diplomatic power. In spite of its economic and financial weight – comparable to that of Canada or Italy – it is not a member of the G7 or the G10.[6] The country has neither permanent executive representation at the IMF – although a Spaniard was elected managing director in May 2004 – nor a permanent seat on the UN Security Council, and lacks the ability to project military force much beyond its borders. Nuclear weapons are constitutionally forbidden (Gaviria 1996). Arguably, the recent rise in outward direct investment has generated more duties for Spanish diplomats, but also new opportunities. The executives of Spanish firms recognize the policy consequences of their decisions to invest abroad. Thus Francisco González of BBVA has argued that, because of foreign investments, Spain is now "a much more important country from an institutional point of view."[7] Iberdrola's Iñigo de Oriol has made similar remarks.[8]

Most foreign-policy analysts see the rise in foreign direct investment as an opportunity for Spain to play a greater role in the world. For instance, Fernando Delage, the deputy director of the leading foreign-relations journal *Política Exterior,* writes:

Spanish diplomacy has to not only defend the interests of its firms (and learn how to tell when those business interests do not coincide with the political goals of the government): it also has to develop a policy oriented towards the strengthening of civil society, the nurturing of the middle classes and the consolidation of democracy in the region . . . But Latin America is not just an opportunity for Spanish firms. It is the territory in which to show its aspirations; in fact, the only one that can turn Spain into a global power (Fernando Delage 2003:569–70).[9]

---

[6] The G7 includes Canada, France, Germany, Italy, Japan, the United Kingdom, and the United States. The G10 includes the G7 plus Belgium, Holland and Sweden. Spain, Luxemburg, and Switzerland joined the G10 in the negotiations leading up to the Basle II accord for banking capital adequacy (see chapter 5).

[7] *Diario de Sesiones del Senado: Comisión de Asuntos Iberoamericanos* 141 (7 June 2001):17.

[8] *Diario de Sesiones del Senado: Comisión de Asuntos Iberoamericanos* 206 (15 November 2001):1–14.

[9] "La diplomacia española no sólo tiene que defender los intereses de sus empresas (y saber distinguir cuándo esos intereses empresariales no coinciden con los objetivos politicos del gobierno): tiene que desarrollar también una política orientada al reforzamiento de la sociedad civil, la creación de clases medias y la consolidación de la democracia en el

The dangers are, according to him and many other analysts, to focus excessively on Latin America, and to rely too much on the US, which has its own agenda for the region.

Spain nowadays enjoys – or can enjoy – a diplomatically meaningful presence in Latin America, not because of its historical ties to the region but thanks to the activities of Spanish firms and, less importantly, the increase in development assistance. During 2001 and 2002 the Spanish Congress and Senate held multiple hearings on the Argentine crisis and its ramifications for Spain, at which several foreign-affairs officials and company executives made presentations and fielded questions. Senators displayed an enormous interest in how the foreign activities of Spanish firms affected the country's policy options in Latin America and elsewhere.[10] Even the population appears to consider the newly acquired international presence of Spanish firms as the most important reference point for foreign policy-making, ahead of non-governmental organizations, religious organizations, and the armed forces (Del Campo and Camacho 2003).

Foreign policy means

Discussions of Spanish foreign policy, however, may end up being little more than academic in nature if the means and the mechanisms are not there to pursue the broader and more ambitious goals that may now lie within the country's reach given the enhanced global stature of its firms. There is indeed agreement about one issue regarding foreign policy-making: the resources devoted to it are grossly insufficient. At the end of 2001 Spain had 738 diplomats (200 of them stationed in Madrid), compared to about 9,000 for the US, 2,180 for France, 1,538 for the UK, 1,461 for Germany, 1,050 for the Netherlands, and 934 for Italy (Fernando Delage 2003:564). The number of diplomats has

continente . . . Pero América Latina no es sólo una oportunidad para la empresa española. Es el terreno en el que demostrar sus aspiraciones; en realidad, el único que puede hacer de España una potencia global."

[10] See *Diario de Sesiones del Congreso de los Diputados* 137 (12 February 2002); *Diario de Sesiones del Senado: Comisión de Asuntos Iberoamericanos* 141 (7 June 2001), 148 (12 June 2001), 155 (26 June 2001), 177 (4 October 2001), 206 (15 November 2001), and 241 (27 February 2002).

barely changed over the last three decades, and it is only 70 percent higher than at the start of the Civil War back in 1936. Most other elite civil - service corps – university professors, tax inspectors, judges, etc. – are now several times more numerous than seventy years ago.[11]

It does not help matters that almost half (41 percent) of all diplomats are originally from Madrid, while regions like the Basque Country, Catalonia and Valencia, known for their entrepreneurial firms, many of which have become multinationals (see chapter 3), contribute few of them. Rare is the Spanish diplomat with a business background. Few serve on corporate boards upon retirement from the service (Valdivielso del Real 2003). In interviews with analysts, policy-makers and businesspeople, I learned that there is a gulf separating the training, worldviews, and yearnings of the foreign-policy and business communities in Spain. They do not seem to understand each other; yet they have to cope with the new reality of massive Spanish investments abroad. While this criticism is true to a large extent, it is also undeniably true that the top brass at the Ministry of Foreign Affairs is not only well versed in global economic and financial affairs, but also attentive to the interests of the largest Spanish multinationals. Smaller firms, by contrast, tend not to be on the radar screen of foreign policy-makers.

Another serious limitation in Spanish foreign policy-making, especially in an era of economic and financial globalization, is the scarcity of specialized research in the areas of international relations, area studies, strategic studies, and the international economy. There are some three dozen institutions and associations devoted to the study of some part of the world or aspect of international relations (Sorroza Blanco 2003; Pereira Castañares 2003), but only two or three have enough funding. The university system produces little research on

[11] In May 2004 some officials in the Rodríguez Zapatero government leaked to the press a plan to merge the diplomatic corps with the 450-strong corps of "Técnicos Comerciales del Estado," which due to the transfer of services to the autonomous regions have a much reduced workload. Although difficult to implement in practice due to the very different training of the two corps, this measure could enhance the economic and financial stature of Spain's foreign service (*Expansión*, 4 May 2004). Observers also point out long-standing rivalries as an obstacle.

international relations or specific parts of the world. Spanish research on Europe, the Maghrib or Latin America is not generally cited by researchers in other countries.

Perhaps the three organizations that have taken the presence of Spanish business abroad most seriously into account are Estudios de Política Exterior SA, the Real Instituto Elcano for International and Strategic Studies, and the CIDOB. Estudios de Política Exterior SA is a private research and publishing organization founded in the mid-1980s. It publishes a specialized journal, *Política Exterior.* Some of its experts advise several of Spain's largest multinationals. Elcano is named after the commander of the first expedition to circumnavigate the globe (1519–22). Founded in 2001, it is supported by contributions from the Ministries of Foreign Affairs, Defense, Economy, and Education as well as from companies, some of which are major multinational corporations (BBVA, Grupo Prisa, Indra, Santander, Telefónica). A host of other multinationals collaborate with the Institute, including Iberia, Repsol-YPF, and Unión Fenosa. The Institute's research priorities and activities reflect the importance of Europe, Latin America, the United States, and the Maghrib to Spanish foreign policy. It undertakes research from economic, political, and sociological perspectives. Barcelona-based CIDOB or Center for International Relations and Cooperation was originally founded in 1973 and is now affiliated with the University of Barcelona. A very active center in terms of research and teaching, most of its funding comes from the governments of Barcelona, Catalonia, and Spain.

Clearly, the recent dynamism of Spanish society and economy has produced new challenges and opportunities for foreign policy-making. In particular, the international projection of Spanish firms has enhanced the country's potential for global stature. Whether or not it is realized depends on how Spanish foreign policy is reorganized to deal with the new realities and on the resources and structures made available to undertake it. In the next section, I make a proposal.

A (modest) foreign-policy proposal

Given the new economic and financial interests that Spanish firms and Spanish society have acquired in Latin America, the EU (now extending into Eastern Europe), and the Maghrib, it seems logical to argue for a long-term approach to foreign policy in those areas. The policy would need to contain several key components: (1) an emphasis on initiatives that strengthen institutions, civil society, and economic development; (2) enhanced coordination among the various Spanish government bureaus and agencies that deal with international relations; (3) a greater involvement of Spanish firms, universities, and other relevant social actors in the foreign-policy process; and (4) coordination with the US and the EU, with an emphasis on the latter. Naturally, these considerations do not exhaust the full range of foreign-policy goals that Spain should pursue. There are other very important issues such as the promotion of Spanish language and culture abroad, the quest for peace and security, and the decolonization of the British enclave of Gibraltar, to mention but a few. Let us focus, then, on the aspects of foreign policy that are related to Spain's economic and financial interests.

A non negligible part of Spanish foreign policy is already focused on institution-building, civil society, and economic development in the form of official development assistance. It appropriately targets Latin America and the Maghrib as preferential areas. In 2002 the average official development assistance level (ODA) for the twenty-two OECD countries engaged in it was 0.41 percent of gross national income; Spain allocated the equivalent of 0.26 percent ($1.7 billion).[12] The amount of funds should be increased, but the finer policy point is to link the allocation of funds, especially the non-reimbursable portion, to the pursuit of Spanish interests, economic or otherwise (i.e. cultural, linguistic, humanitarian, etc.). This can only be accomplished if the second component of the proposed approach is present, namely, if there is increased coordination among various agencies within the Ministry of Foreign Affairs (those in charge of development aid and the different area secretaries, for instance), and among the ministries of the Economy, Culture, and Foreign Affairs, as well as the central bank, all of which have a say in different aspects of Spain's international relations. Interviewees favoring one major political party or the other agreed that lack of coordination among state agencies presently poses major problems for foreign policy-making. Some would point out rivalries among the various elite corps with a say in international economic affairs as a key impediment to effective policy-making.

[12] http://www.oecd.org//dataoecd/3/2/22460411.pdf.

The third component is to involve Spanish firms, universities, and other relevant actors more deeply in foreign policy-making: something that institutions like the newly founded Real Instituto Elcano or the CIDOB seek to accomplish. Company participation in the policy process needs to be accompanied by corporate programs to promote social, political, and economic development in the countries in which they operate. Multinationals from other countries have established foundations and other philanthropic mechanisms to help out. Spanish firms are beginning to do so, but much remains to be done if the country's, and their own, image and international projection are to improve. Another important aspect is to get not just the largest firms involved but also the medium-sized multinationals. There are nearly one thousand Spanish firms with foreign operations, and foreign policy-making needs to take all of them into account, not just the largest ones. Many of the hundreds of midsized multinationals are critical of Spanish foreign policy. They tend to rely on their respective regional governments rather than the national one when it comes to opening doors in foreign countries.

Lastly, Spanish foreign policy, as it relates to economic and financial issues, must keep the US and the major European countries in mind, for the rather obvious, though not always recognized, reason that these countries also have interests in Latin America and the Maghrib. The long-term strategy here should be to look for ways to become less dependent on Washington, Berlin, or Paris. In the short run, however, ignoring the importance of the US in Latin America, France in the Maghrib or Germany in Eastern Europe would be blatantly unrealistic. Spanish firms have (or would like to acquire) a presence in each of those three regions.

It is crucial to note in closing that this foreign-policy proposal is consistent with the possible occurrence of cross-border corporate mergers in Europe. If some of the large Spanish multinationals merged with their European counterparts, the complexity of Spain's foreign policy could be reduced considerably. In particular, it would make it easier for Spain to work within the EU policy framework and in conjunction with the foreign policy-makers of other European countries in order to cope with the consequences of outward foreign direct investment, especially in Latin America. If Spanish financial, energy, water and oil companies with foreign investments were to merge with other European firms in their industry, there would be another reason for a return to a European-centered foreign policy.

To date, the most important merger between a Spanish multinational and a European one is the case of Altadis, the 1999 combination of the former Spanish (Tabacalera) and French (Seita) tobacco monopolies. The company has activities in thirty-five countries, with major investments in Latin America, the US, and Morocco. In the latter, it entered by acquiring 80 percent of the tobacco monopoly. The deal took place in June 2003, as part of Morocco's second-largest privatization bidding contest, in which BAT, Philip Morris, and Japan Tobacco also participated. It is important to note that French companies have been more active than Spanish ones in the Moroccan privatization process, especially in construction and in automobile assembly, with Renault increasing its stake in Sonaca at around the same time as the tobacco acquisition. The deal also took place at a time when Spanish–Moroccan relations became less tense, and Aznar and his counterpart held a meeting in Toledo.[13]

I personally believe that it is more likely than not that Spanish companies in banking, electricity, oil and gas, telecommunications, and construction will end up looking towards Western and Eastern Europe for further growth. If my prediction proves correct, Spanish foreign policy will be, once again, deeply affected. In this case, however, foreign policy could be reconstituted and streamlined quite easily because the country's historical, cultural, political, economic, and financial overlap with Europe is so much greater than with the US, the Maghrib, or even Latin America. If Spanish firms with major investments in Latin America join forces with one or more of their European counterparts, yet another chapter in foreign policy will need to be written. One thing seems assured: the best perspective will again be a pluralist rather than a realist one.

---

[13] *Economist Intelligence Unit Views Wire*, 2 September 2003; *El País*, 6 June 2003.

8 | Spain's enduring image problem

> Oh, lovely Spain! Renowned,
> romantic land!
>
> > Lord Byron

> It is important to have leading firms.
> Sweden has Volvo and Saab; the Nether-
> lands, Unilever and Shell, and so on, but
> Spain lacks first-rate firms.
>
> > Lester Thurow, best-selling economist
> > and former Dean of the MIT Sloan
> > School of Management (1994)[1]

A country's international image has the characteristics of a public good in that, while all individuals, groups, companies, or organizations associated with it can potentially benefit, the marginal cost of an additional entity actually benefiting is zero. Images, however, can be harmful as well as beneficial. More often than not, Spain happens to be a country whose international image tends to detract from the worldwide competitiveness and reputation of its companies. The country is faced by a long-standing historical legacy of poor product image quality and weak national reputation. Spain as a country, its products and its companies do not command much "brand equity" or commercial recognition around the world, as a number of studies have demonstrated (Durán 2001; for a review, see Noya 2002:183–218). Spain is internationally perceived as a relatively backward country that produces traditional products or services with little or no technology.

Much of the image problem has to do with the past rather than the present. Spain has been burdened by at least three mutually inconsistent historical perceptions. The first negative legacy is the Black

---

[1] *El País Negocios*, 27 February 1994, p. 27. Needless to say, Sweden no longer owns Saab or Volvo's automobile business, and neither Unilever nor Shell is purely Dutch, but Anglo-Dutch. In spite of the infelicitous choice of examples, Thurow has a point, especially taking into account the predicament of Spanish firms as of 1994.

Legend: the image of an intransigent, dogmatic and violent country, especially in its colonization of the Americas, which dates back to the period of Spanish hegemony in Europe (Noya 2002:48–53). The second is the view of a decadent, though still European, country, an image originally espoused by the Enlightenment. Backwardness is attributed to either the persistence of medieval institutions or, as Montesquieu would have it, to its "way of being": passionate, violent, lazy, arrogant, superstitious (Alvarez Junco 2001:108–9). And the third is the exotic image, originating in the observations of romantic French and English travelers and writers of the eighteenth and nineteenth centuries, who no longer believed Spain to be part of Europe. Lord Byron ("Oh, lovely Spain! Renowned, romantic land!"), Washington Irving ("Tales of the Alhambra"), Alexandre Dumas ("Europe starts at the Pyrenees"), Prosper Mérimée ("Carmen") and many, many others reified the "oriental" character of Spain (despite its location at the western edge of Europe), a term that "could be translated as meaning beauty, melancholy, ruins, knightly honor, hedonism or intense passions" (Alvarez Junco 2001:200).

Over the centuries, foreigners came to see Spain as "the country of indolence, a result of the hot climate, no doubt, but also of the values of the nobility and the disdain for useful occupations; the country of ignorance, superstition and Catholic intolerance" (Alvarez Junco 2001:107, 200). The Civil War of 1936–9 could have brought about a break with the legacies of the past, but did not, given the outcome. Spain remained a country inhabited by "good" but ignorant and impulsive people.

While the intense social and political changes of the 1960s, 70s, and 80s did much to erase the legacy of intransigence and dogmatism, the remarkable economic progress of the 90s and early 2000s has not yet fully erased the perception of decadence, relative backwardness, and exoticism. Recent public opinion research undertaken in several European countries suggests that foreigners tend not to score Spain and Spaniards high on attributes such as "intelligent," "successful," "hard-working," or "modern." Spaniards are supposed to have a good sense of humor, and to be friendly and warm, but also lazy and disorganized. People in the US or Latin America do not see them in much better terms. Spanish culture, art, and language are perceived as the most highly esteemed things that the country offers to the world (Noya 2002:61–103).

In this chapter I review the impact that outward FDI has had on Spain's international image. First, I will analyze the effects on elites and public opinion in the host countries in which the Spanish multinational firm has come to operate. I will then delve into the perception of Spain and of Spanish firms by the international financial community and business schools. Lastly, I will examine the evolution of the worldwide appeal of Spanish brands in the wake of FDI.

The image in the host countries

Given the inherited image of a backward if noble and friendly country, one would expect the recent surge in foreign direct investment to have an important impact on the perception of Spain and its businesses abroad, at least in those countries in which investments have been proportionally significant (i.e. Portugal and Latin America). After all, the arrival of Spanish firms could be seen as signaling the coming of age of a country long thought to be at the rear of Europe in terms of economic and social development.

At first, FDI did not perceptibly change Spain's economic and business reputation among the public in the host countries. Surveys conducted in Chile, Mexico, Peru, and Uruguay during the 1980s – i.e. before the investment boom – showed Spain to be less preferred as a foreign investor when compared to Japan, the US, and Germany, though more preferred than France, the UK, and Italy. This was true both of public opinion in general and economic leaders in particular. In the late 1990s, after Spanish FDI had taken place, the attitudes were strikingly similar. Spanish firms were perceived as promoting economic growth and technological development, but not as much as their US counterparts. The main criticisms had to do with Spanish firms benefiting from monopolistic situations, and failing to invest as much as expected.

The early complaints about Spanish businesses in Latin America pale by comparison with the staunch criticisms that developed during the late 1990s. The occurrence of severe macroeconomic crises in several Latin American countries during the late 1990s coincided with Spain's most notable successes in Europe, namely, managing to become a founding member of the euro and achieving a GDP growth rate one or even two percentage points greater than the EU average. This combination of events offers an opportunity to assess the deteriorating image of Spanish businesses in Latin America even when the overall reputation of Spain as a country was growing. In Latin America the image of Spain is now inextricably associated with the presence of Spanish firms. In terms of image, if not diplomacy, Spanish multinationals have become Spain's most important ambassadors (Pérez Herrero 2003:328; García Pérez 2003:548; Noya 2002:174–85, 2003).

The public's opinion of Spanish multinationals throughout Latin America worsened rapidly after 1999. Overall, only 30 percent of those interviewed in seventeen Latin American countries in 2003 felt that Spanish investments were "very beneficial" or "somewhat beneficial," compared to 55 percent of respondents in Spain. The most favorable countries tend to be small ones in which Spanish investments are not very important in magnitude (Paraguay, Uruguay, Honduras, Nicaragua, Costa Rica, and El Salvador). In some medium-sized and large countries in which Spanish investments are more important, the attitudes towards Spanish investors are mildly negative (Bolivia, Venezuela, Chile, Ecuador, Colombia, Mexico, Brazil). Attitudes have worsened most intensively in Peru and Argentina, where Spanish investments are important (Latinobarómetro 2003; Noya 2002:177–85; 2003; see also chapter 9).

The reasons for Spain's growing image problem in Latin America are diverse and complex. Undoubtedly, some high-profile mistakes (e.g. Iberia in Venezuela and Argentina) and the relatively isolated cases of corrupt dealings have not helped. It is important to note, however, that attitudes towards the economy have shifted throughout the region, not just those regarding Spanish investment. In particular, popular support for liberalization, deregulation, and privatization has eroded (Latinobarómetro 2003). Focus groups held in several Latin American countries as well as opinion surveys provide evidence on the connections between economic attitudes in general and the deteriorating image problems of Spanish firms with major investments in the region (Alloza and Noya 2004). First, attitudes in Latin America towards foreign investments in general are rather negative, although the positive aspects of contributing capital and technology to local development are acknowledged. They are seen as a force undermining local culture and national sovereignty. This problem affects all firms operating in the region.

Second, most Spanish firms have entered Latin America via acquisition, and invested primarily in highly visible and regulated industries, many of them recently privatized. Acquisitions and privatizations tend to be more politically controversial than greenfield entries (Guillén 2001c). Spanish firms and the privatization processes in which they have participated raised very high expectations that would have been difficult for anyone to meet. Much of the discontent among the public is directly linked to their growing dissatisfaction with liberal economic reforms. The backlash against the "Washington Consensus" has contributed greatly to this process. Between 1998 and 2003 popular support for privatization fell from 51 to 33 percent in Brazil, from 51 to 29 in Chile, from 32 to 12 in Argentina, and from 44 to 22 in Peru (Latinobarómetro 2003). Perhaps the most prominent case is Argentina, where an increasing proportion of the population, fueled in part by the writings and statements of journalists and politicians, believes that Spanish firms actively and knowingly participated in the "plundering" of Argentina's riches during the 1990s (for instance, see Cecchini and Zicolillo 2002).

And, third, Spanish firms have been perceived as "new conquistadors," meaning arrogant actors with clear goals and preconceived notions as to how to run things, often behaving in authoritarian ways without showing much respect for the abilities and accomplishments of local employees and managers. Another feature associated with this negative image is the resentment felt against Spanish firms which have acquired monopolistic or quasi-monopolistic positions in the market, especially in the wake of privatizations (Alloza and Noya 2004). Spanish multinationals, however, are moving in the right direction, namely, modifying their managerial appointment policies in favor of local managers and beefing up their public-relations image throughout the region as long-term investors and philanthropists committed to the host-country's development.

As analyzed in the preceding chapter, the perception of Spanish investors among the Portuguese public has also deteriorated rapidly. The issue here is different than in Latin America. Portugal is a European partner, aligned with Spain on many issues. Portugal, however, is small, and feels that its openness towards Spanish investment has not been reciprocated by its larger Iberian neighbor. The tensions, while real, are unlikely to generate the problems of, say, Argentina or Peru, especially given that the two countries are increasingly collaborating on a number of economic projects like the Iberian electricity market and high-speed railway links.

Spain and Spanish firms face a difficult public-relations problem in Latin America. While the degree of enthusiasm for Spanish FDI falls, decision-makers see the situation in very different terms. The top managers of Spanish multinationals and officials in charge of foreign affairs and economic negotiations – regardless of the party they belong to or sympathize with – tend to think that Spain's "visibility, stature, even power" have been enhanced as a result of investments in Latin America (see chapters 6 and 7). In interviews, they indicated that outward investment helps Spain mature as a country and achieve a higher level of international respectability. The apparent gap between their perceptions and those of the populations of the host countries in which Spanish firms operate, especially in Latin America, will surely require attention in the future.

The international financial community

The international financial community is an important constituency for the Spanish multinationals, especially those that are large and listed on the stock exchange. As noted in chapter 4, the norm is that between 40 and 60 percent of the equity of the largest Spanish multi-nationals is accounted for by foreign institutional investors. Interviews with executives revealed that presentations in London, New York, and Madrid take up a significant chunk of the time of presidents, vice-presidents, and CEOs. I was able to ascertain that they had learned the language of the international financial community, especially all of the key terms in corporate finance, strategic management, and corporate social responsibility, which they use skillfully in order to appear legit-imate and to further the interests of their firms, a major change from ten or twenty years ago. The CEOs of the largest Spanish firms regularly have lunch with the Madrid correspondents of the financial media and with prominent stock analysts. But how does the inter-national financial community perceive them? Are there any significant changes over time? In order to answer this question I will examine how the international financial and business press and equity analysts perceive Spanish companies.

The printed media

The international financial and business press has devoted an increas-ing amount of coverage of Spanish business since the mid-1980s.

I have analyzed over time the intensity and quality of coverage for five key printed media: the *Financial Times*, *The Economist*, *Fortune*, the *Wall Street Journal* and the *Wall Street Journal Europe*. These five publications are undoubtedly influential among executives, government officials, stock analysts, and investment bankers. Figure 8.1 presents a rough indicator of coverage, namely, the proportion of all articles published in a given year in each of the five printed media that contained the words "business" and "Spain," calculated as a percentage of all articles that contained just the word "business." This indicator contains noise in that many articles do not refer to Spanish multinationals, but rather to foreign multinationals doing business in Spain. However, it does measure to what extent Spain is an important subject in international financial circles from a business point of view. It should be noted that the importance of Spain as an economy has changed following an inverted-U shape curve during the last twenty years. In 1985 Spain's GDP amounted to 1.4 percent of the world's, reaching a high of 2.5 percent in 1992, and sliding back to 1.8 percent by the early 2000s, due not to the lack of economic growth in Spain but to the vigorous growth rates experienced by some large developing countries, especially China and India.

The overall picture is that, starting in the late 1980s and early 1990s, the leading printed financial and business media raised the level of attention paid to Spanish business. The peak years in terms of coverage are 1992 – the year of the Barcelona Olympics and the Seville Universal Expo – and 2000, when Spain starts to stand out for its economic growth within the eurozone. The *FT* presently devotes 40 percent more attention than Spain's share of world GDP would warrant, and the *WSJE* and *The Economist* about 140 percent more. By contrast, *Fortune* and the *WSJ* – the two US-centered printed media investigated – devote an amount of attention roughly proportional to Spain's relative economic weight in the world. The five printed media have significantly lowered their coverage of Spanish business since the turn of the century. The correlations in the level of coverage across publications are remarkably high, except for *Fortune*, which has been more idiosyncratic (see figure 8.1).

Aside from the intensity of coverage, the international financial and business media have shifted their views of Spanish firms several times since they started to make headlines around the world for their foreign expansion. Four distinct phases can be identified: the initial surprise

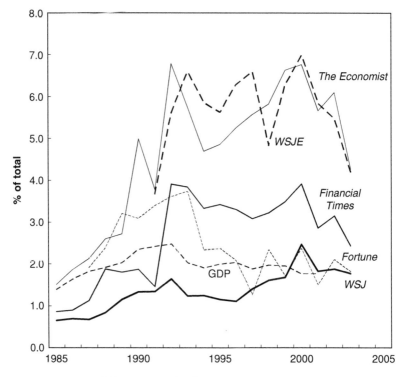

Figure 8.1. Spanish business in the financial printed media, 1985–2003.

Correlations between pairs of time series

	WSJ	FT	Economist	WSJE	Fortune
WSJ					
FT	0.68				
Economist	0.82	0.91			
WSJE	0.13	0.80	0.66		
Fortune	−0.15	−0.02	−0.05	−0.19	
Spain's GDP	0.26	0.29	0.43	−0.62	0.73

Note: The time series were calculated by dividing the number of articles published in a given year that contained the words "business" and "Spain" by the number of articles that contained just the word "business."
Source: Factiva.

and disbelief (until 1996 or 1997), growing understanding and adula-tion (1997–2000), severe warnings about Latin American exposure (2001–2), and realization that the Spanish firms are long-term invest-ors with a shot at European leadership in their respective industries (2003 onwards).

International financial and business journalists at first assessed the Spanish firms' international investments with a mixture of surprise and disbelief, mainly because the likes of Telefónica, Repsol, or San-tander were coming out of the blue sky, with no hitherto known proprietary technologies or brands, and they were bidding aggressively for assets that firms from other more reputable countries were not willing to buy, or at least not for the amounts offered by the Spaniards. This was particularly evident in the case of the Latin American privat-izations. At most, the media would point out the diversification op-portunities afforded to investors by Spanish companies with an international presence and a solid, established presence in the Spanish market, now part of the EU. But news stories would stop short of referring to the Spanish multinationals as up-and-coming international competitors, mainly because of their relatively weak or dubious tech-nological, marketing, and managerial capabilities (e.g. *Fortune*, 27 September 1991; *The Economist*, 30 April 1994, 14 December 1996; *FT*, 30 June 1995, 20 October 1998; *WSJ*, 23 May 1996; *WSJE*, 24 May 1996).

It was during the early 1990s that terms such as "Eldorado," "colonization," "invasion," and, most famously, "new conquista-dors" (or even "acquistadors") were used to convey the perception of a primitive but determined, daring and audacious cadre of firms taking over a number of Latin American companies which nobody else wanted to buy. A good illustration of the "bold" process by which Spanish firms became a prominent presence throughout Latin America comes from the following characterization in the *WSJ* of how in 1995 Telefónica ended up presenting a bid for the Peruvian state telephone monopoly in an amount "more than twice those of US companies GTE and Southwestern Bell":

Ignacio Santillana, Telefónica Internacional's chief executive, likes to tell a story that explains the difference. The day the bids were to be submitted, he says, the five-member Telefónica team went for a stroll in downtown Lima and stopped for a shoe-shine. By contrast, the American bidders arrived in armored cars with bodyguards. "Telefónica had a very different idea of risk," Mr. Santillana says (*WSJ*, 23 May 1996).

Interviews with current or former Madrid correspondents of the international printed media indicated that many of the initial prejudices and misconceptions about Spanish firms and managers did not even get into print. Both the correspondents and the editors in London and New York played a role in creating a distorted image that grossly underestimated the Spanish firms at the beginning of what would be a decade-long effort to consolidate a foreign presence that eventually turned several of them into serious European contenders.

The continued and intensified foreign expansion of Spanish firms into the late 1990s, with no apparent pitfalls or spectacular mistakes (except Iberia's), did much to refurbish the initial image. *Fortune* (3 April 2000), for instance, included three Spanish executives (Telefónica's Villalonga, and Santander's Botín and Corcóstegui) among a celebrity-packed list of seventeen names of what it called "the new European business elite," noting not only the firms' Latin American successes but also their new higher profile within Europe. While the problems of integrating foreign and domestic acquisitions were duly noted, the media recognized the inescapable need for Spanish firms to look for growth abroad and their largely successful process of internationalization (*The Economist*, 23 January 1999). By the time Repsol made its "calculated but bold" acquisition of Argentina's state-owned YPF, the international media were ready to recognize that the decision was appropriate in terms of both the host region and the complementary assets and capabilities of the target (*WSJ*, 21 January 1999, 30 April 1999; *FT*, 22 January 1999, 30 April 1999). Some stories even added that the deal was "to catapult the Spanish oil, gas and chemical group into the major league of world oil companies" (*WSJE*, 3 May 1999), an exaggerated assessment for sure (see chapter 4). In a story also centered on Repsol's move, the *WSJE* summarized the emerging consensus among the international financial printed media about the rational motivations and the facilitating factors behind the surge in Spanish outward investment:

European monetary union has driven interest rates in Spain down to around 3 percent today from double-digit rates four years ago. As a result, Spanish companies are flush with cash. The Spanish energy groups are too small to gobble up counterparts in, say, Italy or France; in fact, if they don't gain scale through acquisitions in Latin America, they risk being bought themselves. Analysts say the Spanish expansion into Latin America is wise. European markets offer little in the way of future growth as deregulation and competition for consumers drives down profit margins (*WSJE*, 4 May 1999).

Many other glowing news stories followed. Particularly adulatory was *Business Week*'s long article on "Spain's Surge," featured on the cover of its European edition (22 May 2000). Interestingly, when Citibank acquired Mexico's largest bank, Banamex, the media pointed out that the move simply enabled the American financial group to match the Spanish banks' earlier forays into Mexico as well as other Latin American countries. Implicitly, they were portraying Citibank as a follower rather than a leader (*WSJ*, 18 May 2001; *WSJE*, 22 February 2001).

In parallel to the growing recognition of the sound international strategy and enhanced stature of the large Spanish multinationals, attention also started to be paid during the late 1990s to smaller, "pocket-size" multinationals, such as those discussed in chapter 3 (e.g. *FT*, 19 January 1998; see also 16 July 2002), whose international presence had been noted in the 1980s, but forgotten during the 1990s. It is also at this time that Inditex becomes a darling of the international financial printed media, especially in the months prior to its IPO in 2001, noting its competitive strengths and chances of becoming a major global player (e.g. *The Economist*, 19 May 2001; *Fortune*, 4 September 2000). Dozens of news stories appeared in the *FT*, and the *WSJ*, mostly written in a positive vein, until the company's share price started to plummet during 2003 in the wake of missed growth and profit targets and forecasts.

Turmoil in emerging markets, starting with the Brazilian devaluation of 1999 and intensifying with the Argentine economic crisis and default in early 2002, provoked a major shift in the media's assessment of Spanish firms, abandoning the adulatory tone of the late 1990s. Some of the coverage of the effects of the Latin American crisis was plainly hostile: "After years of boasting about their expanding empire in Latin America, Spain's biggest companies are now suffering because of it" (*The Economist*, 5 January 2002). But most of the news stories were even-handed, reporting with admirable objectivity. They first issued warnings about the dire consequences of crises and defaults in Latin America (*FT*, 16 October 2001, 22 December 2001; *WSJ*, 20

July 2001), and later reported falling earnings and stock prices as a
result of the Argentine collapse. (Madrid's Ibex-35 stock index fell by
almost 30 percent during 2002.) The media routinely admonished
Spanish companies for concentrating too many of their investments
in such a volatile region (*The Economist*, 5 January 2002; *FT*, 1
February 2002, 3 September 2002, 8 October 2002, 31 October
2002, 18 November 2002; *WSJ*, 23 July 2002, 14 August 2002; 29
September 2002). In a representative piece, the *WSJE* (18 June 2001)
pointed out in a front-page article that

> in the worst-case scenario, a financial meltdown in Argentina would shake
> investor confidence in Spain and cast doubt on its companies' strategies for
> the region. Depressed share prices at home and a recession in Latin America
> eventually could retard Spain's own economic growth.

Interestingly, in 2003, after the worst of the crisis in Argentina and
elsewhere in Latin America had passed, seeing that Spanish firms were
staying the course (while those from other countries decided to exit)
and making appropriate provisions and write-offs (see chapter 6), the
situation was seen in a rather different light:

> While Europe's economy continues in the dumps, Spain's largest companies
> are getting some welcome relief from an unexpected place: Latin America,
> one of last year's biggest economic basket cases. . . So far this year, the
> Madrid Stock Exchange has been one of the best performing markets in
> Europe – a feat that many analysts attribute in part to the changing fortunes
> of Brazil (*WSJ*, 2 June 2003 and *WSJE*, 2 June 2003).

By mid-2003, then, the international printed media had changed their
tune once again, now praising Spanish firms for weathering the storm
in Latin America successfully and for managing to turn themselves
into European and even global players in their own right (e.g. *WSJ*, 16
September 2003; *FT*, 22 January 2004). In early 2004, BBVA's decision to make a tender offer for the 41 percent it did not own in
Mexico's Bancomer was greeted with reserved optimism by the *FT*
(3 February 2004) and quite open enthusiasm by the *WSJ* (3 February
2004), which suggested the operation could be a stepping-stone into
the US market. Also in early 2004, Telefónica's acquisition of Bell-
South's mobile telephone operations throughout Latin America was
received by the printed media with respect, while pointing out some of
the problems related to integrating the new operations with existing
ones and securing permission from regulators in ten affected countries

(*WSJ*, 9 March 2004). The media took good notice that, when completed, the $4,000 to 5,000 million deal would turn Telefónica into the world's number four mobile operator, behind two Chinese companies and Vodafone. The *FT* (9 March 2004) assessed the deal as follows: "the Telefónica quest for world domination continues to look much less quixotic than those of some of its rivals."

This necessarily brief analysis reveals that, by and large, the international financial and business printed media have not been overly unfair to the Spanish multinationals, although they have tended to underestimate their capabilities and accomplishments, and to exaggerate the dangers and the risks of their international expansion. The media have not been able to resist the temptation of swinging back and forth between positive and negative assessments in cycles of two to three years, reflecting the changing fortunes of the Latin American region in which much of the investment has taken place. It is, however, the duty of the companies to communicate their long-term goals and strategy clearly, especially to a constituency with such a large impact on investor sentiment and behavior.

The equity analysts

Equity analysts are a second, influential part of the international financial and business community. They produce reports on listed companies that include calculations of the likely evolution of their stock prices and recommendations as to whether to buy, hold or sell their stock. Figure 8.2 plots the proportion of all equity research reports stored on the Investext database that have to do with a Spanish company. The figure presents two separate time series, based on two different sets of analyst organizations, because coverage of organizations with a focus on parts of the world other than Europe increased from the first to the second series. Hence, the proportion of reports that examine Spanish companies is greater in the first than in the second series. The organizations whose reports are part of the database include Morgan Stanley, Lehman Brothers, Credit Suisse First Boston, Daiwa Securities, Beta Capital, and many others. Unlike the international printed media, research analysts cover relatively few Spanish firms with less frequency than would be warranted by either Spain's GDP or, especially, the number of listed companies as a percentage of the world total.

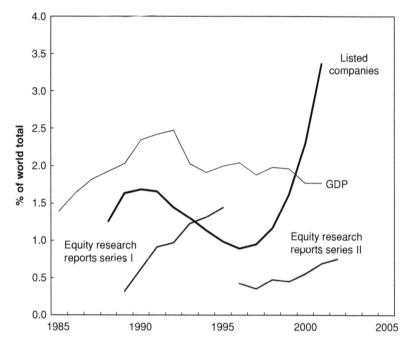

Figure 8.2. Equity research analysts' coverage of Spanish companies, as a percentage of the world's total, compared to the number of listed companies and GDP, 1985–2002.
Note: The two series are based on two different sets of research organizations, and hence give different assessments of the number of reports that refer to Spanish companies. In particular, coverage of research organizations with a focus on parts of the world other than Europe increased from the first to the second series.
Source: Investext Plus.

Stock analysts tend to cover more frequently and intensively the largest companies. The top five Spanish multinationals account for a quarter of the 5,000 or so reports on Spanish firms contained in the database. Table 8.1 presents an analysis of the recommendations of a subsample of the reports (N = 1,932), those published by the thirty-eight leading American, European and Asian research organizations on twenty-six Spanish firms with at least twenty reports each. Between 1990 and 2002 the coverage of these firms increased exponentially. Since the mid-1990s, more than half of the reports offered overly

Table 8.1. *Stock analysts' recommendations concerning Spanish companies, 1990–2003 (in percentages)*

	1990	1991	1992	1993	1994	1995	1996	1997	1998	1999	2000	2001	2002	2003	Row total N
Recommendation															
Strong buy	0	0	0	0	0	2	0	3	0	0	8	0	4	0	42
Buy	33	40	79	54	55	28	47	47	40	62	57	56	40	40	916
Outperform	0	30	13	23	28	36	13	9	15	9	4	6	10	10	195
Accumulate	0	0	0	0	0	0	6	25	12	7	7	2	2	1	63
In line	0	0	0	0	0	0	0	0	0	0	0	0	2	2	20
Hold	50	0	4	15	2	8	16	6	18	16	13	19	18	19	325
Neutral	0	30	4	0	6	26	9	6	7	4	8	11	12	17	228
Underperform	17	0	0	0	0	0	0	0	4	1	0	3	5	7	67
Reduce	0	0	0	0	0	0	6	3	3	0	0	1	3	3	40
Sell	0	0	0	8	9	0	3	0	1	1	2	1	3	1	36
TOTAL	100	100	100	100	100	100	100	100	100	100	100	100	100	100	100
TOTAL N	6	10	24	13	53	50	32	32	68	90	215	426	534	379	1932

Note: Data based on analysts' reports published by thirty-eight investment banks from Spain, Europe, North America, and Asia, assessing twenty-six Spanish companies.
Source: Investext Plus.

positive recommendations (e.g. "strong buy," "buy," "outperform," or "accumulate"). The best years were 1999 and 2000. A decline in the quality of the recommendations started in 2001, due to uncertainty in the markets and the impact of the Argentine crisis. The proportions of most favorable recommendations fell substantially during 2002 and 2003, even though many of the large Spanish multinationals outperformed their European counterparts during 2003 (see chapter 6). Overall, the assessments of the equity research analysts have fluctuated over time much less than those of the international financial press.

The business schools

Business schools are important economic institutions. Through teaching and research, they create and diffuse not only knowledge but also reputation. One key way in which they affect the images of both companies and countries is by publishing case studies, technical notes, and teaching notes that are then used in teaching programs around the world, especially postgraduate ones like the master's in business administration (MBA). The typical MBA student, for instance, is exposed to anywhere between 60 and 300 case studies before graduation, depending on the school. By the end of 2003, the American Association of Collegiate Schools of Business had accredited 467 institutions, 55 of them outside the United States. Most of them (434) offered postgraduate education courses. With over 120,000 postgraduate management students taking classes around the world each year, case studies have a strong impact in terms of managerial perceptions and images of companies and countries. In fact, many companies and executives consider it an honor to be approached by a business school professor with the purpose of writing a teaching case on their company or on themselves. In many instances, however, the research on which the case is based does not involve contact with the company. Business graduates tend to attach a higher prestige to companies or countries discussed in class, with implications for their choice of job after graduation.

The European Case Clearing House (ECCH) manages a worldwide database that includes teaching materials published by Harvard Business School (or HBS, the inventor of the case method, accounting for 46 percent of the entire database), the Darden School at the University of Virginia, IESE, IMD, INSEAD, the Kennedy School of Government (KSG), the Richard Ivey School of Business, and a long list of other schools that publish smaller numbers of cases. I have undertaken two types of analyses with the data. First, I have identified the number of case studies, technical notes, and teaching notes that make references to specific countries in the world. Second, I have analyzed the case studies published on Spanish firms. In the analyses that follow, I equate the prominence of countries or companies in the ECCH database with their image, implicitly assuming that "any publicity is good publicity." My colleagues' and my own experiences indicate that months after taking a class, graduate management students may not recall whether a company was effective or successful, but they will remember discussing it in class.

Business school cases and the prominence of countries

The data on the references to selected countries appear in Table 8.2. It is important to keep in mind that the search engine used to generate the table considered the countries mentioned in the abstract of the case only. About half of all cases in the database did not include references to any specific country. Another feature of the data is that they speak to where the action in the case takes place, and not necessarily to the nationality of the firm being discussed, which is the subject of the next analysis. With these limitations in mind, it is possible to make some revealing remarks. First, the number of cases (22,419) is certainly tilted towards the Anglo-Saxon world: the United States, Canada, the United Kingdom, and Australia account for nearly half of all references to countries in the 11,000 or so cases of the total of 22,419 that make a reference to at least one country. This bias is most likely due to the leading position of English-speaking countries in the world of business education and the ease with which researchers and case writers can access information about companies based in them.

Second, Spain appears at first sight to fare extremely well, with references in 383 cases, just behind France and Germany, and ahead of the United Kingdom, Switzerland, the Netherlands, and Italy. It is crucial to realize, however, that 314 of those 383 cases (82 percent) are published by Spanish business schools, especially by IESE. If one excludes cases published by a home-country school from the calculations, Spain is cited in just sixty-nine cases, eighteen published by HBS

Table 8.2. References to selected countries in the European Case Clearing House (ECCH) database, end of 2003, by publisher

Country	Total ECCH	HBS	INSEAD	IESE
United States	3,304	1,664	154	45
Canada	1,434	309	162	44
Europe as a region	1,146	309	162	44
India	710	66	22	0
Japan	526	297	40	8
China	466	137	67	8
France	427	77	156	15
Germany	385	130	52	18
Spain	383	18	21	292
United Kingdom	327	183	25	9
Switzerland	199	51	24	2
Netherlands	184	40	20	4
Mexico	174	77	4	4
Italy	158	64	11	14
South Africa	143	31	8	8
Australia	142	45	2	1
Ireland	135	11	2	0
Russia	123	43	13	0
Sweden	118	19	11	4
South Korea	88	37	13	1
Poland	86	19	16	7
Brazil	83	35	4	0
Argentina	75	35	0	3
Taiwan	72	23	14	0
Chile	33	9	2	3
Portugal	16	2	4	3
Peru	15	4	0	0
Colombia	11	6	0	1
TOTAL CASES	22,419	10,342	1,159	955

Note: The ECCH database includes cases from all over the world, in spite of its name.

About half of the cases in the ECCH database do not make a reference to a specific country in the abstract.

Multiple references to countries are counted separately for each country.

Source: European Case Clearing House (www.ecchatbabson.org).

and twenty-one by INSEAD, Europe's leading business school. This means that Spain is cited in fewer cases than any of the European countries listed except Portugal. Still, the fact that Spanish business schools like IESE and Instituto de Empresa are responsible for the inclusion on the ECCH database of, respectively, 292 and 9 case studies citing Spain is important because business professors around the world search it when developing their courses.

Third, the pattern over time is remarkable. Only 27 percent of the 383 cases that make a reference to Spain were published before 1994. In the 1994–98 five-year period, 205 cases were published with references to Spain (54 percent of the total of 383). In the next five years (1999–2003), the number fell to 72 (19 percent of 383). Thus it appears that interest in Spain on the part of case writers peaked in the mid-1990s, *dropping* by 65 percent between 1994–1998 and 1999–2003, whereas the total number of cases in the ECCH database *increased* by 22 percent. This is certainly an alarming trend because countries other than Spain – most notably Asian ones – are becoming more prominent in the database of business school cases, while the rest of Europe continues to attract much more attention than Spain. These conclusions, however, need to be tempered by an analysis of the prominence of Spanish companies in the database, because it could well be that, due to their international expansion, Spain as the home country is not being cited, although their operations in other parts of the world are.

Business school cases and the prominence of companies

Spanish multinational firms have received scant attention by business school case writers. Table 8.3 shows the data, in which subsidiaries are attributed to the parent company. Excluded are cases with disguised company names or Spanish companies owned by foreigners at the time the case was written. A total of 268 cases on Spanish companies are included in the ECCH database (1.2 percent of the world's total), of which 82 percent were published by IESE, followed by HBS, INSEAD, Instituto de Empresa, and ICFAI, the Indian business school, with less than 4 percent each. Other foreign schools have published one to three cases based on Spanish firms (KSG, Ivey, Darden, London Business School, IMD, Wharton). These represent, however, a very tiny proportion of their total case production. More than two-fifths of the cases

Table 8.3. *Spanish companies with three or more cases in the European Case Clearing House (ECCH) database, end of 2003, by publisher*

Company	Total	HBS	Kennedy School	INSEAD	ICFAI (India)	IESE	Instituto de Empresa	EADA
Telefónica	17	1	2	3	3	6	1	
Acenor	9					3		
Banco Popular Español	6			2		4		
Inditex (Zara)	6	3		1		1		
Autopistas del Maresme	4					4		
Bankinter	4	1				3		
Grupo Santander	4					3		
Hospital Sta. Cruz y S. Pablo	4					4		
Miguel Torres	4					3		
Mondragón Corp Cooperativa	4					4		
Repsol	4	1				1	2	
Mutua Guipuzcoana de Seguros	3					3		
Seat	3					3		
TOTAL SPANISH FIRMS	268	10	3	8	4	217	8	4
GRAND TOTAL OF CASES IN DATABASE	22,419	10,342	773	1,159	n.a.	955	9	5

Notes: The ECCH database includes cases from all over the world, in spite of its name. Cases based on subsidiaries are attributed to the parent company.
Cases with disguised company names are excluded. Cases of Spanish companies controlled by foreigners at the time the case was written are excluded.
Source: European Case Clearing House (www.ecchatbabson.org).

on Spanish firms were published prior to 1994, and just about another two-fifths between 1994 and 1998. Since 1999 there has been a marked decline in the attention devoted to Spanish firms as the subject of teaching cases.

Few Spanish *multinational* firms have captured the imagination of case writers. Only 49 of the total of 268 cases (18 percent) are based on a Spanish firm with significant foreign operations. Telefónica has received by far the most attention, including ten cases on the company as a whole, two each on Terra-Lycos and Telefónica de Argentina, and one each on Telefónica Móviles, Páginas Amarillas, and Telefónica I+D (its R&D arm). After telecommunications, banking is the most frequently studied industry. However, two banks with little by way of foreign operations – Banco Popular Español and Bankinter – are the subjects of more cases than Santander (four cases) and BBVA (one) combined. Among the large Spanish multinationals, only Repsol-YPF (four cases), Mondragón Corporación Cooperativa (four), Endesa (two), Unión Fenosa (two), Agbar (one) and Iberia (one) are the subject of cases. Not a single case on the construction firms is available from this database. Medium-sized Spanish multinationals perhaps receive more relative attention than their larger counterparts: Inditex (six cases), Miguel Torres (four), Antonio Puig (one), Chupa Chups (one), Indo Internacional (one) and TelePizza (one).

An analysis of the various management topics discussed in the cases reveals that the recent internationalization of Spanish firms has not yet attracted much attention. Only 39 of the 268 cases (14 percent) have to do with international business, i.e. with the management of multinational enterprises. The most common topics include strategic management (discussed in 51 percent of the cases), followed by general management (46 percent), human resource management (24 percent), marketing (23 percent), finance (also 23 percent), organization (15 percent), production (13 percent), leadership (11 percent), and technology (9 percent).

Equally discouraging are the results in terms of the geographical area covered in the case. In 240 of the 268 cases Spain was the location or one of the locations in which the action took place (91 percent). Latin America was discussed in only 11 percent of the cases, and Europe or the United States in barely 4 percent. Thus the focus of most of the cases on Spanish companies remains the home country or an activity located in the home country.

This brief analysis of the prominence of Spain and of Spanish companies in the ECCH database of business teaching cases reveals that the massive increase in FDI over the last decade has failed to enhance their traditionally low profile. After somewhat of a spurt during the mid-1990s, the present trend is not auspicious at all. As the next section will show, the international prominence of Spanish brands also leaves a lot to be desired.

The branding problem

While over the last two decades Spain has become a major exporting power and the quality levels of Spanish-made goods and services have improved remarkably, the reputation of Spanish companies, brands, and offerings is far from being well established in the global market-place (Durán 2001; Noya 2002; Casilda Béjar 2002:387–406; Chislett 2003:197–203). Buyers around the world are more willing to pay a higher price for a French wine or train, an Italian garment, fashion accessory or bottle of olive oil, a British mobile phone contract, a room in a Swiss hotel, an American movie or fast-food meal, a Japanese or Korean electronic gadget, or a German machine-tool or insurance policy than for the equivalent Spanish good or service.

There are many sides to this problem. First, while Spain is a major manufacturer and exporter of a wide array of widgets, well over half of them are sold on international markets under a foreign brand name, and it is the latter that seems to carry the day in terms of reputation. Second, Spanish service-sector firms, though internationally competitive, have not managed to acquire a strong reputation for quality and reliability. And, third, few if any Spanish brands have been leveraged across product or service categories, resulting in a reduced name recognition and value.

Javier Noya (2002:185–218) has recently published a comprehensive overview of the international image of Spanish goods and services, drawing on data from a wide variety of empirical studies. His conclusions are rather discomforting. First, the level of awareness of Spanish goods and services is not very high, in spite of the fact that Spain is a member of the European Union, a major exporter of a wide range of goods and services, and the second most important tourist destination in the world. Buyers do not tend to associate Spanish products with Spain. When asked, most people associate the "Made in Spain" label with products such as foods, wine, leather, furniture, clay, and (but only in some countries), automobiles. Second, Spanish products are only perceived of being of relatively "good quality" in emerging economies and not in the most advanced countries. Third, the international business elite in foreign countries holds Spain and its products in higher esteem than the general population. Fourth, the product attributes most frequently associated with Spanish goods and services include: cheap, low quality, little variety, traditional, primitive, authentic, and robust. Spanish products tend not to score highly on technology, innovativeness, environmental friendliness, originality, creativity, sophistication, design, good taste, modernity, reliability, exclusivity, finish, or touch. In general, Spanish goods and services are perceived as ranking lower than those from the most advanced countries in Europe, Japan or the United States, but higher than those from the emerging or developing countries. These relative perceptions have not changed significantly since 1990.

Spain and the most valuable global brands

An interesting and widely used indicator of international brand reputation is value. Every year *Business Week* publishes the ranking of the hundred most valuable *global* brands, calculated by the marketing consultancy Interbrand, as the present value of future profits attributable to the brand, adjusted for risk. Not a single Spanish brand has ever made it onto this list, primarily because, though certainly possessing market value, Spanish brands do not have significant distribution in the three key geographical regions of the Americas, Europe and Asia, one of the two criteria used for inclusion in the ranking. (The other is having one-third of sales outside the home country.) The ranking is dominated by US brands (sixty-three), followed by France and Japan (seven each), Britain and Germany (six each), and Switzerland (three). The only newly industrialized country with a brand on the list is South Korea (Samsung).

Table 8.4 shows the 2003 ranking. I have inserted in bold type the sixteen most valuable Spanish brands, also calculated by Interbrand. If Telefónica, Santander, BBVA, Zara, Banco Popular, and El Corte Inglés had a significant presence not just in Spain, Europe, and Latin America but also in North America and Asia, then Spanish brands would probably be on a par with those from countries like Britain,

Table 8.4. The hundred most valuable global brands, compared to Spain's most valuable, 2003

#	Brand	$bn	Industry	Country
1	Cola-Cola	70.4	Beverages	US
2	Microsoft	65.2	Software	US
3	IBM	51.8	Computing	US
4	GE	42.3	Electrical equipment	US
5	Intel	31.1	Computing	US
6	Nokia	29.4	Electronics	FI
7	Disney	28.0	Entertainment	US
8	McDonald's	24.7	Restaurants	US
9	Marlboro	22.2	Tobacco	US
10	Mercedes	21.4	Automobiles	US
11	Toyota	20.8	Automobiles	DE
12	HP	19.9	Computing	US
13	Citibank	18.6	Finance	US
14	Ford	17.1	Automobiles	US
15	Amex	16.8	Finance	US
16	Gillette	16.0	Personal care	US
17	Cisco	15.8	Computing	US
18	Honda	15.6	Automobiles	JP
19	BMW	15.1	Automobiles	DE
20	Sony	13.2	Electronics	JP
	Telefónica	12.6	Telecoms	ES
21	Nescafé	12.3	Beverages	CH
22	Budweiser	11.9	Beverages	US
23	Pepsi	11.8	Beverages	US
24	Oracle	11.3	Software	US
25	Samsung	10.8	Electronics	KR
26	Morgan Stanley	10.7	Finance	US
27	Merill Lynch	10.5	Finance	US
28	Pfizer	10.5	Pharmaceuticals	US
29	Dell	10.4	Computing	US
30	Merck	9.4	Pharmaceuticals	US
31	J. P. Morgan	9.1	Finance	US
32	Nintendo	8.2	Entertainment	JP
33	Nike	8.2	Sports goods	US
34	Kodak	7.8	Reproduction	US
35	SAP	7.7	Software	DE
36	GAP	7.7	Apparel	US

Table 8.4. (*continued*)

#	Brand	$bn	Industry	Country
37	HSBC	7.6	Finance	UK
38	Kellogg's	7.4	Foods	US
39	Canon	7.2	Reproduction	JP
40	Heinz	7.1	Foods	US
41	Goldman Sachs	7.0	Finance	US
42	Volkswagen	6.9	Automobiles	DE
43	IKEA	6.9	Furniture	SE
44	Harley-Davidson	6.8	Automobiles	US
45	Louis Vuitton	6.7	Luxury goods	FR
46	MTV	6.3	Entertainment	US
47	L'Oreal	5.6	Personal care	FR
48	Xerox	5.6	Reproduction	US
49	KFC	5.6	Restaurants	US
50	Apple	5.6	Computing	US
51	Pizza Hut	5.3	Restaurants	US
52	Accenture	5.3	Consultancy	US
	Santander	5.2	Finance	ES
53	Gucci	5.1	Luxury goods	IT
54	Kleenex	5.1	Personal care	US
55	Wrigley's	5.1	Beverages	US
	BBVA	4.7	Finance	ES
56	Colgate	4.7	Personal care	US
57	Avon	4.6	Personal care	US
58	Sun Microsys	4.5	Computing	US
59	Philips	4.5	Electronics	NL
60	Nestlé	4.5	Foods	CH
61	Chanel	4.3	Luxury goods	FR
62	Danone	4.3	Food and drink	FR
63	Kraft	4.2	Foods	US
64	AoL	4.0	Internet	US
65	Yahoo!	3.9	Internet	US
66	Time	3.8	Publishing	US
67	Adidas	3.7	Sports goods	DE
68	Rolex	3.7	Luxury goods	CH
69	BP	3.6	Oil and foods	UK
70	Tiffany	3.5	Luxury goods	US
71	Duracell	3.4	Batteries	US
72	Bacardi	3.4	Beverages	BM US

Table 8.4. (*continued*)

#	Brand	$bn	Industry	Country
73	Hermès	3.4	Luxury goods	FR
74	Amazon.com	3.4	Internet selling	US
75	Caterpillar	3.4	Heavy equipment	US
76	Reuters	3.3	Information	US
77	Levi's	3.3	Apparel	US
78	Hertz	3.3	Car rental	US
79	Panasonic	3.3	Electronics	JP
80	Ericsson	3.2	Electronics	SE
81	Motorola	3.1	Electronics	US
	Zara	3.0	Apparel	ES
82	Hennessy	3.0	Beverages	FR
83	Shell	3.0	Oil	UK NL
84	Boeing	2.9	Aerospace	US
85	Smirnoff	2.8	Beverages	UK
86	J&J	2.7	Personal care	US
87	Prada	2.5	Apparel	IT
88	Möet Chandon	2.5	Beverages	FR
89	Nissan	2.5	Automotive	JP
90	Heineken	2.4	Beverages	NL
91	Mobil	2.4	Oil	US
92	Nivea	2.2	Personal care	DE
	Banco Popular	2.2	Financial	ES
93	Starbucks	2.1	Restaurants	US
94	Burger King	2.1	Restaurants	US
95	Polo Ralph Lauren	2.1	Apparel	US
96	Fedex	2.0	Transportation	US
97	Barbie	1.9	Toys	US
98	Wall Street Journal	1.8	Publishing	US
99	Johnnie Walker	1.7	Beverages	UK
	El Corte Inglés	1.7	Retailing	ES
100	Jack Daniels	1.6	Beverages	US
	La Caixa	1.0	Finance	ES
	Repsol	0.8	Oil	ES
	Iberdrola	0.5	Utilities	ES
	Caja Madrid	0.4	Finance	ES
	Iberia	0.4	Air transport	ES
	El País	0.4	Publishing	ES

Table 8.4. (*continued*)

#	Brand	$bn	Industry	Country
	Mapfre	0.3	Insurance	ES
	San Miguel	0.2	Beverages	ES
	Fortuna	0.2	Tobacco	ES
	Leche Pascual	0.2	Foods	ES

Note: Spanish firms are not ranked by *Business Week* because they lack significant distribution in the Americas, Europe, and Asia. In some cases, the owning company does not generate more than a third of its sales from outside the home country, Spain, the second excluding reason used by *Business Week*.
Source: Business Week (4 August 2003), pp. 71–78; *Expansión Empresas* (19 December 2003).

France and Germany, and well ahead of South Korea, Italy, Sweden, the Netherlands, and Switzerland. However, this is unlikely to happen any time soon, except in the cases of Zara, by far the most valuable nearly global Spanish brand, and possibly Telefónica, which, if ranked by *Business Week*, would fall within the world's top twenty-five. There are other Spanish brands with a truly global appeal that do not make it onto *Business Week*'s ranking because their value is relatively small, namely, Chupa Chups, Cola-Cao, Freixenet, Lladró, Mango, and Panda Software, among others. One could also add Carbonell (olive oil), Iberia (airline), Fagor (appliances), and Seat (automobiles) to a list of brands with good recognition in certain parts of the world though not globally (Noya 2002:192–4). Thus the international expansion of Spanish firms is unlikely to render their brands truly valuable in the global marketplace unless their presence extends beyond Europe and Latin America.

The distribution of the world's most valuable brands by industry offers some further insight into which brands tend to command high value globally. The industries with the most global brands are beverages (twelve among the top hundred), computing and software (ten), automobiles (eight), consumer electronics (seven), financial services (seven), personal-care products (seven), luxury goods (six), information and publishing (six), foods (five), restaurant chains (five), apparel (four), entertainment (three), and oil (three). Intriguingly, not a single telecommunications brand appears on *Business Week*'s ranking, even though Vodafone is surely a highly valuable brand with global appeal. Telecommunications aside, there are internationally strong and visible Spanish companies and brands in just two of these industry groupings, namely, financial services and apparel. Spanish firms are too small relative to their foreign competitors in beverages, personal care, luxury goods, information and publishing, foods, restaurant chains, and oil. No internationally significant Spanish firm exists in computing and software, automobiles, consumer electronics and entertainment, which together account for a quarter of *Business Week*'s top hundred global brands.

Further foreign direct investment might raise the relatively low global profile of Spanish brands, though only if it extends into the rest of Europe, North America, and South and East Asia in addition to Spain and Latin America. As revealed by the analysis of the top hundred global brands by country and industry, Spanish brands may well gain in visibility during the years ahead, especially in telecommunications, financial services, and apparel. This prospect, however, is far from assured.

The future of Spain's image

The evidence as to whether FDI has improved Spain's international image or merely reinforced some of the negative stereotypes inherited from the past is mixed. International financial journalists have increased their coverage of Spanish firms, but their views continue to be relatively skeptical about their capabilities and volatile over time. Equity research analysts and, especially, business school faculty around the world pay less attention to Spanish firms than would be warranted given the country's weight in the global economy. On the more positive side, the views of equity analysts have not oscillated over time as much as those of the financial press. Spanish brands continue to be perceived as relatively traditional and of low quality. As analyzed in the previous chapter, Spanish foreign policy has failed to raise the country's international profile in a way that is sustainable over time and consistent with the views and desires of the population.

This rather disheartening panorama is grossly inconsistent with the reality of a country that is, and will be for the foreseeable future, among the world's ten largest economies and foreign investors, a country that is quickly approaching the European Union's average standard of living. One thing seems clear: Spanish multinational firms, and Spain as a country, face a huge international image problem which tends to constrain their economic performance in the global market-place. Image and reputation translate into economic value and well-being, but Spain does not seem to be able to break out of the mold of its unique but largely negative historical legacy.

9 Public opinion, the labor unions, and the multinationals

> The proprietor of stock is properly a citizen of the world, and is not necessarily attached to any particular country.
>
> Adam Smith, *The Wealth of Nations*
> (1976: 848–9)

THE sudden rise in Spanish outward FDI has had social as well as economic, financial, and diplomatic consequences. In this chapter I use various types of information to ascertain the social impact of the activities of Spanish multinational firms. I begin by documenting the historical roots of the debate over the multinationals in Spain. I then proceed to analyze public opinion data obtained from representative surveys of the Spanish population at two points in time (1995 and 2003). Next, I turn to the attitudes and responses by the Spanish labor unions, drawing on interviews with their leaders and on their publications and documents. The attitudes of the Spanish population and labor unions have evolved from being hostile or skeptical toward foreign investment to being quite favorable. Lastly, I examine the effects on the labor market, especially in terms of job creation for highly educated professionals.

Multinational enterprises are a contentious type of organization, and those originating from Spain are no exception. The main reason has to do with the multinationals' unrivaled ability to develop technology, reap economies of scale, avoid high wages, reduce transaction costs, shift from saturated to emerging markets, exploit tax loopholes, and leverage their power in negotiations with governments, labor unions, local communities, suppliers, and customers. As Gilpin (1987:231–45) has pointed out, the multinational firm is controversial because of the very reasons that give rise to its existence, namely, its monopolization of some intangible asset (Hymer 1960), and its footloose ability to exploit product life-cycle dynamics by shifting production around the world in order to reduce costs (Vernon 1966, 1979), as indicated in chapter 2.

Critics of the multinational enterprise range from those accusing it of being an "octopus," an "agent of imperialism," a "dog of capitalism," or a "cultural dictator," to those convinced that it is a "dinosaur" on the verge of extinction because of its unwieldy size, bureaucratic inertia, and inability to adapt and innovate. The apologists of the multinational, perhaps fewer in number and less adept at finding colorful metaphors, call it a "dolphin," a "leader of modernization," a "job creator," or a "boon to mankind." The classical economic thinkers already recognized the advantages that capital enjoys from being mobile. Thus Adam Smith wryly observed in *The Wealth of Nations* that "the proprietor of stock is properly a citizen of the world, and is not necessarily attached to any particular country" (Smith 1976:848–9). Karl Marx, for his part, pointed out that capitalists do not only benefit from their ability to shift investments from one location to another but also from their expansion into underdeveloped areas: "The rate of profit is higher [in the colonies] due to backward development, and likewise the exploitation of labor" (Marx 1967:3:238).

Political, industrial, intellectual, and labor elites have historically displayed a propensity to engage in praise or (more often) criticism of the multinationals. Far from being a mere "bread and butter" issue, the presence of foreign multinationals is seen by many as colliding with pride and dignity. Debates over multinationals frequently escalate to tackle questions of economic policy, national sovereignty, property rights, labor exploitation, and even cultural identity (Vernon 1971). Different actors have different views or ideological images of the multinationals. Such ideologies provide ways of constructing reality, identifying problems and opportunities, and guiding proactive or reactive action (Guillén 1994). As cultural systems, ideologies provide blueprints for action and have immediate consequences on the behavior of people and on the policies and activities of organized actors such as labor unions. "Whatever else ideologies may be – projections of unacknowledged fears, disguises for ulterior motives, phatic expressions of group solidarity – they are, most distinctively, maps of problematic social reality and matrices for the creation of collective conscience" (Geertz 1973:220).

Spanish foreign investment ideologies in historical perspective

Spanish attitudes and ideologies towards foreign investment have always been affected by political dynamics. Historically, conservatives and other right-wingers have frequently sided with the detractors of the multinationals, while liberals and leftists have more often than not welcomed them with varying degrees of enthusiasm. This pattern was first established as far back as the anti-Napoleonic counterrevolution and the struggles between liberals and conservatives to impose their views throughout the nineteenth century. Liberal intellectuals saw in foreign investors not only a most welcome source of capital and entrepreneurship but also a way to counterbalance the return to the old regime and to introduce liberalism, or at least more tolerant political practices. For example, the usually irreverent and caustic writer and journalist Mariano José de Larra stated in 1833:

A foreign investor who rushes to an unknown country so as to risk his own money, brings new capital into circulation, contributes to society, which benefits immensely from his talent and money. If he loses, he is a hero; if he wins, it is only fair that he receives the reward for his hard work, because he is giving us something we would otherwise not get.[1]

Similarly, in one of his historical novels of the *National Episodes* series, Benito Pérez Galdós presented foreign investment as a way, however costly, to break with the country's geographical and cultural and political isolation:

Oh, Northern Railway Company, fortunate escape route to the European world, divine breach for civilization! Blessed be one thousand times the gold of the French Jews and Protestants that made your existence possible; lucky the ones who paved your way through the crust of the old Spain . . . For a thousand reasons we praise you, Northern Railway Company, and even if

---

[1] De Larra (1993:198–9): "Un extranjero que corre a un país que le es desconocido, para arriesgar en él sus caudales, pone en circulación un capital nuevo, contribuye a la sociedad, a quien hace un inmenso beneficio con su talento y con su dinero. Si pierde, es un héroe; si gana, es muy justo que logre el premio de su trabajo, pues nos proporciona ventajas que no podíamos acarrearnos solos."

you did *not* achieve organizational perfection . . . everything shall be pardoned for the immense benefits that you have conferred upon us.[2]

The railway celebrated by Pérez Galdós in 1907 connected Madrid to southern France and then Paris, and was the usual escape route for Spanish political exiles. It was built with the financial assistance of the Peréire brothers.

After welcoming foreign investment in railways, utilities, and certain manufacturing industries, the dominant mood in the country turned decisively against foreign investors and traders towards the end of the nineteenth century. Anti-foreign sentiment, coupled with import-substitution dreams, was to reach a climax in the aftermath of the Civil War of 1936–9, when the Franco dictatorship became dominated by nationalist policy-makers. Foreign interests in railways, mining, and telecommunications were nationalized, and a series of tight financial controls made foreign investment virtually impossible (Campa and Guillén 1996a). The limitations of the import-substitution model became apparent by the mid-1950s. Starting in 1959, liberal economic reforms substituted steep tariff barriers for non-tariff barriers to trade, and encouraged the arrival of multinationals in capital-intensive industries. During the 1960s Spain was among the fastest-growing economies in the world, matching Japan's rates, in part thanks to foreign investment.

Debates about outward FDI started in the eighteenth century when the economists of the Enlightenment considered the need to promote trading companies (*compañías de comercio*). Unlike the Netherlands, Portugal or Britain, the Spanish Empire had failed miserably to capitalize on the economic and trading potential of its colonies, mainly because of the creation of the Seville-based monopoly. Some economists, Jerónimo de Ustáriz and Bernardo de Ulloa in particular, argued that the trading companies would not be beneficial because they would tend to reduce competition. They thought that Spain, given its policy traditions, would be unable to regulate them properly.

---

[2] Pérez Galdós (1986:43–4): "¡Oh ferrocarril del Norte, venturoso escape hacia el mundo europeo, divina brecha para la civilización! Bendito sea mil veces el oro de judíos y protestantes franceses que te dio la existencia; benditos los artífices que te abrieron en la costra de la vieja España . . . Y por mil razones te alabamos, ferrocarril del Norte y si *no* fuiste perfecto en su organización . . . todo se te perdona por los inmensos beneficios que nos trajiste."

Others, however, while acknowledging the need to safeguard competition, urged the government to provide incentives for the creation of
trading companies. Among them were the Marquis of Santa Cruz de
Marcenado – a diplomat, officer, and author – who persuaded Charles
III to set up the Philippines Trading Company. Some of the most
liberal economists also saw the need for the government to create
them. Thus, Bernardo Ward argued that "well managed trading companies help increase and expand trade to foreign and distant lands;
and when large amounts of capital are required, they serve to establish
well-funded operations." Similarly, Pedro Rodríguez Campomanes,
while opposed to trading privileges in the domestic market, was
enthusiastic about their potential contribution to trade between the
metropolis and the colonies (Viñas Mey 1922:250, 253).

The debate over the trading companies quieted down considerably
during the nineteenth century, especially after the loss of most of the
American colonies in the wake of the Napoleonic Wars. With the rise
of textile and clothing production in Catalonia starting in the 1860s,
however, new calls were made for the establishment of trading companies in order to secure raw materials at privileged prices and access
to protected colonial markets (Viñas Mey 1922). The controversy
resurfaced again during the early twentieth century after the loss of
Cuba, Puerto Rico, and the Philippines in 1898. The protectionist
employer association FTN (Fomento del Trabajo Nacional) and the
Africanist League became champions of the trading companies and
asked the government to invoke the Law for the Protection of National Industry to promote investments in Spanish Morocco. Francisco
Cambó, the Minister of Finance responsible for the infamous protectionist tariff of 1922 (which remained in place until 1960), was in
favor, though interest waned quickly (Guirao 1922).

The political turbulence of the 1930s, the Civil War, and the economic hardships of the 1940s and 50s relegated outward FDI to the
background. The brief spur during the 1960s came to an end with the
economic crisis of the 1970s. It was during the 1980s, especially after
the formation of the PSOE government in 1982 that the debate, at
least in government circles, regained some prominence. The generation of politicians that dominated the economic and social policy-
making of the new government was moderate in orientation and
relatively liberal in terms of economic ideas. Social-democratic figures
such as Miguel Boyer, Josep Borrell, José María Maravall, Oscar

Fanjul (later to become the founding president and CEO of Repsol), and Javier Alvarez Vara (who presided over CASA) understood that one of Spain's main limitations was the lack of companies of international stature. The debate had to do with how to improve the situation. Borrell, for instance, frequently argued that spending money trying to beef up state-owned enterprises so as to help them in their international projection would deliver inferior results compared with spending state funds on healthcare, education, and infrastructure. As Maravall argued in an interview, their fascination with the Swedish model did not prevent them from realizing that private enterprise plays a key role in the economy in all of Scandinavia.

The Socialist governments of 1982–96 embarked on a policy journey that would lead to the restructuring of state-owned companies, the gradual privatization of most of them (not without keeping a golden stake to guarantee the state's continued influence in corporate governance), and the internationalization of their operations as a way to give them enhanced stature in an increasingly deregulated European marketplace. By the early 1990s, the official policy of the two holdings of state-owned firms (Teneo and INI) had become to "promote in a variety of ways the international presence of the member companies, either individually or in collaboration with third parties" (Sidro 1993:16). As analyzed in chapter 4, state-owned firms spearheaded the rise in outward FDI during the 1980s and 90s, a trend that continued and intensified as the Popular Party governments of José María Aznar (1996–2004) implemented one of the most ambitious deregulation and privatization programs in Europe. Interestingly, the rapid internationalization of Spanish firms has taken place with the quiet consent of the population and the labor unions, which have not seen in this process a threat to their interests.

Public opinion and foreign investment

The Spanish population views the international expansion of Spanish firms quite favorably, even in the face of a persistently high unemployment rate, which peaked at just above 24 percent of the active population in 1994, precisely when outward FDI started to gather speed (see figure 1.1). Responses to the same set of questions obtained through public opinion surveys conducted in 1995 and 2003 show a favorable shift in attitudes towards Spanish direct investment abroad (Table 9.1).

Table 9.1. Attitudes of the Spanish population aged eighteen and above towards foreign direct investment, 1995 and 2003 (in percentages)

Question	1995	2003
1. How many multinationals does Spain have?		
a. Many.	3	9
b. Some.	18	44
c. Just a few.	45	30
d. None.	11	4
DK/NA	23	13
2. Are you in favor of Spanish firms investing abroad?		
a. Very in favor.	11	33
b. Somewhat in favor.	39	42
c. Somewhat opposed.	18	11
d. Very opposed.	16	8
DK/NA	15	6
3. With which of the following three sentences do you agree the most?		
a. Spanish-owned firms should not invest abroad given the high unemployment rate in Spain.	38	22
b. Spanish-owned firms should invest abroad because it indirectly contributes to job creation in Spain.	35	48
c. The most important role of the firm is to make a profit regardless where it creates jobs.	15	21
DK/NA	12	9
4. Spanish investments in Latin America have been:		
a. Very beneficial to the host countries?	n.a	16
b. Somewhat beneficial to the host countries?	n.a	40
c. Of little benefit to the host countries?	n.a	20
d. Not at all beneficial to the host countries?	n.a	4
e. No effect.	n.a	2
DK/NA	n.a	18
5. How would you evaluate the impact of the increasing presence of Spanish firms abroad on the country's international image?		
a. Very positive.	n.a	13
b. Quite positive.	n.a.	44
c. Neither positive nor negative.	n.a.	16
d. Quite negative.	n.a.	12
e. Very negative.	n.a.	6
DK/NA	n.a.	9

Table 9.1. (continued)

Question	1995	2003
6. Would you like to work for a foreign multinational firm?		
a. Yes	6	47
b. No	93	43
DK/NA	1	10
7. Would you like to work for a Spanish multinational firm?		
a. Yes	5	72
b. No	94	21
DK/NA	1	7

Source: CIRES 1995 and BRIE November 2003 surveys (see the Appendix for further details).
Note: Wording of questions:
1. Los países más avanzados cuentan con empresas multinacionales propias. ¿Cree Vd. que España cuenta con muchas, algunas, unas pocas o ninguna multinacional propia?
2. A menudo se habla de que la empresa española debe invertir en países extranjeros para promocionar nuestras exportaciones e incluso para fabricar a menor coste, si bien hay quien piensa que esto puede disminuir el empleo en España. ¿Está Vd. muy a favor, algo a favor, algo en contra o muy en contra de que empresas españolas realicen inversiones en el extranjero?
3. De las tres frases siguientes, ¿con cuál estaría Vd. más de acuerdo? Más de acuerdo con . . . A. La empresa de propiedad española no debería invertir en el extranjero dado el elevado desempleo existente en España. B. Conviene que la empresa española invierta en el extranjero porque así se contribuye indirectamente a aumentar el empleo en España. C. La función primordial de la empresa es generar beneficios con independencia de dónde se creen los puestos de trabajo.
4. ¿Cómo cree que ha sido la inversión de capitales españoles en América Latina, muy, algo, poco o nada beneficiosa?
5. ¿Cómo valora Vd. la creciente presencia de empresas españolas en el extranjero para la imagen de España en el mundo: muy positiva, algo positiva, ni positiva ni negativa, algo negativa o muy negativa?
6. ¿Le gustaría a Vd. trabajar para una empresa multinacional extranjera?
7. ¿Y para una empresa multinacional española?

Awareness of the phenomenon of Spanish investment abroad has increased markedly since the mid-1990s. In 1995, at the beginning of the boom in outward FDI, only 3 percent of survey respondents thought that Spain had many multinational firms, and 18 percent thought that the country had "some." A majority of 56 percent thought that there were "just a few" or no Spanish multinationals. By the end of 2003 the perception was the opposite: more than half (53 percent) thought that Spain had "many" or "some" multinational firms.

Spaniards have traditionally been weary of multinational firms and very critical of capital flight. However, the overall attitudes towards Spanish direct investments abroad have been relatively positive. In 1995, 50 percent were either "very" or "somewhat" in favor, and only 34 percent "somewhat" or "very" opposed. By 2003, the proportions had shifted to 75 and 19 percent, respectively. Thus, for every Spaniard who opposes foreign investment by Spanish firms, there are four who are in favor. This shift in attitudes is also reflected in the responses to three well-known statements about the role of the business firm in society. When asked with which of three statements they agreed the most, respondents showed an increasingly positive attitude over time. The zero-sum statement that "Spanish-owned firms should not invest abroad given the high unemployment rate in Spain" was the most popular back in 1995 (38 percent). But by 2003, nearly a majority of the respondents (48 percent) agreed with the non-zero-sum argument that "Spanish-owned firms should invest abroad because it indirectly contributes to job creation in Spain." Finally, the Friedman-esque statement that "the most important role of the firm is to make a profit regardless of where it creates jobs" was chosen by 21 percent of respondents in 2003, up from 15 percent in 1995. In sum, Spaniards seem to have given the country's multinational firms a strong vote of confidence in their decision-making as to where in the world to make investments.

Interestingly, a majority (56 percent) of respondents in 2003 were persuaded that Spanish investments in Latin America have been either "very" or "somewhat" beneficial to the host-countries, compared to just 24 percent who thought them to be "a bit" or "not at all" beneficial. These perceptions by Spaniards are much more positive than those expressed by respondents in Latin America (30 and 37 percent, respectively). A majority of Spaniards (57 percent) believe that Spanish investments abroad have improved the country's international image, and an additional 16 percent that it has neither improved nor damaged it.

By far the most important attitudinal changes among the Spanish population have had to do with the desire to work for multinational firms. While in 1995 just 6 percent of respondents said they would like to work for a foreign multinational firm and only 5 percent for a Spanish-owned multinational firm, by 2003 the proportions had reached 47 and a whopping 72 percent, respectively. Only about 20 percent of respondents now reject working for a multinational, whether foreign or Spanish-owned. It is interesting to note that more Spaniards would be willing to work for a Spanish-owned multinational than for a foreign-owned one, a topic which I will analyze below in the context of the impact of foreign investment on the managerial labor market.

It is important to bear in mind that the 2003 respondents (and probably those interviewed in 1995 as well) had in mind not a representative sample of the population of Spanish multinational firms, but the largest and most visible ones. In fact, when asked to mention the names of Spanish multinationals, most respondents referred to Telefónica, Repsol-YPF, Grupo Santander, and/or BBVA. Thus, the attitudes of the population are disproportionately shaped by the investments and international presence of this handful of large firms.

Only a tiny part of the attitudinal changes reported above are related to the coming of age of a younger generation of Spaniards with better educational credentials and a more positive attitude towards globalization in general; the bulk of the differences observed in the eight years between 1995 and 2003 represent a genuine shift in attitudes. Statistical analyses of the data show that the higher the socioeconomic status of the respondent, the more favorable the attitudes toward foreign investment, although the effects are not large (CIRES 1995:884–5). Thus the Spanish population has warmed to the phenomenon of outward foreign direct investment and has come to espouse remarkably favorable attitudes.

The labor unions' point of view

Another useful way of gauging the social response to foreign direct investment is to examine the attitudes and actions of the labor unions, which in Spain have played an important role as social actors before, during, and after the transition to democracy in 1975–8. The relationship between foreign or domestic multinational corporations and organized labor has frequently been adversarial, and the case of Spain is no exception to the rule. Spanish leftist labor unions harbored anti-foreign ideologies during the 1950s and 60s under the authoritarian regime of General Franco. Since the 1970s, however, they have come to adopt openly favorable attitudes towards foreign multinationals in a context of democracy and integration with Europe. Unions have heralded multinationals as political and economic partners, and as the ideal agents to help create jobs, transfer technology, and assist in modernizing the country. Only the much diminished anarchist unions have refused to welcome foreign investment, given their rejection of collective bargaining and European integration. Democracy, liberal economic policies, and union friendliness have prompted a massive arrival of long-term foreign direct investment. The reaction of the unions to rapidly growing outward foreign direct investment by Spanish firms since 1992 has also been quite moderate, even supportive.

This section analyzes the evolution of the unions' views about foreign investment. I begin by documenting the quite dramatic shift in attitudes toward foreign multinationals from the 1950s to the 90s, which provides the background to the discussion of their position concerning outward FDI since the mid-1990s. The evidence is based on union publications, congress proceedings, and interviews with several union officials.[3]

The unions and inward FDI

The evolution of the ideological stand of the labor unions since the 1960s has been both remarkable and momentous for the unfolding of foreign investment in Spain, and it has generally been consistent with the liberal and leftist inclination to accept the multinationals provided the right political conditions were in place. The socialist (UGT), communist (CCOO), Christian-socialist (USO), and anarchist (CNT) unions opposed the Franco dictatorship – albeit following different strategies – and participated in the return to democracy during the late 1970s. These (clandestine) unions organized protests and strikes, and lobbied foreign governments, unions, and international organizations in their attempts to undermine the compulsory corporatist system of

---

[3] This chapter relies on some material published previously (Guillén 2001c, chapter 5). See also Guillén (2000) for the article version of the argument.

joint, vertical representation of workers and employers prevalent since the 1940s (Fishman 1990; Guillén 1994:175–85). Up until shortly after the dictator's death in 1975, union leaders, members, and sympathizers suffered unspeakable acts of repression, including torture and murder. Many were tried and jailed for military rebellion. The limited and tightly controlled mechanisms for collective bargaining introduced by Franco in the late 1950s so as to better sustain a capitalist, export-led model of growth and help the regime appear more liberal to the outside world allowed clandestine unionists to challenge, among other things, the presence of the foreign multinationals.

As in many other newly industrialized countries, the Spanish unions took offense at the multinationals during the 1960s for being the agents of capitalist imperialism, providing support to the Franco dictatorship,[4] and failing to observe basic labor rights. "¡Ay España, quién te quiere y quién te USA!" (Poor Spain! Who loves you, and who USes you!), read a famous bumper sticker. Thus, the multinationals would sit back and watch how the Labor Ministry jailed strikers, only to sack them forty-eight hours later for not showing up for work. Given that strikes were illegal, workers were temporarily suspended or summarily fired by the labor authorities anyway. In response to such practices, the clandestine unions would contact their counterpart labor organizations in the home country of the multinational so as to expose its outrageously inconsistent behavior. In one example among many involving American or European multinationals, the United Auto Workers distributed a leaflet in the US criticizing the Chrysler Corporation for being "more francoist than Franco himself" in its treatment of striking workers at its Madrid plant in January 1969. This tactic proved successful more often than not.[5]

[4] *Boletín de la Unión General de Trabajadores de España en el Exilio* (January 1955): 6–7; (February 1955): 7–8; (December 1959): 4–5; and (January–February 1960): 9.
[5] The leaflet was reproduced, translated into Spanish, in *Boletín de la Unión General de Trabajadores* (July 1970): 3. Other similar instances of repression took place at FIAT, Philips, Montefibre, Solvay, Authi, Lilly, Kodak, Sears, General Electric, Uniroyal, Olivetti, Firestone, Danone, and Atlas Copco. See *UGT: Boletín de la Unión General de Trabajadores de España* (hereafter *UGT*), (January 1972): 4; (March 1973): 14; (January 1974): 5; (May 1974): 7; (July–August 1974): 9; (September

Given this behavior and the widespread suspicions about the motives of multinationals doing business in a protected market and under
a dictatorial regime, labor leaders proposed to monitor and curtail the
activities of these companies in a variety of ways. They calibrated their
criticisms and recommendations very carefully lest the multinationals'
job-creation activities in Spain would be endangered. Thus the socialist union UGT's "Minimalist Program" of 1972 contained a rather
mild and vague proposal to "rigorously control foreign capital
invested in Spain."[6] This union's worker training courses included a
remarkable session on how to deal with foreign firms: "*Multinational
enterprises are a consummate, irreversible fact. The time to quarrel
over whether we should reject or accept their existence has passed.
What we can discuss is the way in which the working class ought to
deal with them.*"[7]

By the early 1980s, economic and political conditions were ripe for
the unions' unmitigated acceptance of foreign multinationals. Spain
adopted a democratic constitution in 1978, and was yearning to join
the European Union, which it did in 1986. Unlike in many Latin
American and East Asian countries, labor unions participated in the
entire process of political transition, and their views were quite influential in shaping economic and social policy-making (Bermeo 1994a,
1994b; Fishman 1990). Thus multinationals were no longer the collaborators of a dictatorial regime; nor could they easily take advantage of the working class, which was relatively well organized,
protected by favorable labor legislation, and politically enfranchised
into a democratic worker representation system. As the union leaders
of the time indicated in interviews with the author, the transition to
democracy and the empowerment of the labor organizations made it
possible to abandon the "inordinate fears" about the multinationals.[8]

1974): 3, 6; (November 1974): 4, 7–10; (December 1974): 16; (March
1975): 10–17; (April 1975): 12–16; (July-August 1975): 18; (October
1975): 21–3; (March 1976): 6; (April 1976): 16; (June 1976): 21;
(December 1976), I:2. See also *Unidad Obrera*, the official publication
of CCOO de Madrid, 9 (1st fortnight, June 1977); 12 (15–30 September
1977): 4; *Acción: Periódico Obrero de Barcelona y Provincia* (1971–4).
[6] *UGT* (July 1972): 9.
[7] *UGT* (September 1974): 8, 12. Emphasis added.
[8] Interviews with Nicolás Redondo, Madrid, 24 June 1998, and Marcelino
    Camacho, Madrid, 22 June 1998. Redondo was secretary-general of

The communist CCOO would not wait much longer than its socialist counterpart to openly express its acceptance of foreign investment, although with some strings attached:

Foreign investments are in principle acceptable if informed by the following principles: prioritization of labor-intensive industries . . . avoidance of investments in technologies that are obsolete in the home country of the multinational . . . promotion of investments in industries in which Spain lacks technological know-how or suffers from underinvestment . . . absorption of the technology being transferred . . . reinvestment of profits . . . release of operational information to the government and the unions . . . respect for workers' rights in all the subsidiaries of the multinational worldwide.[9]

The unions' new favorable attitudes toward foreign investors were due not only to the transition to democracy – which guaranteed a respect for workers' rights and greater accountability, as demanded by CCOO in the above excerpt – but also to their own shift from a populist to a modernizing mentality. As Álvarez-Miranda (1996: 219–48) has documented, during the 1970s the Spanish left abandoned its long-standing isolationist and anti-capitalist proposals to embrace pro-European views (*europeísmo*), a development that helped pave the way for the massive arrival of foreign investment since 1985. Spanish labor unions behaved as moderate and fairly constructive agents during the 1970s and 1980s, rejecting the extremes of populism, and accepting wage growth below inflation in the face of massive unemployment (Bermeo 1994a, 1994b:116; Fishman 1990; Hamann 1998). The modernizing mentality of the unions came to dominate discussions of topics such as economic policy-making, industrial restructuring, and foreign investment. In a sharp departure from the mentality of the 1960s, the communist and socialist unions began to argue in the late 1970s that the small size of the Spanish market required an integration with Europe, a greater export and competitive effort, and a rejection of the import-substitution model.[10]

UGT from 1976 to 1994. Camacho was secretary-general of CCOO between 1976 and 1987. See also: *Unidad Obrera* 25 (1st fortnight, October 1979): 10–11; *UGT Metal* (1980:5, 15–21).

[9] *Gaceta Sindical* (hereafter *GS*) (April 1981): 17.

[10] See CCOO's publications: *Unidad Obrera* 28 (2nd fortnight, November 1979): 10–11; *II Congreso de la Confederación Sindical de CCOO: Informe general y resoluciones aprobadas*, in *Cuadernos Gaceta Sindical*

Thus the unions had shifted their ideological position, joining the liberals in the country against the isolationist and anti-foreign position defended by the conservatives and right-wingers.

Spanish organized labor became utterly persuaded that foreign multinationals could bring to Spain jobs, technology, and even socio-political improvements. Thus union leaders came not only to the conclusion that "few countries in the world, not even the richest ones, can afford to do without the experience, technology, and capital of the multinational enterprises," but also to accept the proposition that multinationals could make a key positive political and social contri-bution: a type of employer that was, or could be, much more sensible, progressive, and democratic than the average Spanish entrepreneur. Thus foreign multinationals became a factor of "modernization of the weak and unequivocally reactionary domestic entrepreneurial com-munity," or, as the leader of the communist CCOO put it in an interview with the author, "Spain needed the multinationals because of the lack of a viable domestic bourgeoisie. Without a dynamic bourgeoisie there is no chance of making the transition from pre-industrial feudalism to industrial capitalism, and without capitalism there can be no transition to the socialist and communist society."[11] Tellingly, the socialist and communist unions have actively partici-pated in efforts to court foreign investors, including General Motors, Volkswagen, and DuPont.[12] And the multinationals have responded like true partners by stepping up their investments in Spain and

---

1 (1981): 15; *III Congreso de la Confederación Sindical de CCOO*, Special Issue of *GS* (1984): 37. Also, by UGT, *Resoluciones del XXXII Congreso* (Madrid, 1980), pp. 111–12, and Redondo's interview in *Aragón/Express*, 3 November 1979, p. 13. Interviews with Carlos Martín Urriza, staff economist of CCOO, Madrid, 30 June 1998, and Jesús Pérez, executive secretary of UGT, and Antonio González, director of the technical staff of UGT, Madrid, 1 July 1998, also confirmed the modernizing mentality of the unions.

[11] *Unión*, 4 September, 1981, supplement p.3; *GS* (May 1981): 49; *Unión Sindical* (May 1979): 12; interview, Marcelino Camacho. Camacho was a metal-worker at Perkins Hispania, a subsidiary of International Harvester.

[12] Among the multinationals successfully courted by the unions were Gen-eral Motors, Volkswagen, and DuPont. See: UGT Metal report(1980); Interview, Nicolás Redondo.

spending on training per worker three times as much as domestically owned firms (Mineco 1994:269, 290–4).

Naturally, the emerging consensus among union leaders that multinationals could indeed become political and economic partners was not easy to sustain during economic downturns, when multinationals scaled back their investment plans or even divested.[13] Jobs are, of course, the key issue for the unionists as well as for most of the population given that unemployment stubbornly stayed at over 15 percent of the active population from the early 1980s to the late 90s. Employment represents a goal which could even justify state subsidies and other emoluments to attract, or prevent from leaving, job-creating foreign investments. Thus in 1993 the official journal of the socialist union UGT argued that Spain ought to "subordinate institutional [i.e. state] support for the multinationals to the preservation of production inside Spain's borders, so that foreign subsidiaries do not degenerate into mere distributors of foreign products once they have captured market share."[14] In fact, the labor unions have often voiced their preference for greenfield investments, and their criticism of foreign acquisitions of Spanish companies and speculative investments in the stock market.

We are witnessing neither the unfolding of industrial activity nor investments in firms so as to create jobs, but rather the arrival of money to speculate in the stock market and to gain control of firms at low prices . . . We welcome the arrival of foreign money, but aimed at founding new firms and creating jobs instead of at buying firms.[15]

---

[13] *UGT* (June 1978): 30; *GS* (January 1987): 47; *Unión*, 1 August 1981, p. 1, 4 September 1981, p. 4, 4 September 1981, supplement, p. 3, and 4 November 1981, p. 3. *Gaceta Sindical* (digital edition) 312(bis) (12 April, 2002): 3, 331(bis) (27 September, 2002): 3. See also *The Journal of Commerce*, 4 April 1994, p. 7A; *International Herald Tribune*, 2–3 April 1994; *Época*, 5 June 1995, pp. 24–8. A particularly severe series of plant closures took place in late 2003 and early 2004, affecting more than 10,000 direct workers (*El País*, 15 March 2004). The unions, however, did not blame the multinationals as much as they did the government for not investing in R&D.

[14] *Unión* (September 1993): 22.

[15] *GS* (September 1987): 5, 17–19. Emphasis added. See also (January 1991): 20, (January 1992): 4, (June 1997): 13; *Unidad Obrera* 29 (1st forthnight, December 1979): 8–9, 142 (September 1992): 6–13.

The roles of democratic consolidation and of a modernizing mentality in prompting the socialist and communist unions to adopt a
favorable ideological image of the multinational firm stand in sharp
contrast with the unreconstructed mentalities and arguments of the
anarchist union, the CNT, which has become a marginal organization.
Still, it is methodologically important to present not just the views of
the unions that did change their assessment of foreign investment from
the 1960s to the 90s, but also those of unions that have remained
uncompromisingly intolerant.

First of all, one should bear in mind that anarchist unions reject social
productivity pacts and development policies seeking to accelerate economic growth, are weary of collective bargaining, and are deeply
distrustful of the state, even a democratic one. Accordingly, the CNT's
image of the multinational enterprise remains anchored in the past.
"Workers depend on the decisions made at the powerful foreign capitalist complex. Hundreds of thousands of workers labor, and more of
them will in the future, under the authority of a foreign employer: paces
of work, human relations policies, collective bargaining."[16]

Second, Spanish anarchists reject the defense of foreign multinationals on the basis of their contributions to employment, because in their
view jobs created by multinationals also help increase the power of the
government and the police, and they happen to be highly polluting.[17]
Third, they have repeatedly exposed the hasty efforts by the various
dictatorial and democratic governments in Spain to offer favorable
investment terms, including subsidies and lax regulations, and have
more persistently sounded the alarm over foreign acquisitions of
Spanish firms as a by-product of EU membership.[18] Fourth, the anarchists have been much more critical of the manipulative potential of
the new managerial and organizational techniques brought to Spain
by the multinationals, especially Japanese ones:

Today, directly from Japan, the world's *second* largest exporter of
stupidities, comes a new managerial activity called "quality circles". In
simple terms, workers must know . . . Thus, besides those of us who favor

[16] CNT: *Órgano de la Confederación Nacional del Trabajo* (hereafter
CNT) (October 1978): 6–7. See also: (February 1990):18, 205; (July
1996):4, 217–18; (January 1997).
[17] CNT (February 1990): 18.
[18] CNT (March 1979):6; (January 1981):5; (April 1985): 12.

the abolition of the ownership of the means of production are those who not only work for somebody else's profit but also must "brainstorm" in order to propose to the management "brilliant" ideas that make the firm even stronger.[19]

It is important to underline in closing that the anarchists cannot be blamed for ideological inconsistency. They have denounced the economic and political development of the Soviet Union, China, and Cuba as much as they have criticized the capitalist countries. This "Neither Trilateralist Capitalism nor Bureaucratic Socialism" attitude has prompted some noted anarchist political economists like Abraham Guillén (no relation to the author) to apply the same logic of criticism normally levied against the multinationals headquartered in the capitalist countries to the generally neglected phenomenon of Soviet industrial and service foreign investment. In his remarkable 1987 article, "Soviet Capitalism: The Last Stage of Imperialism," Guillén published a list of seventy-two Soviet multinational corporations with foreign investment holdings in twenty-two capitalist countries.[20] Unlike their socialist and communist counterparts, the anarchist unions did not alter their views and strategies after the return to democracy, and have dismissed modernizing attitudes and policies as oppressive and inherently undesirable. In short, the famous anarchist motto of "No god, no king, no owner, no religion, no state," might be appended with the phrase, "no multinationals." With the one exception of the rather marginal anarchist union, Spanish organized labor has come to accept and celebrate foreign investment as part of its modernizing mentality. As the multinationals' collaboration with the Franco dictatorship and their abusive industrial relations practices receded into the past, the unions began to welcome foreign investors as job creators and technology providers. Democracy and the abandonment of populist attitudes in favor of modernizing ones by the unions paved the way for the full acceptance of foreign multinationals as partners in economic development.

[19] *CNT* 78(1985): 7. Emphasis added. This piece comments on the introduction of quality circles at Nissan Motor Ibérica. See also another article (January 1994: 6–7), criticizing Toyota's lean production.

[20] *CNT* (April 1987):8–9. Abraham Guillén (1913–93) went into exile in Buenos Aires after having been a political commissar in an anarchist militia during the Spanish Civil War of 1936–9.

The unions and outward FDI

The unions' reaction to outward FDI by Spanish firms during the 1990s was characterized by moderation and even some support. The unions did take notice of the fact that, for the first time in recent history, Spanish outward FDI exceeded inward FDI during 2000.[21] They seem to regard this remarkable development as business as usual. The reasons are four-fold. First, by the 1990s, Spanish unions had come to realize the importance of inward FDI to the development of the country, and of outward FDI to the international competitiveness of Spanish-owned businesses. Being themselves pro-globalization, however qualified in that it should be driven by solidarity and the observance of labor rights, the unions have acquiesced.[22] Their relatively moderate and modernizing ideology (Bermeo 1994b:116; Fishman 1990; Guillén 2001c), has prompted them to accept, although not necessarily celebrate, the international expansion of Spanish firms. Second, as noted in previous chapters, the overwhelming majority of Spanish outward FDI has been driven by motives that are neither suspicious nor biased against the interests of Spanish workers: (a) horizontal investments mandated by the need to produce a service jointly with the customer, to overcome restrictions imposed by foreign governments, and/or to grow in the wake of rapid deregulation and enhanced competition in Europe (e.g. construction, banking, telecommunications, utilities, information, tourism, security services, etc.); (b) backward vertical investments to secure raw materials not available in Spain (fishing, oil, gas); or (c) forward vertical investments in the form of distribution channels to facilitate Spanish exports (consumer-goods). Only a tiny proportion of Spanish FDI refers to backward vertical operations intended to reduce production costs by exploiting

[21] See, for instance, *Gaceta Sindical* (digital edition) 211 (26 September, 2001): 4.

[22] On the unions and globalization, see the recent statements in *Unión* 111 (23 January 2003): 1, and *Unión Sindical* 139 (February 2003): 8. The anarchist CNT is the only major union which is flatly against economic globalization, although in an asymmetric way: "Against economic globalization, without party and boss, and in favor of proletarian internationalism!!" ("¡Contra la globalización económica, sin partido ni patrón, y por el internacionalismo proletario!!" See *CNT Edición Digital* 266 (11 May 2001). See also 268 (June 2001), 274 (11 December 2001), and 278 (April 2002).

lower wages abroad, e.g. textiles, clothing, toys, and eyewear (see Giráldez Pidal 2002:132).

The third reason is that most Spanish outward FDI has flowed to democratic countries in Latin America and Europe, thus eliminating a main concern of the unions. In fact, they are generally critical of investments in China.[23] And the issue of tax evasion by locating subsidiaries in tax havens has only emerged prominently once, in the case of BBVA in 2002, after the Bank of Spain issued an investigation that eventually led to the dismissal or resignation of most of the executives from the former BBV and the rise to power of the executives from Argentaria (the "A" in BBVA).[24] Lastly, the unions themselves have seen their power diminished during the 1990s, and thus have adopted less confrontational attitudes and practices.

Against the backdrop of an increasing integration of Spain into the European and global economies, the leaders and officials of the dominant communist (CCOO) and socialist (UGT) labor unions have tended to regard outward FDI as "something natural," "to be expected," "reasonable," "necessary," and "generally positive," especially if "social dumping" is not involved. In fact, they have noted that only in certain cases of backward vertical investments by firms in the toy and clothing industries has there been a loss of jobs in Spain as a direct result of outward FDI. The unionists see the process of internationalization of banks and utilities as an opportunity to create larger, more competitive firms, gain market share in foreign markets, and guarantee job security at home.[25] These attitudes and beliefs are certainly "modernizing" and connote a deep understanding of how competition in the global economy takes place. In many ways, this stand is consistent with the unionists' view of inward FDI. The common denominator is that they strongly believe in the "home-country effect," whereby multinationals tend to make "the most important decisions," locate "higher value-adding activities," and "employ more qualified workers" in their country of origin. Therefore, it is regarded as being good for the working class of any country to see its firms expanding throughout the world.[26]

[23] *Gaceta Sindical* (digital edition) 218 (October 5, 2001):1.
[24] *Gaceta Sindical* (digital edition) 312 (April 10, 2002):3.
[25] Interviews with Marcelino Camacho (CCOO), Madrid, 22 June 1998; and with Jesús Pérez and Antonio González (UGT), Madrid, 1 July 1998.
[26] Interview with Carlos Martín Urriza (CCOO), Madrid, 30 June 1998.

As in the case of inward FDI, the unions have reacted to the increasing involvement of Spanish firms in foreign countries by pursuing cross-border monitoring and collective action. Joint organizations and liaison committees have been established, especially with unions representing the workers employed by Spanish firms in Latin America. Thus, the four main unions (CCOO, UGT, USO, and CNT) have expressed their solidarity with the workers employed by the subsidiaries of Spanish firms located in other countries in the event of layoffs, labor conflicts, and strikes,[27] and have sought the support of their unions when faced by problems at home.[28] As part of international associations of labor unions or by itself, CCOO has agreed with Telefónica on a code of conduct to protect the group's 120,000 employees worldwide, with Santander in Brazil that "any restructuring or change would be undertaken in a negotiated way with the unions," and with BBVA on labor relations in Chile, Uruguay, Colombia, and Brazil. According to the union, "the goal is to strengthen competitive and financial success in combination with professional development, training, motivation and integration of employees so as to ensure a positive evolution of labor relations in a climate of consensus."[29]

As in the case of inward FDI, the anarchist CNT has been hostile to Spanish multinationals. The union has criticized in quite scathing terms large firms such as Endesa for not observing the rights of indigenous peoples affected by their electricity-generating dams in Chile; Repsol-YPF for allegedly forcing people in Patagonia to relocate so that the firm can extract oil, and also for benefiting from the activities of the paramilitaries in Colombia; Telefónica for taking advantage of privatizations in Argentina and Brazil; the Spanish

[27] See, for instance, CCOO's criticism of Santander's job cuts at Banespa, one of its Brazilian subsidiaries, in *Gaceta Sindical* (digital edition) 129 (April 19, 2001):3. See also *Unión* 174 (1998):19.

[28] As in the case of the labor conflict at Telefónica in 1999 over working conditions and layoffs, when CCOO sought the solidarity and support of the Grupo Intersindical Iberoamericano de Telefónica. See *Gaceta Sindical* 171 (January 1999):30.

[29] See *Gaceta Sindical* (digital edition) 108 (15 March, 2001):3; 141(9 May, 2001):3; 264 (18 December, 2001):3; 335 (23 October, 2002):3. See also the views of César Alierta, president of Telefónica, in *Diario de Sesiones del Senado: Comisión de Asuntos Iberoamericanos* 155 (June 26, 2001):16.

government for its handling of the Aerolíneas Argentinas fiasco; and Abengoa, Iberdrola and Gas Natural for their investment projects in Central America.[30] It has also rebuked Indo for exporting jobs to lower-wage countries and UGT and CCOO for, according to the anarchists, not acting. CNT has also criticized Inditex, though apparently for no other reason than its very success.[31]

The crisis in Argentina starting in the summer of 2001 has elicited a number of responses from the unions. First, they have urged Spanish firms to commit themselves to staying in the country and preserving jobs.[32] Second, they have criticized, though relatively infrequently, the attempts by Spanish firms to secure special access and privileges from the interim government of President Duhalde and later of President Kirchner.[33] And, third, they have urged the government to put pressure on the IMF to help relieve poverty in Argentina.[34] Union representatives have been dispatched to the region in order to gather information and coordinate union actions. As usual, the CNT has been most strident in its remarks, arguing that Argentina's problems are to be attributed to the misdeeds of the American and Spanish multinationals.

We accuse Spanish multinationals – BBVA, SCH, Telefónica, Iberia, Repsol, Endesa, Aguas de Barcelona, and many more. We accuse them for stealing, for having plundered the wealth of Argentina and other peoples. We accuse them of being undemocratic, for lobbying and bribing governments so that they make decisions against the will of the people. We accuse them of being murderers who are now trying to save their skins in Argentina, even at the

---

[30] *CNT* 237 (August 1998):16; 238 (September 1998):15; 245 (April 1999):16; 259 (June 2002):14; 270 (August 2001):19; 274 (December 2001):5; 278 (April 2002):14, 21; 287 (February 2003):12; 291 (June 2003):22. *CNT* (digital edition) 287 (February 2003), 291 (June 2003).

[31] *CNT* 259 (June 2002):14. "El Grupo Zara y el Pacto Global de la ONU" (18 January 2002) *http://www.cnt.es/Noticias/Not180_zara.htm.*

[32] *Gaceta Sindical* (digital edition) 272 (14 January, 2002):3.

[33] In particular, Santander's President Emilio Botín's lobbying was criticized on the front page of *Gaceta Sindical* (digital edition) 279 (23 January, 2002):1.

[34] *Gaceta Sindical* (digital edition) 303 (Feburary 26, 2002):1; *Unión Sindical* 133 (April 2001):5; *Unión Sindical* 139 (February 2003):8; Federación Obrera Regional Argentina, "Informe de la situación social en Argentina" (2003), reproduced on CNT's website: http://www.cnt.es/noticia.php?id=296.

expense of the population and its misery. We accuse the Spanish government
of complicity with the Spanish firms. We accuse former President Felipe
González and the current Aznar government of unashamedly lobbying in
favor of these multinational firms and against the Argentine people.[35]

Leaving aside the anarchist CNT, analysis of the contents of the
main publications of the unions reveals that the sharp rise in outward
FDI has not aroused the kinds of passions that inward FDI generated
back in the 1960s and 70s. The reasons for this – the unions' modernizing ideology, the nature and destination of the investments, and their
own eroded power base – produce a situation in which the unions see
outward FDI, for the most part, as a non-issue.

The impact on the managerial labor market

An important social aspect of the rise of the Spanish multinational
company has been the multiplication of jobs for Spanish university
graduates both in Spain and in the foreign countries in which the firms
have invested. In a country with the highest, though receding, unemployment rate in the OECD, and with massive *under*employment
of university graduates, the creation of tens of thousands of new,
highly skilled, white-collar jobs has created somewhat of a revolution,
especially in Madrid, which is home to many of the large Spanish
multinationals (Cuadrado Roura 2003).

The foreign expansion of Spanish firms has generated the need for
expatriate managers. It is estimated that there are between 5,000 and
7,000 Spanish expatriate managers, most of them in Latin America,
the rest of the European Union, and the United States (Ugalde 2002).

---

[35] *CNT* (digital edition) 276 (February 2002): "Acusamos a las Empresas
Multinacionales Españolas, BBVA, BSCH, Telefonica, Iberia, Repsol,
Endesa, Aguas de Barcelona . . . y muchas más: Las acusamos de Ladro-
nas, por haber expoliado durante todos estos años la riqueza del pueblo
argentino y de muchos otros. Las acusamos de Antidemocráticas, por
presionar y sobornar a los gobiernos para que actúen en contra del
pueblo. Las acusamos de Asesinas, por pretender ahora salvar sus naves
en Argentina, aun a costa de mayor miseria de la población. Acusamos al
Gobierno Español de complicidad con las empresas españolas. Acusamos
al ex presidente Felipe González y al actual gobierno de Aznar de presionar descaradamente en beneficio de estas empresas transnacionales y
en contra del pueblo argentino."

However, the total figure for Spanish managers working abroad for a Spanish-owned firm is probably three times greater because some multinationals have staffed foreign positions by hiring new employees with no preexisting contractual link to the parent company, only to the foreign subsidiary. These managers, while working abroad, are not considered "expatriates" in the technical sense of the term.

Spanish expatriates, strictly defined as managers who are shifted from a domestic position to a foreign one within the same firm or business group, tend to be younger, better educated, and more proficient in foreign languages, though naturally less experienced than older generations of Spanish managers (Suárez-Zuloaga 2001; Watson Wyatt 2003; Deloitte and Touche 2003). These characteristics are even more accentuated among Spanish managers who are hired for a foreign position without having been previously employed at the parent company.

Executive search firms and expatriate consultancies operating in Spain indicated in interviews that Spanish multinational firms face several challenges when sending executives abroad to staff their foreign subsidiaries. First, the pool of "global" managers in Spain has expanded slowly, with lack of proficiency in foreign languages still the main stumbling-block. Second, Spanish executives are reluctant to move abroad for cultural and family reasons. (An important side-effect is that assignments in Latin America, except for risky Colombia and Venezuela, are preferred to those in countries in which Spanish is not the official language.) Third, most Spanish executives are deeply concerned with their return to Spain, and rightly so because, lacking appropriate planning, companies tend to cut their compensation package upon completion of the expatriate assignment and they rarely reassign the expatriate to a position of similar status in the managerial hierarchy back home. Finally, in many industries (the main exceptions being banking and consulting) a foreign assignment is not seen as an opportunity to advance one's career but just the opposite. Unlike most well-established multinationals, Spanish firms with investments abroad tend not to see foreign assignments as a necessary part of a manager's career.[36] It is striking to note that these problems parallel

---

[36] *El País Negocios*, 11 March 2001, 4 August 2002, 23 February 2003. *Expansión Empleo*, 22 February 2003; *Expansión*, 27 November 1997; *Capital Humano* 171 (November 2003):85.

those observed for expatriates from other countries, except that more established American and European multinationals do have better expatriate programs in place (Gates 1994; Conway 1995). In spite of these problems, however, the market for expatriate managerial assignments seems to be expanding rapidly, as more and more Spanish multinationals seek outside candidates for foreign positions, especially in Latin America, the rest of the European Union, the United States, and Eastern Europe.

Many Spanish multinational firms, especially medium-sized ones, lack programs to develop international managers, and they have failed to make it possible for women managers to succeed in their organizations, in spite of the fact that women make up more than half of university graduates, obtain better grades than men, and tend to be more willing to accept expatriate managerial positions. Another interesting aspect is that Spanish firms are trying to reduce their use of expatriate managers in Latin America due to a combination of causes, including the cost of persuading and compensating managers to accept positions in a volatile region, and a growing local perception of Spanish managers as arrogant economic colonizers.

Interviews with specialists and consultants in this area indicated that Spanish companies had learned the hard way that managing an expanding group of expatriate executives is no easy task from legal, fiscal, organizational, and psychological points of view. They say that, except for the six or eight largest, most Spanish multinationals still lack a well-developed policy and that they are reluctant to spend the money that is required to make it work. And they suggest that the largest multinationals decided to implement a comprehensive expatriate policy only after they ran into trouble, including not just expatriate failure to adapt but also legal problems involving the fiscal obligations of the expatriates. Obviously, Spanish multinationals in such highly visible and sensitive industries as banking, utilities, or telecommunications cannot afford the negative publicity that tends to be associated with legal procedures, especially those involving taxes.

A final aspect related to the managerial market is perhaps of more consequence than the proliferation of expatriate positions. Headhunters and expatriate consultants indicated in interviews that more and more Spanish managers now prefer to work in Spain for a Spanish multinational than for a foreign one. The reason is that they perceive their professional opportunities as constrained by the location of global headquarters. Given their preference not to work abroad, a foreign multinational offers limited promotion potential. In sum, the expansion of the market for expatriate managers and of the global headquarters of Spanish firms has meant something of a revolution, especially for young Spanish managers, a most welcome development given the underemployment of many university graduates.

The social acceptance of the Spanish multinational firm

The Spanish population and labor unions have reacted favorably and unemotionally to the steep increase in the presence of Spanish multinationals abroad. The key fact that helps put such a response in context is the nature of the impact of outward FDI on social and labor conditions within Spain. Few foreign investments undertaken by Spanish firms have sought to take advantage of lower wages, while highly qualified jobs have been created in Spain, especially in Madrid. In addition, by the early 1990s the presence of foreign multinational firms in Spain was already taken for granted. Thus there has been no major reason for Spaniards to feel that Spanish firms ought to stay in Spain and forgo opportunities abroad.

It is from the point of view of the social aspects of Spanish outward FDI that one can firmly assert that the country has indeed become a "normal" one. Spaniards are no longer systematically fearful of foreigners doing business in Spain; neither are they suspicious of Spanish firms investing and creating jobs abroad. The country has become part of the global economy in an "interdependent" way, the only viable one for an economy equivalent to 2 percent of the world's total. Multinational firms – foreign and domestic – have become a normal, unproblematic part of the Spanish landscape.

10 | *Europe, Spain, and the future of Spanish multinational firms*

> That they invent things? Let them invent!
> The electric bulb illuminates here as much
> as where it was invented.
>
> > Miguel de Unamuno (1906)[1]

> It suffices to take a look at a map to see that
> the natural strategic advantages of Spain are
> so formidable that if the country is strong
> then it will play a major role in global
> affairs, but if weak it will attract the
> attention of the strong.
>
> > Salvador de Madariaga (1931)[2]

THE last fifteen years or so have witnessed a major transformation of Spanish businesses. After decades of protectionism and isolation, virtually all of them are now exposed to the winds of international competition; nearly a thousand have invested abroad in order to exploit the opportunities inherent in operating across borders. As a result, Spain has become one of the ten largest foreign direct investors in the world, with key consequences for the country's economy, financial system, diplomacy, image and society, as well as for Europe. Moreover, this process of foreign expansion is applauded by the population and by the labor unions. Unless jobs are destroyed in the home country, Spanish multinational firms can continue to rely on a considerable amount of social goodwill in support of their quest for international competitiveness (see chapter 9).

---

[1] "¿Que ellos inventan cosas? ¡Invéntenlas! La luz eléctrica alumbra aquí tanto como donde se inventó." From a letter to philosopher José Ortega y Gasset (Robles 1987: 42).

[2] "Basta una ojeada al mapa para mostrar que las ventajas estratégicas naturales de España son tales que, si fuerte, ha de representar en el mundo un papel de primer plano, y, si débil, ha de ser constante objeto de atención por parte de los fuertes" (quoted in Rubio 2003: 557).

Looking towards the future, Spanish multinational firms face three distinct challenges which also affect the country and Europe as a whole. These have to do with the sustainability of their foreign expansion, the need to improve their image, and the implications for Spain's and Europe's roles in the world. Let me analyze each of them in turn.

The sustainability of foreign expansion

How sustainable is the foreign presence of Spanish firms, focused as it is on a few industries and a few parts of the world? The answer to this question can be broken down into two interrelated issues. The first has to do with the extent to which their current foreign operations will continue to be profitable, while the second with whether Spanish firms will continue to be "Spanish" in the sense of keeping their centers of decision-making located within the country. As analyzed in chapter 6, one-third to one-half of the profits of the large Spanish multinationals come from Latin America. Those streams of profit are subject to wide fluctuations. Although Spanish firms with operations in the region have managed recent crises rather well, their long-term well-being is under constant threat. From my perspective, the best way for Spanish firms to manage this exposure is to reduce the relative weight of their Latin American operations by expanding in other parts of the world, especially Western and Eastern Europe.

The issue of managerial control is linked to the dependence on Latin American growth and profits in a paradoxical way. On the one hand, growth in a profitable albeit risky part of the world militates against takeovers or even makes the Spanish firms more capable of launching takeovers themselves due to their greater size. On the other, if those investments turn sour, Spanish firms could see their share prices plummet and they could become easy prey. I find the geographical concentration of Spanish foreign direct investment more problematic than its industry focus. I am not concerned about the importance of foreign investments in service sectors. Quite the contrary, services hold the key to the future because Spain is a service economy. Having said that, manufacturing remains an important part of Spain's economy, but I am confident that many Spanish firms have made the necessary investments to remain competitive. The geographical concentration, however, is problematic because Latin America represents no more than 8 percent of the global economy (Spain, 2 percent). If the largest Spanish multinationals remained strong in just Spain and Latin America, they would be missing from 90 percent of the global economy, hardly a desirable prospect.

Among all the peculiarities of the foreign expansion of Spanish firms perhaps the most salient has to do with its relatively small presence in the rest of Europe, which accounts for about 20 percent of the global economy. Spain has been a member of the EU since 1986, a bloc that guarantees the free movement of goods, capital, and people. Spain also is a founding member of Economic and Monetary Union (EMU). British, French, Dutch, German, Italian, and Swedish firms have long invested in Spain. They are active in service as well as manufacturing industries. Spanish firms, with only a few exceptions, do not enjoy a comparable presence in those European countries. As analyzed in chapter 5, part of the problem lies in the fact that the largest Spanish multinationals operate in highly regulated, and hence highly politicized, industries such as banking, telecommunications, and energy. In several cases, nationalism has stood in the way of the Spanish multinationals making acquisitions in Europe. I suspect that it is only a matter of time before a wave of mergers and acquisitions in the leading European service sectors takes place. If Spanish firms are not ready for it, others will be.

I fully realize that if Spanish firms do acquire a presence in Europe as well as in Latin America, they will only be strong in about one-third of the global economy. However, it takes time for firms to expand internationally, and Spanish firms need the time to acquire the requisite skills. If they join forces with their European counterparts, they will be in a much better position to pursue growth in other parts of the world. Their present organizational and managerial capabilities are perhaps appropriate for expansion in the United States and Canada, which account for almost 25 percent of the global economy. The biggest challenge will be Asia, which accounts for over one third. The three largest economies – China, Japan, and India – pose unique problems for foreign firms. Medium-sized Spanish firms in manufacturing and in services have a small presence in China, but almost none in Japan or India. The greatest stumbling-block lies in managerial personnel. It is unclear whether large Spanish firms will be in a position to expand in Asia within the foreseeable future; unless, that is, they merge with other European firms.

In the case of the large Spanish multinationals, I see expansion in Europe through mergers and acquisitions as a necessary step toward further expansion in the United States, Canada, or Asia. Without the skills and managerial personnel of their European counterparts, it is likely that Spanish firms will remain strong in the 10 percent of the world represented by Spain and Latin America, and largely absent from the rest. A different scenario might encounter the medium-sized multinationals analyzed in chapter 3, many of which are family-owned or -controlled. Some of them already have a presence on four continents. Their biggest challenge will be to find an ownership and governance structure than enables them to continue growing.

Intangible assets and Spain's international image

The sustainability of Spain's foreign investment also depends on the ability of companies to develop intangible assets such as brands, technology, and managerial know-how. It is well known that Spain allocates meager resources to R&D – no more than 1 percent of GDP – much less than most countries in the OECD except for Portugal, Greece, Hungary, Poland, Turkey, and Mexico. Countries such as Japan, Germany, Finland, South Korea, and the United States spend three times as much as Spain; France and the UK twice as much (MCT 2003). Spain is the only "advanced" country that spends more on lotteries than on R&D. In fact, lottery expenditure (which excludes casinos and slot machines) stands at nearly twice R&D expenditure: 1.8 percent of GDP (Garrett 2001).

Another peculiarity of the Spanish case is that business firms are relatively less involved in R&D than their European, Japanese, Korean, or American counterparts. While in the OECD as a whole businesses contribute two-thirds of total R&D expenditure, in Spain they only contribute about half. The reasons why Spanish firms do not spend enough on R&D are not well understood. At first sight, it seems like a lack of vision with negative consequences for their long-term competitiveness. The reality, however, is complex. One cannot generalize to the entire spectrum of Spanish firms. As observed in chapters 1 and 4, two-thirds of Spanish foreign investment has been undertaken by firms in service sectors such as banking, transportation, telecommunications, electricity, water, hotels, mass media, and security services. In these activities companies tend to buy the technology rather than create it. Their international competitiveness derives from their marketing, managerial, and organizational skills. For instance, Spanish high-technology manufacturing firms devote 11 percent of value added to R&D, compared to 5 percent for high-technology service firms (MCT 2003: 73). Still, Spanish service-sector firms compare relatively well with their foreign competitors. For instance, Telefónica devotes 1.8 percent of total revenues to R&D, an amount that, while low for manufacturing firms, is appropriate for its industry given that Deutsche Telekom spends 1.7 percent and British Telecom 1.5 (*Actualidad Económica*, 1 August 2003). As discussed in chapter 3, large Spanish firms are not the most active in R&D. Rather, it is medium-sized firms, often family-owned, which invest the most. Foreign firms established in Spain do not stand out for their R&D activities either.

The consequences of the gap in resources allocated to R&D translates into a situation in which, during 2001, for every patent filed by a Spanish resident in order to secure protection in Spain, non-residents file forty-six patents, up from nineteen in 1990. Spain imports 60 percent more high-technology products than it exports (MCT 2003: 71–3). The country's technological dependence is on the increase.

It seems rather obvious that spending on R&D must be raised, as the new head of the government has promised, and that businesses need to contribute more to that effort. There is another aspect that requires attention. According to the Heritage Foundation, the US Chamber of Commerce, the National Patent Protection System and the US Trade Representative Watch List, Spain is among a large group of countries – mostly developing – with weak protection of intellectual property rights (Zhao 2004). This may be an important reason why foreign firms prefer not to do R&D in Spain, thus depriving local firms of spillover effects.

I also believe that much of Spain's image problem, as analyzed in chapter 8, is inextricably related to the perception that Spanish companies and products tend to be low-tech and lack sophistication. The central and autonomous regional governments in Spain can spend money improving the country's image through advertising. Countries like South Korea and Taiwan, by contrast, have focused on allocating money to R&D and not to public relations. That is the example for Spain to follow. Aside from this, Spanish companies do need to work on projecting a better, more accurate image with international financial journalists. They also need to facilitate the job of equity analysts and business school faculty so that more research reports and teaching cases are written about Spanish firms.

Spain's role in the world

The writer, historian, and diplomat Salvador de Madariaga (1886–1978) put it succinctly in the quote that appears at the beginning of this chapter. Because of its strategic relevance, Spain either plays a major role on the diplomatic chessboard – as it did during the sixteenth and seventeenth centuries – or becomes a pawn in global affairs. Madariaga was an astute observer from afar of his country's predicament. A world traveler, educated in Paris at the Ecole Polytechnique and the Ecole des Mines engineering schools as well as at Oxford, and the Spanish Republic's ambassador to the US just before the Civil War of 1936–9, he was a liberal who yearned for the return of democracy to Spain, and who cared about his country's international stature. He formulated his prescient argument a few years before the Civil War, which would be proved correct: the conflict was prolonged and intensified by the intervention of Nazi Germany and the Soviet Union.

It is sad to realize that the aftermath of the horrific 11 March, 2004 terrorist massacre in Madrid also illustrates his point. With José María Aznar (1996–2004) Spain became more attuned – the critics would say subservient – to US policy. After Rodríquez Zapatero's surprise win, the country has ostensibly oscillated towards the Berlin–Paris axis. Leaning on the former or the latter is no guarantee that Spanish economic and financial interests will be observed, although I would consider the European option more compatible with them, as I explained in chapter 7. Still, because of the zigzags in foreign policy, Spain is now farther away from the goal of being a respected country in the world than it was ten years ago. The reality is more of a comparatively weak country with a fluctuating foreign policy: the worst of all possible scenarios. Spain yearns to participate in the global diplomatic tennis match as a key player, but, if it fails to commit itself to a sustainable and popular foreign policy, it runs the risk of becoming merely the ball hit back and forth by more powerful countries.

The foreign investments of Spanish firms are both a constraint and an opportunity for foreign policy-making. They are a constraint because foreign policy needs to keep them in mind so as to advance, or at least not interfere with, the international activities of Spanish companies. They represent an opportunity because they infuse bilateral relationships with substance and meaning. The analysis of Spanish foreign policy in chapter 7 suggested that Spain must use Europe as leverage in its pursuit of vital cultural and economic interests around the world. Let me turn to this most important topic.

Implications for Europe

Spain is a country fully integrated with Europe in terms of trade and foreign investment. Although Latin America has been the most important destination for Spanish multinationals, their process of international expansion has repercussions not just for Spain but also for Europe. These fall into three categories. First, within the European context, Spain is no longer a relatively poor country with powerless firms. Second, Spanish financial and economic interests outside Europe are not necessarily the same as those of other European countries, hence further complicating the pursuit of a common European relationship vis-à-vis third countries. And third, while two decades ago Spanish firms were not, or could not be, active actors in the European mergers and acquisitions landscape, the situation is today much changed.

Spain has closed almost half of the per capita income gap that separated it from the EU when it joined as a full member in 1986. In that year Spain's per capita GDP at purchasing power parity was 72 percent of the EU-15 level; in 2003 it was roughly 85 percent. Given that the Spanish economy continues to grow faster than the EU average, the country is likely to bridge the gap even more. True, part of this superior performance is owing to the generous EU transfers from richer members, which have fueled infrastructure investments. A thriving Spanish economy has come hand in hand with ever larger and more internationally oriented service-sector firms, as analyzed in chapters 4 and 5. Thus, Spain and its firms have gained economic weight within the EU, something that brings both opportunities and risks. The opportunity is for Spain to become a more important player in key decisions and to participate in the probable Eastern European boom. The risk is to fail to defend the country's interests. As Leopoldo Calvo-Sotelo, the head of government in 1981–2, famously stated, the

EU is not a "love machine," but a "measuring machine." Europe might expect a more assertive Spain, but Spain needs to play its cards carefully and tactfully, especially in an expanded Union, because it is large enough to be influential but too small to accomplish anything by itself.

Perhaps the main reason why Spain needs to exercise caution in its European policy is because its global cultural and economic interests do not overlap much with those of the large EU countries, let alone the new Eastern members. In addition to the interests inherited from the past, Spain has acquired new ones, especially in Latin America and North Africa (the Maghrib). No other European country has so much at stake in these two regions as Spain does, with the only possible exception in the Maghrib of France, a country that is often a competitor of Spain's. The EU's expansion to the East offers little help in this regard, unless Spain can forge other types of ties with the newly admitted members.

In the area of European mergers and acquisitions, Spanish firms in several service sectors are likely to become important players. As I suggested in chapters 4 and 7, Spain's role in Europe could benefit from cross-border mergers in at least two ways. The first would be to make it possible for the large Spanish multinationals to enhance their stature and consolidate their chances of remaining viable competitors. The second would be a way out of Spain's difficult predicament as a country with vital cultural and economic interests in two parts of the world – Europe and Latin America – that often seem to contradict each other. If half a dozen large Spanish firms were to acquire, or merge with, some of their European counterparts, then Spain would find it easier to make both sets of interests compatible with each other. This "Europeanization" of Spain's Latin American economic interests might be attractive to other countries like Italy, France, or Germany, given that their manufacturing (though not service) firms are already major investors across the Atlantic. In this way, Europe would benefit from an enhanced presence in Latin America, and Spain from increased embeddedness in one of the world's largest and safest economic areas. Naturally, the Spanish government and public – and the companies themselves – should be ready to accept the need, in some cases, to relinquish national control of the firms in whole or in part. It will be very hard indeed for all of the Spanish multinationals to play a role globally without becoming part of greater European entities. Thus

Spanish companies stand the best chance of expanding furthest around the world as "European" firms, perhaps controlled and managed not only by Spaniards.

While during the last fifteen years Spanish firms of all sizes have grown to become serious international competitors, their future is far from assured. Medium-sized multinationals – often family-owned or -controlled – face formidable hurdles in the global economy, especially because they compete in manufacturing industries in which their foreign counterparts are much bigger and possess a longer history of innovation and international growth. The future of the large Spanish multinationals is not certain either. They have a well-established presence only in Spain and Latin America. Their next step should be to consolidate their European positions, perhaps as a springboard to further expansion in North America and Asia. This analysis also applies to Spain as a country. Although its Latin American interests are substantial, the country needs to work hard to forge a set of relationships in Europe that make it possible to pursue its overall agenda. A Spain firmly rooted in Europe will help improve both its international stature and Europe's leadership in the world.

Appendix: Data and sources

This appendix lists the large-sample surveys of firms and the interviews conducted for this book, as well as the newspapers and magazines consulted, and the libraries and archives visited.

Large-sample surveys

1. A survey of 120 firms – twenty of the largest firms from ten manufacturing industries in Spain – using a closed-item questionnaire, conducted during 1993 in collaboration with Professor José Manuel Campa of New York University with funding from the Carnegie Bosch Institute for Applied Studies in International Management.
2. A survey of 1,150 exporting firms in Spain with twenty-five or more employees using a closed-item questionnaire, conducted by the Spanish Institute for International Trade (ICEX) in 1992.
3. A survey of 1,200 respondents representative of the adult population in Spain. The sample is a cross-section of the Spanish population aged eighteen and over. The sampling error is 2.89 percent for $p = 0.50$ with a confidence level of 95.5 percent. Conducted by Professor Juan Díez Nicolás, director of the CIRES survey research institute, and known as CIRES 1985. Questions on attitudes toward foreign investment were included in a larger survey of economic and political attitudes in June of 1995.
4. A survey of 1,204 respondents representative of the adult population in Spain. The sample is a cross-section of the Spanish population aged eighteen and over. The sampling error is 2.90 percent for $p = 0.50$ with a confidence level of 95.5 percent. Conducted by the Real Instituto Elcano, and known as BRIE November 2003. Questions on attitudes to foreign investment

were included in a larger survey of attitudes towards international relations, conducted in October–November 2003.

Formal interviews and conversations

(*denotes interviews conducted by research assistant Laura Chaqués, Ignacio Madrid, or Carlos Pereira. Those in Argentina, Chile, or Mexico were conducted by Adrian Tschoegl and the author. All other interviews were conducted by the author.)

Miguel A. Aleixandre, export manager, Sáez Merino, Valencia, 1 December 1994.*

Marta Alvarez-Novoa, partner, director of the Expatriate Management Department, Ernst and Young, Madrid, 9 February 2004.

Luis Amor, marketing director, Pascual Hermanos, Valencia, 30 September 1994.*

Evaristo Arias, international manager, Campofrío, Madrid, 12 June 1994.*

Eduardo Arrotea Molina, general manager, Telefónica de Argentina, Buenos Aires, 24 March 1995.

Andrés Aymes Blanchet, vice-chairman, BBV Probursa, Mexico City, 14 May 1998.

Víctor Barallat, director of strategy and investor relations, Banco Santander, Madrid, 25 June 1998.

Jorge Barbat, partner, SpencerStuart España, Madrid, 25 November 2003.

Francisco Barberá, export director, Géneros de Punto Ferrys, Canals, Valencia, 30 September 1994.*

Francesc Bayó, researcher, CIDOB, Barcelona, 16 March 2004.

Germán Bejarano, general director of international economic relations, Ministry of Foreign Affairs, Madrid, 5 June 2003.

Antonio Bernardo Sirgo, CEO, Duro-Felguera, La Felguera, Asturias, 29 December 1993.

Josep Lluís Bonet, general manager, Freixenet, Sant Sadurní d'Anoia, Barcelona, 8 November 1994.*

Carlos Budnevich, Banco Central de Chile, 4 May 1998.

José María de Areilza, former advisor to Prime Minister Aznar on US affairs, 6 October 2003.

Marcelino Camacho, secretary-general of Comisiones Obreras, CCOO (1978–87), Madrid, 22 June 1998.

Alfredo Canal, partner, Boyden: Global Executive Search, Madrid, 18 November 2003.

Juan Luis Cebrián, CEO of Grupo Prisa, and former director of *El País*, Madrid, 24 October 2003.

Jesús Centenera, international manager, Indas, Pozuelo de Alcorcón, Madrid, 10 November 1994.*

Claudio Chamorro, head of research, Superintendencia de Bancos e Instituciones Financieras, Santiago, Chile, 6 May 1998.

William Chislett, freelance journalist, former Madrid correspondent of *The Times* (1974–8) and of the *Financial Times* in Mexico (1978–84), Madrid, 15 September 2003.

Ángel Corcóstegui, CEO and vice-president, Banco Central Hispano, Madrid, 17 June 1998.

Miguel Ángel Cortés, Secretary of State for International Cooperation, Ministry of Foreign Affairs, Madrid, 6 February 2004.

Rodolfo A. Corvi, assistant general manager, BBV Banco Francés, Buenos Aires, 7 May 1998.

Fernando Delage, researcher and consultant, Estudios de Política Exterior, Madrid, 8 and 12 January 2003.

Alejandro Díaz de León Carrillo, Banco de México, Mexico City, 13 May 1998.

Peru Egurbide, chief foreign relations correspondent, *El País*, Madrid, 16 February 2004.

Oscar Fanjul, former chairman and CEO of Repsol (1986–96) and vice-chairman of Omega capital, Madrid, 25 September 2003.

Jaime Ferrer Colom, partner, Boyden: Global Executive Search, Madrid, 18 November 2003.

Antonio Ferrero, international manager, Nutrexpa, Barcelona, 2 November 1994.*

Jaime Ferry, CEO, Fábricas Asociadas de Muñecas Onil (FAMOSA), Onil, Alicante, 10 January 1995.*

William Floistad, export manager, Osborne, Cádiz, 28 November 1994.*

Fernando Florenzano, CEO, Cobra, Madrid, 8 June 1994.

Carlos M. Fedrigotti, president, Citibank Argentina, Buenos Aires, 8 May 1998.

Mikel Gabilondo, export manager, Comercial Ufesa, Vitoria, 20 September 1994.*

Ricardo Augusto Gallo, vice-president, Banco de Boston, Buenos Aires, 22 March 1995.

Joaquim Garcia, planning director, La Seda de Barcelona, Barcelona, 14 November 1994.*

Manuel García Aranda, director of training and publications, Spanish Institute for Foreign Trade (ICEX), Madrid, 17 June 1994.

Jesús García-Luengos, lawyer and consultant, Madrid, 26 November 2003.
Richard Gardner, US Ambassador to Spain, Cambridge, MA., 18 October 1994.
Javier Gavito Mohar, vice-president, Comisión Nacional Bancaria y de Valores, Mexico City, 4 January 1998.
Julio J. Gómez, president, Asociación de Bancos de la República Argentina, Buenos Aires, 8 May 1998.
José Luis Gómez Navarro, researcher and consultant, Estudios de Política Exterior, Madrid, 8 January 2003.
Antonio González, director of the technical staff of UGT, Madrid, 1 July 1998.
J. Guiridi, manager, Azkoyen, Peralta, Navarra, 28 December 1994.*
Alejandro Henke, deputy director, Superintendency of Financial Institutions, Banco Central de la República Argentina, 7 May 1998.
Diego Hidalgo, entrepreneur, Cambridge, MA, 27 October 1994.
John Hardiman, formerly CEO of Ford Europe, Cambridge, MA, 13 October 1994, 8 March and 5 May 1995, and 1 May 1996.
Sixto Jiménez, CEO, Viscofán, Pamplona, 19 December 1996.*
Gabriel Kuri Labarthe, general manager, Casa de Bolsa Santander México, Mexico City, 14 May 1998.
Emilio Lamo de Espinosa, director, Real Instituto Elcano de Estudios Internacionales y Estratégicos, Madrid, 9 June 2003.
Francisco León, Citibank, Santiago, Chile, 5 May 1998.
Joshua Levitt, Madrid correspondent of the *Financial Times*, Madrid, 8 October 2003.
Ernesto Livacic, Superintendencia de Bancos e Instituciones Financieras, Santiago, Chile, 4 May 1998.
José Lladó, president, Técnicas Reunidas, Madrid, 26 January 2004. Former Minister of Trade and Minister of Transportation in the late 1970s, and former Spanish ambassador to the US (1978–82).
Jorge Llorens, general manager, Isolux-Wat, 13 June 1994.
Antonio López García, president, Amper, Madrid, 9 June 1994.
Enrique L. Mallea, general manager, YPF Gas, Buenos Aires, 6 October 1996.
José María Maravall, Minister of Education (1982–8), Cambridge, MA, 27 October 1993, and Madrid, 9 June 1994.
Francisco Martín, General Director, Banco Santander, Cambridge, MA, 27 April 1994.
Carlos Martín Urriza, Staff Economist of CCOO, Madrid, 30 June 1998.
Ricardo Martínez Rico, director of the undersecretary's staff, Ministry of Trade and Tourism, Madrid, 15 June 1994.

Raimundo Monge, chief financial officer, Banco Santander, Santiago, Chile, 5 May 1998.

Francisco Novela, CEO, Comelta, Madrid, 6 September 1994.*

Melchor Ordóñez, CEO, La Casera, Madrid, 9 June 1994.

A. Pajares, manager, Bodegas Miguel Torres, Barcelona, 4 January 1995.*

Tomás Pascual Gómez-Cuétara, adjunct to the presidency, Leche Pascual, Madrid, 1 June 1994.

Eladio Pérez, CEO, Agemac Tecnoseveco, Vilanova del Camí, Barcelona, 7 November 1994.*

Jesús Pérez, executive secretary of UGT, Madrid, 1 July 1998.

José María Planells, CEO, Anecoop, 29 November 1994.

Francisco Pons López, CFO, Indo, Hospitalet d'Llobregat, Barcelona, 27 October 1994.*

Enrique Pourteau, vice-president, YPF, Buenos Aires, 26 October 1995.

Gonzalo Ramos Puig, general director of international finance, Ministry of the Economy, Madrid, 13 June 2003.

Juan Carlos Rebollo, CFO, Grupo Antolín-Irausa, Burgos, 15 November 1994.*

Nicolás Redondo, secretary-general of Unión General de Trabajadores, UGT (1976–94), Madrid, 24 June 1998.

Luis Reig, general manager, Ficosa International, Barcelona, 11 November 1994.*

Jaime Requeijo, vice-president, Banco Zaragozano, 14 June 1995.

José Luis Rhodes de Diego, CEO, Patentes Talgo, Madrid, 6 June 1994.

Fernando Rodrigo, Professor of International Relations, Universidad Autónoma de Madrid, 8 January 2003.

Luis Javier Rodríguez García, director of the Inspection Bureau for Credit and Savings Institutions, Banco de España, Madrid, 17 June 1998.

Juan Rodríguez Inciarte, general director, Banco Santander, Cambridge, MA, 27 April 1994.

José Luis Rodríguez del Saz, director of communications and public relations, BBV, Madrid, 22 June 1998.

Enrique Ruete, CEO of Banco Roberts, Buenos Aires, 22 March 1995.

Eduardo Sánchez Junco, CEO of Hola SA, Madrid, 21 June 1995.

Ignacio Santillana, former CEO of Telefónica Internacional, Philadelphia, 21 February 1997.

Jesús Sarasa, CEO, Agropecuaria Navarra Sociedad Cooperativa, Pamplona, 20 December 1994.*

Aarón Silva Nava, general manager for accounting projects, Comisión Nacional Bancaria y de Valores, Mexico City, 13 May 1998.

Félix Solís, president, Bodegas Félix Solís, Valdepeñas, Valladolid, 26 October 1994.*

Gloria Sorensen, staff economist, BBV Banco Francés, Buenos Aires, 7 May 1998.

Arturo Tagle, advisor to the president, Banco de Chile, Santiago, Chile, 6 May 1998.

Ramón Talamás, CEO, Cirsa, Barcelona, 17 November 1994.*

Ramón Tamames, professor, formerly Member of Parliament, Madrid, 21 June 1995.

José Antonio Ugarte, president, Ulma Sociedad Cooperativa, Oñati, Guipúzcoa, 13 December 1994.*

José María Vázquez Quintana, president, Telefónica Investigación y Desarrollo, Cambridge, MA, 15 March 1994.*

Ángel Velasco, CEO, Ansa-Lemforder, Burgos, 14 October 1994.

José Viñals, general director of international affairs, Bank of Spain, Madrid, 11 June 2003.

Carlta Vitzthum, Madrid correspondent of the *Wall Street Journal*, Madrid, 23 September 2003.

Carlos Yarza, manager, Fagor Electrodomésticos Sociedad Cooperativa, Mondragón, Guipúzcoa, 23 October 1994.*

José Miguel Zaldo, CEO, Grupo Tavex (Algodonera San Antonio), Madrid, 24 September 1994.*

Guillermo Zamarripa Escamilla, general manager for development and economic studies, Comisión Nacional Bancaria y de Valores, Mexico City, 13 May 1998.

José Antonio Zamora Rodríguez, general technical secretary, Ministry of Commerce and Tourism, Madrid, 15 June 1994.

Mario Zubía, CEO, Urssa Sociedad Cooperativa, Vitoria, 1 November 1994.*

Newspapers and magazines

Acción: Periódico Obrero de Barcelona y Provincia
Boletín Económico de ICE
Boletín de la Unión General de Trabajadores
Boletín de la Unión General de Trabajadores de España en el Exilio
Cinco Días
CNT: Órgano de la Confederación Nacional del Trabajo
The Economist
El País
Expansión
Financial Times

Gaceta Sindical
Información Comercial Española
Política Exterior
UGT: Boletín de la Unión General de Trabajadores de España
Unidad Obrera
Unión
Unión Sindical
Wall Street Journal
Wall Street Journal Europe

Archives and libraries

Asociación Española de Fábricas de Equipos y Componentes para Automoción (Sernauto), Library, Madrid.
Asociación Española de Normalización y Certificación (AENOR), Madrid.
Baker Library, Harvard Business School, Boston, MA.
Biblioteca Nacional, Madrid.
Library of the Banco de España, Madrid.
Library of the Comisión Nacional del Mercado de Valores, Madrid.
Library of the Consejo Económico y Social, Madrid.
Library of the Fundación Fondo para la Investigación Económica y Social, Madrid.
Library of the Fundación Pablo Iglesias, Alcalá de Henares, Madrid.
Library of the Fundación Primero de Mayo, Madrid.
Library and database of the Instituto Nacional de Comercio Exterior (ICEX), Madrid.
Library of the Instituto Nacional de Estadística, Madrid.
Library and archives of the Instituto Nacional de Industria, Library and Archives, Madrid.
Library of the Ministerio de Economía y Hacienda, Madrid.
New York Public Library, New York City.

References

Adams/Jobson. 1996. *Adams/Jobson's Wine Handbook 1996*. New York: Adams/Jobson Publishing.

AFI (Analistas Financieros Internacionales). 2004. *Investor Perceptions of Regulatory and Institutional Risks in Latin America*. Washington, DC: Inter-American Development Bank.

Aguilar Fernández-Hontoria, Eduardo. 1985. "Cinco años de liberalización de las inversiones directas españolas en el exterior, 1980–1984." *Información Comercial Española* (August–September):51–70.

Aharoni, Yair. 1966. *The Foreign Investment Decision Process*. Boston: Harvard Business School.

Alguacil, M. T. and V. Orts. 2002. "A Multivariate Cointegrated Model Testing for Temporal Causality Between Exports and Outward Foreign Investment: The Spanish Case." *Applied Economics* 34:119–32.

Alloza, Angel, and Javier Noya. 2004. "Capital disonante: La imagen de las inversiones españolas en América Latina." Real Instituto Elcano Document. http://www.realinstitutoelcano.org/documentos/86.asp.

Alonso, José Antonio, and Vicente Donoso. 1994. *Competitividad de la empresa exportadora española*. Madrid: ICEX.

——— 1995. "La internacionalización de la empresa y el apoyo público." *Economistas* 64:194–203.

Álvarez-Miranda, Berta. 1996. *El sur de Europa y la adhesión a la Comunidad: Los debates políticos*. Madrid: CIS and Siglo XXI.

Alvarez, Mª. J., N. Lado and M. Samartín. 2003. "Are Spanish Banks and Insurance Companies Re-Discovering Latin America? A Revision of the Theories on the Internationalisation Process." *International Journal of Bank Marketing* 21(3):109–21.

Alvarez Junco, José. 2001. *Mater dolorosa: La idea de España en el siglo XIX*. Madrid: Taurus.

Amsden, Alice. 1989. *Asia's Next Giant: South Korea and Late Industrialization*. New York: Oxford University Press.

Amsden, Alice H., and Takashi Hikino. 1994. "Project Execution Capability, Organizational Know-How and Conglomerate Corporate

Growth in Late Industrialization." *Industrial and Corporate Change* 3 (1):111–47.

Andersen Consulting. 1994. *Worldwide Manufacturing Competitiveness Study: The Second Lean Enterprise Report.* London: Andersen Consulting.

Archibugi, Daniele, and Mario Pianta. 1992. *The Technological Specialization of Advanced Countries.* London: Kluwer Academic Publishers.

Ariño, Gaspar ed. 2004. *Privatizaciones y liberalizaciones en España: Balance y resultados, 1996–2003.* 2 vols. Granada: Ediciones Comares.

Arregui Giménez, Andrés. 1994. "Internacionalización de las empresas de servicios públicos." *Información Comercial Española* 735 (noviembre):131–9.

Auto-Revista. 1986. "25 años de automoción en España." *Auto-Revista* 1455 (28 December – 4 January):19–40.

Azagra Blázquez, Pedro. 2002. "Internacionalización empresarial: ¿vencedores y vencidos?" *Información Comercial Española* 799:201–7.

Aznar, José María. 2004. *Ocho años de gobierno: Una visión personal de España.* Barcelona: Planeta.

Bajo, Oscar. 1991. "Determinantes macroeconómicos y sectoriales de la inversión extranjera directa en España." Información Comercial Española 696–7 (August–September):53–74.

Bajo, Oscar, and Simón Sosvilla. 1992. "Un análisis empírico de los determinantes macroeconómicos de la inversión extranjera directa en España, 1961–1989." *Moneda y Crédito* 194:107–48.

Baklanoff, Eric N. 1996. "Spain's Economic Strategy toward the 'Nations of its Historical Community': The 'Reconquest' of Latin America." *Journal of Interamerican Studies and World Affairs* 38(1) (Spring): 105–27.

Balfour, Sebastian, and Paul Preston. 1999. "Introduction." Pp. 1–12 in *Spain and the Great Powers*, edited by Sebastian Balfour and Paul Preston. New York: Routledge.

Ball, C. A. and A. E. Tschoegl. 1982. "The Decision to Establish a Foreign Bank Branch or Subsidiary: An Application of Binary Classification Procedures." *Journal of Financial and Quantitative Analysis*, 17 (3):411–24.

Barney, Jay. 1986. "Strategic Factor Markets: Expectations, Luck, and Business Strategy." *Management Science* 32(10):1231–41.

Barros, P. P. 1995. "Post-Entry Expansion in Banking: The Case of Portugal". *International Journal of Industrial Organization* 13:593–611.

Bartelsman, Eric J. and Mark Doms. 2000. "Understanding Productivity: Lessons from Longitudinal Microdata." *Journal of Economic Literature* 38(3) (September):569–94.

Bartlett, Christopher A. and Sumantra Ghoshal. 1989. *Managing Across Borders: The Transnational Solution.* Boston: Harvard Business School Press.

Bátiz-Lazo, B., A. B. Mendialdua, and S. Urionabarrenetxea Zabalandikoetxea. 2003. "Growth of the Spanish Multinational in the 1990s." Working paper, Open University Business School.

Baum, D. J. (1974). *The Canadian Banks in the Commonwealth Caribbean: Economic Nationalism and Multinational Enterprise of a Medium Power.* New York: Praeger.

Beltrán i Fos, Enric, and Valentín Martínez Montero. 1994. "Las inversiones exteriores de las empresas industriales alimentarias." *Información Comercial Española* 735 (noviembre):119–30.

Bengtsson, L., U. Elg and J.-I. Lind. 1997. "Bridging the Transatlantic Gap: How North American Reviewers Evaluate European Idiographic Research." *Scandinavian Journal of Management* 13(4):473–92.

Ben-Porath, Yoram. 1980. "The F-Connection: Families, Friends, and Firms and the Organization of Exchange." *Population and Development Review* 6(1) (March):1–30.

Berger, Allen N. et al. 2000. "Globalization of Financial Institutions: Evidence from Cross-Border Banking Performance." Pp. 23–125 in *Brookings-Wharton Papers on Financial Services.* Washington, DC.

Bermeo, Nancy. 1994a. "Sacrifice, Sequence, and Strength in Successful Dual Transitions: Lessons from Spain." *Journal of Politics* 56(3) (August):601–27.

———. 1994b. "Spain: Dual Transition Implemented by Two Parties." Pp. 89–127 in *Voting for Reform*, edited by Stephan Haggard and Steven B. Webb. Washington, DC: World Bank.

Blázquez, Jorge, and Miguel Sebastián. 2003. "El impacto de la crisis argentina sobre la economía española." Pp. 356–70 in *Anuario Elcano América Latina 2002–03.* Madrid: Real Instituto Elcano.

Boix, Carles. 1998. *Political Parties, Growth and Equality: Conservative and Social Democratic Economic Strategies in the World Economy.* New York: Cambridge University Press.

Boldt-Christmas, M., S. F. Jacobsen and A. E. Tschoegl. 2001. "The International Expansion of Norwegian Banks." *Business History* 43(3):79–104.

Boldt-Christmas, Martin, Siv Fagerland Jacobsen, and Adrian E. Tschoegl. 2001. "The International Expansion of the Norwegian Banks." *Business History* 43(3) (July):79–104.

Bolsa de Madrid. 1981. *La industria del automóvil en España.* Madrid: Bolsa de Madrid.

1986. *La industria de equipos y componentes para automoción en España*. Madrid: Bolsa de Madrid.

Bonet, José Luis. 1993. "La competitividad del cava: El caso Freixenet." *Papeles de Economía Española* 56:399–401.

Botín, Emilio. 2002. "La experiencia internacional de Santander Central Hispano." *Información Comercial Española* 799:119–25.

Breton, A. and R. Wintrobe. 1978. "A Theory of 'Moral' Suasion." *Canadian Journal of Economics* 11:210–19.

Broughton, Alan, and Arnaud Ripert. 1997. *European Banking: Spain, The Spanish Banking System*. New York: Morgan Stanley.

Brufau Niubó, Antonio. 2002. "El grupo Gas Natural en Latinoamérica." *Información Comercial Española* 799:173–9.

Buch, C. and G. Delong. 2003. "Determinants of Cross-Border Bank Mergers." In *Foreign Direct Investment in the Real and Financial Sector of Industrial Countries*, edited by H. Herrmann and R. Lipsey. Frankfurt: Springer Verlag.

Buckley, Peter, and Mark Casson. 1976. *The Theory of the Multinational Corporation*, London: Macmillan.

Bueno Campos, Eduardo. 1987. *Dirección estratégica de la empresa*. Madrid: Pirámide.

Campa, José Manuel, and Mauro F. Guillén. 1996a. "Spain: A Boom from Economic Integration." Pp. 207–39 in *Foreign Direct Investment and Governments*, edited by John H. Dunning and Rajneesh Narula. New York and London: Routledge.

1996b. "Evolución y determinantes de la inversión directa en el extranjero por empresas españolas." *Papeles de Economía Española* 66:235–47.

1999. "The Internalization of Exports: Firm and Location-Specific Factors in a Middle-Income Country." *Management Science* 45(11) (November):1463–78.

Campillo, Manuel. 1963. *Las inversiones extranjeras en España, 1850–1950*. Madrid: Manfer.

Cantwell, John. 1989. *Technological Innovation and the Multinational Corporation*. Oxford: Basil Blackwell.

Cardim de Carvalho, F. J. (2000). "New Competitive Strategies of Foreign Banks in Large Emerging Economies: The Case of Brazil." *BNL Quarterly Review* 213:135–69.

Cardone-Riportella, C. and L. Cazoria-Papas. 2001. "The Internationalisation Process of Spanish Banks: A Tale of Two Times." *International Journal of Bank Marketing* 19(2):52–67.

Cardoso, Fernando Henrique, and Enzo Faletto. [1973] 1979. *Dependency and Development in Latin America*. Berkeley, CA: University of California Press.

Casado, Montserrat. 1995. "La capacidad tecnológica de la economía española: Un balance de la transferencia internacional de tecnología." *Información Comercial Española* 740 (abril):153–70.

Casanova, Lourdes. 2002. "Lazos de familia: La inversión española en América Latina." *Foreign Affairs en Español* (web edition, summer issue).

Casilda Béjar, Ramón. 2002. *La década dorada: Economía e inversiones españolas en América Latina, 1990–2000.* Alcalá, Madrid: Servicio de Publicaciones de la Universidad de Alcalá.

Casson, Mark. 1985. "Transaction Costs and the Theory of the Multinational Enterprise." Pp. 20–38 in *The Economic Theory of the Multinational Enterprise*, edited by Peter J. Buckley and Mark Casson. New York: St. Martin's.

Castellvi, Miguel. 1973. "Cataluña abre la puerta del Rosellón." *Actualidad Económica* (30 June):8–13.

Cátedra SCH. 2003. *La internacionalización de la empresa española como protagonista de la apertura de nuestra economía.* Madrid: Universidad Antonio de Nebrija.

Caves, Richard E. 1989. "International Differences in Industrial Organization." Pp. 1127–250 in *Handbook of Industrial Organization*, edited by R. Schmalensee and R. D. Willig. Amsterdam: North Holland.

———. 1996. *Multinational Enterprise and Economic Analysis.* New York: Cambridge University Press.

Cecchini, Daniel, and Jorge Zicolillo. 2002. *Los nuevos conquistadores: El papel del gobierno y las empresas españolas en el expolio de Argentina.* Madrid: Foca.

Centro de Estudios Latinoamericanos (CESLA). 2002. *Efectos de la crisis argentina en la empresa espagñola.* Madrid: Universidad Autónoma de Madrid, CESLA.

CEPES. 2003. *Anuario de la economía social 2002.* Madrid: CEPES.

CESLA. 2002. *Efectos de la crisis argentina en la empresa española.* Madrid: Universidad Autónoma de Madrid.

Chang, Sea-Jin. 2002. *Financial Crisis and the Transformation of Korean Business Groups: The Rise and Fall of Chaebols.* Stanford: Stanford University Press.

Chislett, William. 2003. *Spanish Direct Investment in Latin America: Challenges and Opportunities.* Madrid: Real Instituto Elcano de Estudios Internacionales y Estratégicos.

———. 2004. "Spain and Portugal: From Distant Neighbours to Uneasy Associates." Working paper no. 46. Madrid: Real Instituto Elcano.

Choi, S.-R., A. E. Tschoegl, and C.-W. Yu. 1986. "Banks and the World's Major Financial Centers, 1970–1980." *Weltwirtschaftliches Archiv* 122(1):48–64.

Choi, S.-R., D. Park, and A. E. Tschoegl. 1996. "Banks and the World's Major Banking Centers, 1990." *Weltwirtschaftliches Archiv* 123(4):774–93.

2003. "Banks and the World's Major Banking Centers, 2000." *Weltwirtschaftliches Archiv* 139(3):550–68.

Church, Roy. 1993. "The Family Firm in Industrial Capitalism: International Perspectives on Hypotheses and History." *Business History* 35(4) (October):17–43.

CIRES. 1995. *La realidad social en España, 1993–1994.* Madrid: CIRES.

Claessens, S., and M. Jansen eds. 2000. *The Internationalization of Financial Services: Issues and Lessons for Developing Countries.* Boston: Kluwer Academic Press.

Claessens, S., A. Demirgüç-Kunt and H. Huizinga. 2000. "How Does Foreign Entry Affect the Domestic Banking Market?" In *The Internationalization of Financial Services: Issues and Lessons for Developing Countries*, edited by S. Claessens and M. Jansen. Boston: Kluwer Academic Press.

Clancy, Rockwell. 1998. "Consumidores y banca en Latinoamérica: La grieta de la confianza." *Mercado* (September):177–82.

Clarke, G., R. Cull, L. D'Amato and A. Molinari. 2000. "The Effect of Foreign Entry on Argentina's Domestic Banking Sector." In *The Internationalization of Financial Services: Issues and Lessons for Developing Countries*, edited by S. Claessens and M. Jansen. Boston: Kluwer Academic Press.

Clifton, Judith, Francisco Comín, and Daniel Díaz Fuentes. 2003. *Privatization in the European Union.* Dordrecht, the Netherlands: Kluwer Academic Publishers.

COCINB. 1973. *Las inversiones españolas en el exterior.* Barcelona: Cámara Oficial de Comercio, Industrial y Navegación de Barcelona.

Conway, Bryony. 1995. *Expatriate Effectiveness: A Study of European Expatriates in South-East Asia.* New York: John Wiley.

Cooke, William N. 1997. "The Influence of Industrial Relations Factors on U.S. Foreign Direct Investment Abroad." *Industrial and Labor Relations Review* 51(1):3–17.

Cuadrado Roura, Juan R. 2003. "Madrid, centro nacional e internacional de servicios." *Economistas* 21(95):65–72.

De Erice, Sebastián. 1975. "Comentarios al régimen legal de las inversiones españolas en el extranjero." *Información Comercial Española* 499 (March):77–90.

De Larra, Mariano José. 1993. *Artículos.* Madrid: Cátedra.

De Paula, Luiz Fernanco Rodrigues. 2003. "Los determinantes del reciente ingreso de bancos extranjeros a Brasil." *Revista de la CEPAL* (April): 169–88.

Del Arenal, Celestino. 2003. "EEUU y la política latinoamericana de España." *Política exterior* 17(93):183–93.

Del Campo, Salustiano, and Juan Manuel Camacho. 2003. *Informe IN-CIPE 2003: La opinión pública española y la política exterior.* Madrid: INCIPE.

Delage, Fernando. 2003. "Una política exterior para el siglo XXI." Pp. 563–73 in *La política exterior de España, 1800–2003*, edited by Juan Carlos Pereira. Barcelona: Ariel.

Deloitte and Touche. 2003. *La gestión internacional de recursos humanos en España.* Madrid: Deloitte and Touche.

Demirgüç-Kunt, A. and H. Huizinga. 1999. "Determinants of Commercial Bank Interest Margins and Profitability: Some International Evidence." *World Bank Economic Review* 13(2):379–408.

Dietsch, M. and A. Lozano Vivas. 1996. "How the Environment Determines the Efficiency of Banks: A Comparison between French and Spanish Banking." Wharton Financial Institutions Center Working paper no. 97–29.

Díez Medrano, Juan. 2003. *Framing Europe: Attitudes to European Integration in Germany, Spain, and the United Kingdom.* Princeton, NJ: Princeton University Press.

Dopico, Luis G. and James A. Wilcox. 2002. "Openness, Profit Opportunities and Foreign Banking." *Journal of International Financial Markets, Institutions and Money* 12(4–5) (October–December): 299–320.

Dufey, G. and B. Yeung. 1993. "The Impact of EC 92 on European Banking." *Journal of Financial Management*, 2(3–4):11–31.

Dunning, John H. 1979. "Explaining Changing Patterns of International Production: In Defence of the Eclectic Theory." *Oxford Bulletin of Economics and Statistics* 41:269–96.

   1981. "Explaining the International Direct Investment Position of Countries: Towards a Dynamic or Developmental Approach." *Weltwirtschaftliches Archiv* 119:30–64.

   1988. *Explaining International Production.* London: Unwin Human.

   1993. *Multinational Enterprises and the Global Economy.* Reading, MA: Addison-Wesley.

Dunning, John H. and Rajneesh Narula. 1994. *Transpacific Foreign Direct Investment and the Investment Development Path: The Record Assessed.* South Carolina Essays in International Business no. 10. Columbia, SC: Center for International Business Education and Research, University of South Carolina.

   eds. 1995. *Catalyst for Change: Foreign Direct Investment, Economic Structure, and Governments.* New York and London: Routledge.

Durán Herrera, Juan José. 1992. "Cross-Direct Investment and Technological Capability of Spanish Domestic Firms." Pp. 214–55 in *Multinational Investment in Modern Europe*, edited by John Cantwell. Aldershot, England: Edward Elgar.

Durán Herrera, Juan José ed. 1996. *Multinacionales españolas I*. Madrid: Pirámide.

1997. *Multinacionales españolas II*. Madrid: Pirámide.

1999. *Multinacionales españolas en Iberoamérica*. Madrid: Pirámide.

2001. *Las marcas renombradas españolas*. Madrid: EOI-ICEX.

Durán Herrera, Juan José, and M. P. Sánchez Muñoz. 1984. "La internacionalización de la economía española vía inversión directa 1960–1982." Pp. 347–405 in *Transnacionalización y periferia semiindustrializada*, edited by Isaac Minian. México: CIDE, vol. II.

Durán, Juan José, and Fernando Úbeda. 1996. "El círculo virtuoso tecnológico en el sector de componentes del automóvil español: El caso de Ficosa." Pp. 129–66 in *Multinacionales españolas*, vol. I, edited by Juan José Durán. Madrid: Pirámide.

Economist. 1994. "The Gain in Spain Falls Mainly in Parts." *The Economist*, 5 November, p. 67.

EIU (Economist Intelligence Unit). 1996a. "The Automotive Components Industry in Spain: Foreign Companies Drive Sector Growth." *Europe's Automotive Components Business* (first quarter):71–86.

1996b. "The Automotive Supply Base of South Korea: Achievements and Challenges." *Motor Business Asia-Pacific* (third quarter):104–24.

Engwall, L. and M. Wallenstäl (1988). "Tit for Tat in Small Steps: The Internationalization of Swedish Banks." *Scandinavian Journal of Management* 4:1147–55.

Erice, Sebastián de. 1975. "Comentarios al régimen legal de las inversiones españolas en el extranjero." *Información Comercial Española* 499 (marzo):77–90.

Ettlinger, N. 1997. "An Assessment of the Small-Firm Debate in the United States." *Environment and Planning* 29:419–42.

Evans, Peter. 1979. *Dependent Development*. Princeton, NJ: Princeton University Press.

1995. *Embedded Autonomy: States and Industrial Transformation*. Princeton, NJ: Princeton University Press.

Fazio Vengoa, Hugo. 2000. "América Latina en la política exterior de España." *Historia Crítica* 20 (July–December):55–92.

Fernández, Yolanda. 2003. "La explosión inversora en el exterior." Pp. 209–41 in *1987–2003: Integración económica y financiera de España*, edited by Alfonso García Mora and Francisco J. Valero. Madrid: Escuela de Finanzas Aplicadas.

Fernández Navarrete, Donato. 2003. "El papel del sector exterior en la economía española, 1808–2002." Pp. 129–52 in *La política exterior de España, 1800–2003*, edited by Juan Carlos Pereira. Barcelona: Ariel.

Fernández-Otheo Ruiz, Carlos Manuel. 2003. *Inversión directa extranjera de España en la década final del siglo XX: Nuevas perspectivas*. Madrid: Editorial Biblioteca Fundación José Ortega y Gasset.

Ferré, José María ed. 2000. *España, un actor destacado en el ámbito internacional*. Madrid: Fundación para el Análisis y los Estudios Sociales.

Fishman, Robert M. 1990. *Working-Class Organization and the Return to Democracy in Spain*. Ithaca, NY: Cornell University Press.

Flowers, E. B. 1976. "Oligopolistic Reactions in European and Canadian Direct Investment in the United States." *Journal of International Business Studies* 7:43–55.

Fontrodona Francolí, Jordi, and Joan Miquel Hernández Gascón. 2001. *Les multinacionals industrials catalanes 2001*. Barcelona: Generalitat de Catalunya.

Frank, André G. 1967. *Capitalism and Underdevelopment in Latin America*. New York: Monthly Review Press.

Freres, Christian, and Antonio Sanz Trillo. 2000. "Política exterior de España hacia América Latina desde la Transición: Una visión crítica." Pp. 547–74 in *La política exterior de España en el siglo XX*, edited by Javier Tusell, Juan Avilés, and Rosa Pardo. Madrid: Editorial Biblioteca Nueva.

Fujita, Masataka. 1996. "Small and Medium-Sized Enterprises in Foreign Direct Investment." Pp. 9–70 in *International Technology Transfer by Small and Medium-Sized Enterprises*, edited by Peter J. Buckley, Jaime Campos, Hafiz Mirza, and Eduardo White. London: Macmillan.

Galve Górriz, Carmen and Vicente Salas Fumás. 2003. *La empresa familiar en España: Fundamentos económicos y resultados*. Madrid: Fundación BBVA.

García, Florentino. 1998. "La industria auxiliar de la automoación se acelera." *El País Negocios*, 3 May, 12.

García Blandón, Josep. 2001. "The Timing of Foreign Direct Investment Under Uncertainty: Evidence from the Spanish Banking Sector." *Journal of Economic Behavior and Organization* 45:213–24.

García Canal, Esteban. 1996. "Contractual Form in Domestic and International Strategic Alliances." *Organization Studies* 17(5): 773–94.

García Canal, Esteban, and Ana Valdés Llaneza. 1997. "Tipología de alianzas para la internacionalización: evidencia de las empresas españolas." *Economía Industrial* 314:171–8.

García Canal, Esteban, Ana Valdés Llaneza, and Africa Ariño Martín. 2003. "Effectiveness of Dyadic and Multi-party Joint Ventures." *Organization Studies* 24(5):743–70.

García Canal, Esteban and Mauro F. Guillén. 2004. "Risk Aversion and Imitation as Drivers of Foreign Location Choice in Regulated Industries." Working paper.

García de la Cruz, José Manuel. 1993. "Empresas multinacionales y economía española." PhD thesis series no. 141/93. Madrid: Universidad Complutense de Madrid.

García-Delgado, José Luis, and Juan Carlos Jiménez. 2001. *Un siglo de España. La economía.* Madrid: Marcial Pons.

García Pérez, Rafael. 2003. "España en un mundo en cambio: A la búsqueda de la influencia internacional, 1986–2002." Pp. 539–50 in *La política exterior de España, 1800–2003*, edited by Juan Carlos Pereira. Barcelona: Ariel.

García Ruiz, J. L. 2000. "Internal Organization and Growth in the National Banks: The Case of the Banco Hispano Americano and the Banco Central, 1901–1991." Economic Research Network, Organizations and Markets Working Papers 4.

Garrett, Thomas A. 2001. "An International Comparison and Analysis of Lotteries and the Distribution of Lottery Expenditures." *International Journal of Applied Economics* 15(2):213–27.

Gates, Stephen. 1994. *Managing Expatriates' Return: A Research Report.* New York: The Conference Board.

Gaviria, Mario. 1996. *La séptima potencia: España en el mundo.* Barcelona: Ediciones B.

Geertz, Clifford. 1973. *The Interpretation of Cultures: Selected Essays.* New York: Basic Books.

Ghoshal, Sumantra, and Eleanor Westney eds. 1993. *Organization Theory and the Multinational Corporation.* New York: St. Martin's Press.

Gillespie, Richard, and Richard Youngs. 2000. "Spain's International Challenges at the Turn of the Century." *Mediterranean Politics* 5(2) (Summer):1–13.

Gilpin, Robert 1987. *The Political Economy of International Relations.* Princeton, NJ: Princeton University Press.

Giráldez Pidal, Elena. 2002. *La internacionalización de las empresas españolas en América Latina.* Madrid: Consejo Económico y Social.

Goldstein, Morris. 2001. "IMF Structural Conditionality: How Much is Too Much?" Institute for International Economics Working Paper 01–4.

Goldstein, Morris and Philip Turner. 1996. "Banking Crises in Emerging Economies: Origins and Policy Options." BIS Economic Papers no. 46.

González Cerdeira, Xulia. 1996. "La empresa industrial en la década de los noventa: Actividad tecnológica." Working paper 9609. Madrid: Fundación Empresa Pública.

González, Roberto. 1989. "Las inversiones españolas directas e inmobiliarias en el exterior durante 1988." *Boletín Semanal de Información Comercial Española* (27 February–5 March):869–79.

Granovetter, Mark. 1983. "Small is Bountiful: Labor Markets and Establishment Size." *American Sociological Review* 49(3) (June):323–34.

Grifell-Tatjé, E. and C. A. K. Lovell. 1996. "Deregulation and Productivity Decline: The Case of Spanish Savings Banks." *European Economic Review* 40:1281–303.

Grosse, R. 1997. "Restrictive Business Practices in International Service Industries: Examples from Latin America." *Transnational Corporations* 6(2):29–50.

Grosse, R. and L. G. Goldberg. 1996. "The Boom and Bust of Latin American Lending, 1970–1992." *Journal of Economics and Business* 48:285–98.

Grubel, G. H. 1977. "A Theory of Multinational Banking." *Banca Nazionale del Lavoro Quarterly Review* 123:349–63.

Grugel, Jean. 1995. "Spain and Latin America." Pp. 141–58 in *Democratic Spain: Reshaping External Relations in a Changing World*, edited by Richard Gillespie, Fernando Rodrigo, and Jonathan Story. New York: Routledge.

Guillén, Mauro F. 1989. *La profesión de economista: El auge de economistas, ejecutivos y empresarios en España*. Barcelona: Ariel.

 1994. *Models of Management: Work, Authority, and Organization in a Comparative Perspective*. Chicago: University of Chicago Press.

 2000. "Organized Labor's Images of Multinational Enterprise: Divergent Ideologies of Foreign Investment in Argentina, South Korea, and Spain." *Industrial and Labor Relations Review* 53(3) (April): 419–42.

 2001a. "Is Globalization Civilizing, Destructive or Feeble? A Critique of Five Key Debates in the Social-Science Literature." *Annual Review of Sociology* 27:235–60.

 2001b. "International Business." Pp. 7768–71 in Neil J. Smelser and Paul B. Baltes, eds., *International Encyclopedia of the Social and Behavioral Sciences*. Oxford: Pergamon.

 2001c. *The Limits of Convergence: Globalization and Organizational Change in Argentina, South Korea, and Spain*. Princeton, NJ: Princeton University Press.

Guillén, Mauro F. and Adrian E. Tschoegl. 2000. "The Internationalization of Retail Banking: The Case of the Spanish Banks in Latin America." *Transnational Corporations*, 9(3) (December):63–97.

2002. "Banking on Gambling: Banks and Lottery-Linked Deposit Accounts." *Journal of Financial Services Research* 21(3):219–31.

Guirao, J. Abelardo. 1922. "Nuestros mercados de exportación: Americanismo, Iberismo, Africanismo." *Revista Nacional de Economía* 12 (37):385–401.

Haggard, S. 1990. *Pathways from the Periphery: The Politics of Growth in the Newly Industrializing Countries.* Ithaca, NY: Cornell University Press.

Hamann, Kerstin. 1998. "Spanish Unions: Institutional Legacy and Responsiveness to Economic and Industrial Change." *Industrial and Labor Relations Review* 51(3) (April):424–44.

Hamilton, Gary G. and Nicole W. Biggart. 1988. "Market, Culture, and Authority: A Comparative Analysis of Management and Organization in the Far East." *American Journal of Sociology* 94(Supplement):S52–S94.

Harrison, Bennett. 1994. *Lean and Mean: The Changing Landscape of Corporate Power in the Age of Flexibility.* New York: Basic Books.

Heinkel, R. L. and M. D. Levi. 1992. "The Structure of International Banking." *Journal of International Money and Finance* 16:251–72.

Hennart, Jean-François. 1982. *A Theory of Multinational Enterprise.* Ann Arbor, MI: University of Michigan Press.

Hymer, Stephen. [1960] 1976. *The International Operations of National Firms: A Study of Direct Foreign Investment.* Cambridge, MA: MIT Press.

Jacobsen, S. F. and A. E. Tschoegl. 1999. "The Norwegian Banks in the Nordic Consortia: A Case of International Strategic Alliances in Banking." *Industrial and Corporate Change* 8(1):137–65.

Johanson, Jan and Jan-Erik Vahlne. 1977. "The Internationalization Process of the Firm: A Model of Knowledge Development and Increasing Foreign Market Commitments." *Journal of International Business Studies* 8(1):23–32.

Kerr, Clark, John T. Dunlop, Frederick Harbison, and Charles A. Myers. [1960] 1964. *Industrialism and Industrial Man.* New York: Oxford University Press.

Khan, Mohsin S. and Sunil Sharma. 2001. "IMF Conditionality and Country Ownership of Programs." International Monetary Fund working paper 01/142.

Kindleberger, Charles. 1969. *American Business Abroad.* Cambridge, MA: MIT Press.

Knickerbocker, Frederick. 1973. *Oligopolistic Reaction and Multinational Enterprise.* Boston: Division of Research, Harvard Business School.

Kogut, Bruce. 1983. "Foreign Direct Investment as a Sequential Process."
    In *The Multinational Corporation in the 1980s*, edited by. C. P.
    Kindleberger and D. Audretsch. Cambridge, MA: MIT Press.
Kogut, Bruce, and Nalin Kulatilaka. 1994. "Operating Flexibility, Global
    Manufacturing, and the Option Value of a Multinational Network."
    Management Science 40(1) (January):123–39.
Lamo de Espinosa, Emilio. 2003. "Spain's Atlantic Vocation." Working
    paper. Madrid: Real Instituto Elcano.
Latinobarómetro 2003. *La Democracia y la Economía: Latinobarómetro
    2003*. www.latinobarometro.org.
Leff, Nathaniel. 1978. "Industrial Organization and Entrepreneurship in
    Developing Countries: The Economic Groups." *Economic Develop-
    ment and Cultural Change* 26:661–75.
    1979. "Entrepreneurship and Economic Development." *Journal of Eco-
    nomic Literature* 17:46–64.
Levitt, Theodore. 1983. "The Globalization of Markets." *Harvard Business
    Review* 61(3) (May–June):92–102.
Levy, M. B. 1991. "The Banking System and Foreign Capital in Brazil." In
    International Banking 1870–1914, edited by R. Cameron and V. I.
    Bovykin. New York: Oxford University Press.
López Duarte, Cristina, and Esteban García Canal. 1998. "La estructura de
    propiedad de la inversión directa en el exterior." *Investigaciones Eco-
    nómicas* 22(1):19–44.
    2001. "Acceso a capacidades externas en el proceso de Inversión Directa
    en el Exterior: La elección entre empresas conjuntas y adquisiciones."
    Revista de Economía Aplicada 9(26):5–28.
    2002a. "Adverse Selection and the Choice between Joint-Ventures and
    Acquisitions: Evidence from Spanish Firms." *Journal of Institutional
    and Theoretical Economics* 158(2):304–24.
    2002b. "The Effect of Firm and Host Country Characteristics on the
    Choice of Entry Mode: Some Empirical Evidence from Spanish Firms."
    Journal of Management and Governance 6(2):153–68.
    2003. "Creación de valor en la expansión internacional a través de las
    inversiones directas en el exterior: El caso de las empresas españolas."
    Working paper, University of Oviedo.
Maddison, Angus. 1995. *Monitoring the World Economy 1820–1992*.
    Paris:OECD.
    2001. *The World Economy: A Millennial Perspective*. Paris: OECD.
Makler, Harry M., and Walter L. Ness, Jr. 2002. "How Financial Intermedi-
    ation Challenges National Sovereignty in Emerging Markets." *Quar-
    terly Review of Economics and Finance* 42(5):827–51.

Marichal, C. 1997. "Nation Building and the Origins of Banking in Latin America, 1850–1930." In *Banking, Trade and Industry: Europe, America and Asia from the Thirteenth to the Twentieth Century*, edited by A. Teichova, G. Kurgan-van Hentenryk, and D. Ziegler. Cambridge: Cambridge University Press.

Marín, Juan Pedro. 1982. "La inversión española en el exterior." *Papeles de Economía Española* 11:163–84.

Markides, Constantinos C. and Peter J. Williamson. 1996. "Corporate Diversification and Organizational Structure: A Resource-Based View." *Academy of Management Journal* 39(2) (April):340–67.

Marks, Michael. 1995. "Researching the Origins of Ideas in Foreign Policy: The Case of Spain." *International Studies Notes* 20(1) (Winter): 21–31.

Marois, B. and T. Abdessemed (1996). "Cross-Border Alliances in the French Banking Sector." *International Studies of Management and Organization*, 26(2):38–58.

Marshall, Alfred. 1919. *Industry and Trade*. London: Macmillan.

Martín Aceña, Pablo, and Francisco Comín. 1991. *INI: 50 años de industrialización en España*. Madrid: Espasa-Calpe.

Martínez Carreras, José U. 2003. "El africanismo español." Pp. 357–70 in *La política exterior de España, 1800–2003*, edited by Juan Carlos Pereira. Barcelona: Ariel.

Marx, Karl. [1867, 1885, 1894] 1967. *Capital*, 3 vols. New York: International Publishers.

Mas, I. (1995). "Policy-Induced Disincentives to Financial Sector Development: Selected Examples from Latin America in the 1980s." *Journal of Latin American Studies* 27:683–706.

Maudos, Joaquín, José Manuel Pastor, and Javier Quesada. 1997. "Technical Progress in Spanish Banking, 1985–1994." Pp. 214–45 in *The Recent Evolution of Financial Systems*, edited by Jack Revell. London: Macmillan.

MCT. 2003. *Informe del Ministerio de Ciencia y Tecnología, 2001–2002*. Madrid: Ministerio de Ciencia y Tecnología.

Méndez, Ricardo, and Silvia Marcu. 2003. "La posición geoestratégica de España." Pp. 105–28 in *La política exterior de España, 1800–2003*, edited by Juan Carlos Pereira. Barcelona: Ariel.

Merino de Lucas, Fernando, and Marta Muñoz Guarasa. 2002. "Fuentes estadísticas para el estudio de la inversión directa española en el exterior." *Cuadernos Económicos de ICE* 2751(December):5–15.

MICT. (Ministerio de Industria, Comercio y Turismo. 1991. *Análisis de la situación y perspectivas competitivas del subsector de componentes de automoción*, 4 vols. Madrid: MICT.

MICYT (Ministerio de Industria, Comercio y Turismo). 1992. *Un panorama de la industria española.* Madrid: MICYT.

MIE (Ministerio de Industria y Energía). 1996. *Informe sobre la industria española,* vol. II. Madrid: Ministerio de Industria y Energía.

Miguélez, F., C. Prieto and C. Cataño (with others), 1999. "Employment Relations in the Spanish Banking Industry: Big Changes." In *From Tellers to Sellers: Changing Employment Relations in Banks,* edited by M. Regini, J. Kitay, and M. Baethege. Cambridge, MA: MIT Press.

Mineco. 1994. *La negociación colectiva en las grandes empresas en 1993.* Madrid: Ministerio de Economía y Hacienda.

——— 2003. *La energía en España 2002.* Madrid: Ministerio de Economía.

Mínguez Sanz, Santiago. 1994. "El cava: Su producción y comercialización." *El Campo* 130 (January):111–21.

MIR. 2003. *Anuario estadístico de extranjería 2002.* Madrid: Ministerio del Interior.

Molano, W. T. 1997. "Financial Reverberations: Latin America's Private Banking System during the mid-1990s." New York: SBC Warburg, mimeo.

Molero, José. 1998. "Patterns of Internationalization of Spanish Innovatory Firms." *Research Policy* 27:541–58.

Morán Reyero, Pilar. 1993. "La inversión española en el exterior." *Economistas* 55 (extra):125–33.

Moreno Moré, Juan Luis. 1975. "Quince años de inversiones españolas en el extranjero." *Información Comercial Española* 499 (March):91–107.

——— 1982. "La inversión extranjera en España." *Papeles de Economía Española* 11:141–62.

Moreno, Lourdes and Diego Rodríguez. 1996. "La empresa industrial en la década de los noventa: Actividad Exterior." Working paper 9608. Madrid: Fundación Empresa Pública.

Muñoz, Juan, Santiago Roldán, and Angel Serrano. 1978. *La internacionalización del capital en España, 1959–1977.* Madrid: Edicusa.

Nadal, Jordi. 1975. *El fracaso de la revolución industrial en España, 1814–1913.* Barcelona: Ariel.

Naisbitt, John and Patricia Aburdene. 1990. *Megatrends 2000.* New York: Morrow.

Noya, Javier. 2002. *La imagen de España en el exterior.* Madrid: Real Instituto Elcano.

——— 2003. "La imagen de España en América Latina: Resultados del Latinobarómetro 2003." Madrid: Real Instituto Elcano. http://www.realinstitutoelcano.org/documentos/75.asp.

Nueno Iniesta, Pedro, Nieves Martinez Lapena, and Jose Sarle Guiu. 1981. *Las inversiones españolas en el extranjero.* Pamplona: Ediciones Universidad de Navarra.

Ó hUallacháin, B. 1994. "Foreign Banking in the American Urban System of Financial Organization." *Economic Geography* 70:206–28.

OECD. 1997. *Globalisation and Small and Medium Enterprises.* 2 vols. Paris: OECD.

Oneal, John R. 1992. "The Affinity of Foreign Investors for Authoritarian Regimes." *Political Research Quarterly* 47(3):565–88.

Ontiveros, E., M. Conthe, and J. M. Nogueira. 2004. "La percepción de los inversores de los riesgos regulatorios e institucionales en América Latina." Working paper. Washington, DC: Inter-American Development ment Bank.

Ortega y Gasset, José. 1986. *La rebelión de las masas.* Madrid: Espasa-Calpe. English trans. *The Revolt of the Masses.* New York: W. W. Norton, 1932.

Palacio, Vicente, and Fernando Rodrigo. 2003. "¿Tiene España una política exterior?" *Política Exterior* 17(93):153–65.

Pastor, J. M., S. A. Pérez and J. Quesada. 2000. "The Opening of the Spanish Banking System: 1985–98." in *The Internationalization of Financial Services: Issues and Lessons for Developing Countries,* edited by S. Claessens and M. Jansen. Boston: Kluwer Academic Press.

Pereira Castañares, Juan Carlos. 2003. "Los estudios internacionales en España: La política exterior." Pp. 55–82 in *La política exterior de España, 1800–2003,* edited by Juan Carlos Pereira. Barcelona: Ariel.

Pérez Galdós, Benito. 1986. *La de los tristes destinos.* National Episodes Series no. 40. Madrid: Alianza.

Pérez Herrero, Pedro. 2003. "Las relaciones de España con América Latina durante los siglos XIX y XX." Pp. 319–40 in *La política exterior de España, 1800–2003,* edited by Juan Carlos Pereira. Barcelona: Ariel.

Pérez, Sofía. 1997. *Banking on Privilege: The Politics of Spanish Financial Reform.* Ithaca, NY: Cornell University Press.

Perlmutter, H. 1969. "The Tortuous Evolution of the Multinational Corporation." *Columbia Journal of World Business* 4:9–18.

Perrow, Charles. 1992. "Small Firm Networks." Pp. 445–70 in *Networks and Organizations,* edited by Nitin Nohria and Robert G. Eccles. Boston, MA.: HBS Press.

Peteraf, Margaret A. 1993. "The Cornerstones of Competitive Advantage: A Resource-Based View." *Strategic Management Journal* 14(3) (March):179–91.

Piore, Michael J. and Charles F. Sabel. 1984. *The Second Industrial Divide: Possibilities for Prosperity.* New York: Basic Books.

Porter, Michael E. 1987. "Changing Patterns of International Competition." Pp. 27–57 in *The Competitive Challenge*, edited by David J. Teece. Cambridge, MA: Ballinger.

Portillo, Luis. 1994. "Las empresas japonesas en Europa ante el mercado único y la recesión." *Boletín Económico de ICE* 2411 (2–8 May): 1139–45.

Prahalad, C. K. and Yves L. Doz. 1987. *The Multinational Mission: Balancing Local Demands and Global Vision*. New York: Free Press.

Prial, Frank J. 1996. "Getting a Kick from Champagne." *The New York Times*, 15 September, Section 5, 15, 22.

Prieto Iglesias, José Manuel. 2002. "El compromiso con el conocimiento, clave para la expansion internacional de Unión Fenosa." *Información Comercial Española* 799:189–98.

Raurich, José María Enrique Seoane, y Ferrán Sicart. 1973. *El marco económico de las inversiones catalanas en el Rosellón*. Barcelona: Condal de Estudios Económicos.

Robles, Laureano ed. 1987. *Epistolario completo Ortega-Unamuno*. Madrid: El Arquero.

Rodríguez, J. M. 1989. "The Crisis in Spanish Private Banks: An Empirical Analysis." *Rivista Internationale di Scienze Economiche e Commerciali* 36(10–11):1033–55.

Ross, D. M. 1998. "European Banking Clubs in the 1960s." *Business and Economic History* 27:353–66.

——— 2002. "Clubs and Consortia: European Banking Groups as Strategic Alliances." In *European Banks and the American Challenge*, edited by S. Battilossi and Y. Cassis. Oxford: Oxford University Press.

Rostow, Walt W. 1960. *The Stages of Economic Growth: A Non-Communist Manifesto*. Cambridge: Cambridge University Press.

Rubio, Javier. 2003. "¿Qué Ha Sido la Política Exterior para España?" Pp. 553–562 in *La política exterior de España, 1800–2003*, edited by Juan Carlos Pereira. Barcelona: Ariel.

Sabel, Charles F. and Jonathan Zeitlin. 1985. "Historical Alternatives to Mass Production." *Past and Present* 108 (August):133–67.

Sachs, Jeffrey. 1993. *Poland's Jump to the Market Economy*. Cambridge, MA.: MIT Press.

Sanchez-Peinando, E. 2003. "Internationalization Process of Spanish Banks: A New Stage after the Mergers." *European Business Review* 15 (4):245–61.

Schumacher, Ernst F. 1975. *Small Is Beautiful: Economics as if People Mattered*. New York: Harper and Row.

Secretaría de Estado de Comercio. 1989. *Censo de inversiones directas de España en el exterior a diciembre de 1986.* Madrid: Secretaría de Estado de Comercio.

Secretaría General Técnica. 1995. "La imagen de marca de España." *Boletín Económico de ICE* 2465 (24–30 julio):3–7.

Sernauto. 1996. *La industria española de equipos y componentes para automoción en 1995.* Madrid: Sernauto.

Sidro, Vicente. 1993. "Conquistas internacionales: Las empresas del Grupo han aumentado su presencia en el exterior." *Comunicación Directivos* 40 (November–December):14–17.

Smith, Adam. [1776] 1976. *An Inquiry into the Nature and Causes of the Wealth of Nations.* Oxford: Clarendon Press.

Snodgrass, Donald R. and Tyler Biggs. 1996. *Industrialization and the Small Firm.* San Francisco, CA: International Center for Economic Growth.

Soros, George. 2002. *George Soros on Globalization.* New York: Public Affairs.

Sorroza Blanco, Alicia. 2003. *Directorio de Centros Españoles de Asuntos Internacionales y Estratégicos.* Madrid: Real Instituto Elcano de Estudios Internacionales y Estratégicos.

Stiglitz, Joseph. 2002. *Globalization and its Discontents.* New York: W.W. Norton.

Strohl, Mitchell P. 1993. *Europe's High Speed Trains: A Study in Geo-Economics.* Westport, CT: Praeger.

Suárez-Zuloaga y Gáldiz, Ignacio. 2001. "Los directivos de las multinacionales españolas: en el interior y en la expatriación." *Información Comercial Española* 794 (Octubre 2001):61–74.

Tarrow, Sidney. 2001. "Transnational Politics: Contention and Institutions in International Politics." *Annual Review of Political Science* 4:1–20.

Toral, Pablo. 2001. *The Reconquest of the New World: Multinational Enterprises and Spain's Direct Investment in Latin America.* Aldershot, England: Ashgate.

Tortella, Gabriel. 1994. *El desarrollo de la España contemporánea: Historia económica de los siglos XIX y XX.* Madrid: Alianza.

———. 1995. "The Hispanic American Connection in the Banco Hispano Americano of Madrid." In *Wirstchaft, Gesellschaft, Unternehmen: Festschrift fur Hans Pohl zum 60 Geburstag. Vierteljahrschrift für Sozial-und Wirtschaftsgeschichte,* edited by W. Feldenkirchen, R. Schönert-Röhlk, and Günther Schulz. Beiheft Nr. 120b. Stuttgart: Franz Steiner Verlag.

Toulan, Omar and Mauro F. Guillén. 1997. "Beneath the Surface: The Impact of Radical Economic Reforms on the Outward Orientation of Argentine and Mendozan Firms, 1989–1995." *Journal of Latin American Studies* 29 (May):395–418.

Trigo Portela, Joaquín. 2004. *Veinte años de privatizaciones en España.* Madrid: Instituto de Estudios Económicos.

Tschoegl, Adrian E. 1987. "International Retail Banking as a Strategy: An Assessment." *Journal of International Business Studies* 19(2):67–88.

———. 2000. "Foreign Banks, International Banking Centers and Geography." *Financial Markets, Instruments and Institutions* 9(1):1–32.

———. 2002. "The Internationalization of Singapore's Largest Banks." *Journal of Asian Business* 18(1):1–35.

———. 2003a. "Discussion of 'Determinants of Cross-Border Bank Mergers.'" Pp. 349–64 in *Foreign Direct Investment in the Real and Financial Sector of Industrial Countries*, edited by H. Herrmann and R. Lipsey. Frankfurt: Springer Verlag.

———. 2003b. "Financial Crises and the Presence of Foreign Banks." IBRD Research Project on Systemic Financial Distress and Conference, and WFIC WP 03–35.

Tusell, Javier. 2000. "Prólogo." Pp. 13–28 in *La política exterior de España en el siglo XX*, edited by Javier Tusell, Juan Avilés, and Rosa Pardo. Madrid: Editorial Biblioteca Nueva.

Ugalde, Ruth. 2002. "Latinoamérica ya no es tan apetecible para vivir." *Expansión* (6 November):IV–V.

Unal, H. and M. Navarro (1999). "The Technical Process of Bank Privatization in Mexico." *Journal of Financial Services Research* 16(1):61–83.

UNCTAD (United Nations Conference on Trade and Development). 2003. *World Investment Report 2003.* New York: United Nations.

Valdivielso del Real, Rocío. 2003. "La carrera diplomática española." Pp. 251–66 in *La política exterior de España, 1800–2003*, edited by Juan Carlos Pereira. Barcelona: Ariel.

Varela Parache, Fernando. 1972. "Las inversiones españolas en el extranjero." *Información Comercial Española* 9(104) (August):59–64.

Vasconcelos, M. R., J. R. Fucidji and E. Strachman. 2002. "Foreign Entry and Efficiency: Evidence from the Brazilian Banking Industry." UEM— Universidade Estadual de Maringá, Brazil.

———. 2002. "Concentraçaõ mundial no setor bancário: causas e potenciais efeitos." *Revista Economia Contemporanea* 6(1):26–56.

Vernon, Raymond. 1966. "International Investment and International Trade in the Product Life Cycle." *Quarterly Journal of Economics* 80:190–207.

1971. *Sovereignty at Bay: The Multinational Spread of U.S. Enterprises.*
New York: Basic Books.

1979. "The Product Cycle Hypothesis in a New International Environment." *Oxford Bulletin of Economics and Statistics,* 41(4) (November):255–67.

Vilar, Juan B. and María José Vilar. 2003. "España, de la emigración a la
inmigración." Pp. 217–236 in *La política exterior de España, 1800–
2003,* edited by Juan Carlos Pereira. Barcelona: Ariel.

Villalonga, Belén. 2000. "Privatization and Efficiency: Differentiating
Ownership Effects from Political, Organizational, and Dynamic
Effects." *Journal of Economic Behavior and Organization* 42:43–74.

Viñas Mey, Carmelo. 1922. "Las compañías de comercio y el resurgimiento
industrial de España en el siglo XVIII." *Revista Nacional de Economía*
12(36):239–75.

Watson Wyatt. 2003. *Global 50 Remuneration Planning Report 2002/03.*
Washington, DC: Watson Wyatt.

Wells, Louis T., Jr. 1983. *Third World Multinationals: The Rise of Foreign
Investment from Developing Countries.* Cambridge, MA: MIT Press.

Whyte, William Foote, and Kathleen King Whyte. [1988] 1991. *Making
Mondragón: The Growth and Dynamics of the Worker Cooperative
Complex.* Ithaca, NY: ILR Press.

Williams, B. (1997). "Positive Theories of Multinational Banking: Eclectic
Theory versus Internalization Theory." *Journal of Economic Surveys*
11(1):71–100.

World Bank. 2003. *Argentina – Crisis y pobreza.* New York: World Bank.

Youngs, Richard. 2001. "Spain, Latin America and Europe." Pp. 10–128 in
Spain: The European and International Challenges, edited by Richard
Gillespie and Richard Youngs. London: Frank Cass.

Yu, C.-M. and K. Ito 1988. "Oligopolistic Reaction and Foreign Direct
Investment: The Case of the U.S. Tire and Textile Industries." *Journal
of International Business Studies* 19(3):449–60.

Zaheer, Srilata. 1995. "Overcoming the Liability of Foreignness." *Academy
of Management Journal* 38(2):341–63.

Zhao, Minyuan. 2004. "Doing R&D in Countries with Weak IPR Protection." Stern School of Business, New York University, mimeo.

Index

For EU product safety concerns, contact us at Calle de José Abascal, 56–1°, 28003 Madrid, Spain or eugpsr@cambridge.org.

www.ingramcontent.com/pod-product-compliance
Ingram Content Group UK Ltd.
Pitfield, Milton Keynes, MK11 3LW, UK
UKHW012157180425
457623UK00018B/238